The New
Legal Sea Foods
Cookbook

Also by Jane Doerfer

Going Solo in the Kitchen

The Legal Sea Foods Cookbook
(with George Berkowitz)

The Pantry Gourmet

The New Legal Sea Foods Cookbook

Roger Berkowitz and
Jane Doerfer

Illustrated by Edward Koren

Broadway Books | New York

Broadway Books titles may be purchased for business or promotional use or for special sales.
For information, please write to: Special Markets Department, Random House, Inc.,
1745 Broadway, New York, NY 10019.

PRINTED IN THE UNITED STATES OF AMERICA

BROADWAY BOOKS and its logo, a letter B bisected on the diagonal,
are trademarks of Broadway Books, a division of Random House, Inc.

Visit our website at www.broadwaybooks.com

Designed by Ralph L. Fowler

Library of Congress Cataloging-in-Publication Data

Berkowitz, Roger.
The new Legal Sea Foods cookbook / Roger Berkowitz and Jane Doerfer.
p. cm.
1. Cookery (Fish) 2. Cookery (Seafood) 3. Legal Sea Foods (Restaurant) I. Doerfer, Jane. II. Title.
TX747 .B394 2003
641.6'92—dc21
2002024661

ISBN 0-7679-0691-8

5 7 9 10 8 6

To my late grandmother Anna Wiskind,

in my mind the finest chef I have ever encountered.

She introduced me to the joys of great eating.

A natural-born cook, she never used recipes but

had one ingredient that many people fail to use.

My grandmother cooked with love,

and that was something you could taste.

—RB

To Joanna, Andrew, and Kimberly

—JD

Contents

Acknowledgments

Thank you

- to my "solemate," Lynne, who truly understands my business and is always there for me;

- to my children Matthew, Scott, and Jackie, who learned early on never to take me too seriously;

- to my parents, George and Harriet, who instilled the basic tenets of life and taught me always to strive for the best;

- to the staff at Legal Sea Foods—the key ingredient to our success—you are only as good as the people around you;

- to Jane, a good friend without whose great insight into the many levels of our operation and skill with recipes, this book would not have been written;

- to Edward Koren, a good guy and very funny cartoonist, whose work I have admired for years. Our mutual friendship through the late Tom Winship helped bring us together;

- to John Taylor (Ike) Williams, the quintessential agent;

- to Jennifer Josephy, one of the best cookbook editors in the business, and the creative staff at Broadway Books who fashioned this attractive book.

—Roger Berkowitz

The Legal Sea Foods Heritage

FISH IS MY LIFE. WHEN I WAS GROWING UP, EVERYONE IN OUR FAMILY worked at Legal Sea Foods. My parents, George and Harriet, ran the business. Harriet's mother, Anna, bussed tables. My grandfather Max was the cashier. My brother, Marc, and I helped out after school and on weekends. I swept the floor, stocked the fish cases, sold takeout, scaled and filleted fish, and spent endless hours peeling shrimp. I even met my wife, Lynne, when she was working at Legal Sea Foods, when I was cooking in the kitchen and she was a waitress.

Although I knew every aspect of the business, I planned to work in broadcasting, not at Legal Sea Foods. However, when I graduated from college in 1974 with a broadcast journalism degree, my father asked if I'd be willing to manage our original location in Cambridge, Massachusetts, so he'd be free to open a second restaurant. I expected to do this for a year or two, and move on—but twenty-nine years later, I am still here. I found that no matter how much I tried to deny it, once the food business was in my blood, it became addictive. Very few businesses allow the opportunity to do as many different things as this one, whether it's developing new restaurants, working with people, problem solving, or marketing. Nothing is routine. Every day brings new challenges.

I realized early on that there are no days off in the restaurant world. I logged eighteen-hour days, stretching from dawn, when I bought fish down at the pier, to almost midnight, when I locked up the business. Often I was the first person to arrive and the last person to leave. It was exhausting, hard work, but I can tell you there's no better way to learn the fish business than the way I was trained.

Looking back, it's difficult to believe that our multimillion-dollar business started more than fifty years ago as one tiny fish market in a working-class neighborhood in Cambridge. My father, George Berkowitz, opened Legal Sea Foods in Inman Square, next door to my grandfather's meat and grocery store, which was called Legal Cash Market after the Legal trading stamps that he passed out with the groceries. (In those days, customers saved these stamps to redeem for products; now, stores offer double coupons and other promotions.)

My grandfather, Harry, had a wonderful reputation for stocking only the highest-quality meat and produce. To point up his connection with the Legal Cash Market, my father named his new fish store Legal Sea Foods, and used the same exacting requirements for the selection and handling of fish that my grandfather had for meat.

From the beginning, my father was willing to pay top price to garner the best fish. Very quickly, Legal gained a reputation as *the* place to go in Boston to find the finest selection and quality of fish. My father knew, and taught me, that there were no bargains in the fish business. Top-quality fish always commands top prices. And, if the suppliers know you're their prime customer, they save the "top of the catch" for you. (My motto might be a sign I've hung on my office wall that says, "If you refuse to accept anything but the very best, you will very often get it.")

When my grandfather retired, my parents expanded Legal Sea Foods into the grocery store location, which had so much extra space that they decided to open a restaurant. Their first restaurant venture in Inman Square, Cambridge, was put together for $2,400—and that included buying Frialators, a broiler, and the long tables and benches where people sat and ate family style. I take pride in the handsome table settings Legal now features, but in the beginning we served our food on paper plates with plastic utensils. (There was no money for a dishwasher.) There were also no recipes. We served fish two ways—fried and broiled. In 1967, haddock, our customers' favorite selection, was about fifteen cents a pound wholesale, so we could keep the prices low.

From those humble beginnings as a family fish business, Legal Sea Foods has grown into what I like to call "a family of restaurants." When I took over as CEO and president of Legal Sea Foods in 1992, all of our restaurants were in greater Boston. Now, Legal Sea Foods has expanded along the eastern seaboard to areas such as Washington, D.C., suburban New York City, and south Florida. We've opened nontraditional airport restaurants in Boston and Washington, D.C., and our chowder is served at other airport restaurants nationally. Our locations have quadrupled; we have a staff of nearly 3,000, including executive chefs who offer fish specialties inspired by ethnic as well as regional foods. Thanks to our mail-order division (800–EAT FISH), you can savor a New England clambake and other fish specialties even if you live thousands of miles from Legal Sea Foods.

With all this expansion, our goal has stayed the same. Our customers receive fairly priced, top-quality fish, stored under our famous sanitary conditions, presented with an attention to detail consistent with those of the country's finest restaurants. We've received kudos and awards for the quality of our seafood and our innovative sanitation practices, including *Food Arts'* Silver Spoon Award for our contributions in educating Americans about seafood, and a selection by *Bon Appétit* as one of ten American restaurants that have stood the test of time.

We've also received awards for our sensitivity toward persons with disabilities. We train our employees to be aware of the needs of the disabled, including providing menus in Braille to the blind. We're particularly responsive to persons with allergies. When a customer mentions an allergy—or starts to ask which ingredients are in a dish—it's mandatory that the kitchen pay special attention.

Either the manager or the chef comes to the customer's table and goes over the ingredients included in the dishes the diner has selected. We then take extra steps to insure that there's no cross-contamination with other foods in the kitchen that also might cause an allergic reaction.

A while ago, I went back to school to take the Owner/President Management course for entrepreneurs at Harvard Business School. The program was run by Marty Marshall, a tough curmudgeon similar to the John Houseman character in *The Paper Chase*. At one point in the first session, I was trying to keep my head buried. Unfortunately, I didn't escape. "Berkowitz," he bellowed. "What business are you in?"

My mind started to race. "The restaurant business," I replied.

"You think so," he said. "I want you to do an environmental analysis of your business and turn it in next semester." I spent several weeks doing the research, studying the industry—past, present, and future—and passed in a forty-two-page report complete with graphs and statistics. In front of the class (without opening the report), he waved it in my face and said, "So, Berkowitz, what business are you in now?"

I said, "I'm in the fish business."

He replied, "Good, you did your homework."

I have never forgotten this incident—and it has been the driving force of my life at Legal Sea Foods ever since 1986, when I completed the course. After all, I realized, the key to our success will always be the fish. We're not a restaurant chain that sells seafood. We're a fish company that just happens to run restaurants.

People ask me why we bother to expand. My answer is that each new restaurant gives us yet another opportunity to build on the best of the past even as we head in new directions. Our restaurant menu offerings are a prime example. As always, the core of our menu is simply prepared fresh fish. Now, however, our customers have more options. They still can savor fish simply prepared—or try regional specialties, such as New England Clam Chowder, Baltimore Crab Cakes, or Louisiana Catfish Matrimony. But every Legal Sea Foods restaurant continues to offer the old favorites that customers have been eating for years, such as Smoked Bluefish Pâté or Onion Strings.

We have always had an excellent, fairly priced wine list—and at one time we even had a wine business (see page 178). Our purchasing power allows us to improve the quality of the grapes used to make the wine, while keeping the price down to virtually that charged by a retail wine merchant. We offer flights of fine wine—or even martinis or ports—for the price of one drink. A while ago we added a tea service (including authentic metal Japanese teapots) to the menu.

Ultimately, our challenge is to leverage the buying power we possess as a multimillion-dollar operation to improve what we offer continuously. As I see it, businesses have two choices. Some choose to streamline operations, squeezing efficiencies to make as much money as possible. At Legal Sea Foods, we strive to improve our operations each year. We have the advantage of being a private, family-held business, not a public company that has to give the maximum profit to its stockholders. Thus, we can afford to take a long-term approach that we hope will benefit the consumer.

That includes learning from our employees. As someone who has toiled in every aspect of the restaurant business (no matter how menial), I like to keep in touch with what's happening at each level. We have two advisory councils of employees—one of managers, and another composed of hourly employees, such as our cooks or waiters. They write me a letter on why they'd like to serve on the council, get recommendations from their managers, and then meet with me as a group several times a year to discuss Legal Sea Foods' operations from their perspectives. Each person serves for a year. Some great ideas have come from these sessions. In Baltimore, for example, we opened a seasonal "Crab Joint" in an underutilized area of the restaurant. The Crab Joint is almost a return to our Inman

Square roots. It's very informal. Our customers get some mallets and paper napkins, and they dig into steamed crabs, Maryland style, spread out on newspapers on the tables. The guests enjoy the low-key atmosphere, and so do we. I particularly like the fact that the inspiration sprung from our Baltimore employees.

I remind my staff we all share the same job: the return of the guest, what we call R.O.G. My responsibility is to set the tone so that the managers make their decisions around insuring that this happens. We have succeeded when our guests say, "This meal was great. I can't wait to come back." When this occurs, I tell my staff, then we have all done our jobs.

As you can see, the Legal Sea Foods of the twenty-first century is a constantly evolving business. It seemed only natural after the enormous success of our first cookbook, written by my father, to follow it up with a sequel that explores the new flavors and tastes that our guests have come to enjoy in recent years.

Fourteen years ago, when the first Legal Sea Foods cookbook was published, all of our restaurants offered the same choices. We had kitchen managers rather than chefs. This philosophy changed dramatically in the mid-1990s, when Jasper White joined our staff as Vice President and Executive Chef, a position he held for three years. Jasper White is an exceedingly talented chef, and we were pleased to have him on board. His greatest contribution was to convince me to put chefs and sous-chefs in each restaurant's kitchen, rather than relying upon kitchen managers. This has made a tremendous difference in the choices offered on our menus. With the pooling of all this talent, our customers can now taste the best of the past along with new, creative recipes developed by Executive Chef Rich Vellante and his team of chefs. I encourage each restaurant's executive chef to develop original recipes, usually offered as "specials of the day," many of which are included in this book.

I hope that you enjoy using *The New Legal Sea Foods Cookbook,* and that it becomes a staple in your kitchen.

Selecting and Storing Fish

OUR SLOGAN HAS ALWAYS BEEN, "IF IT ISN'T FRESH, IT ISN'T Legal." Our buyers select the finest fish and shellfish for our restaurants, and we treat it well. It's important that you follow the same standards. Sometimes, that's hard to do because there's no government grading of fish as there is for meat. Meat has to measure up to specific standards, but the only standard for fish is whether or not it is fresh.

In turn, the freshness of fish totally depends upon how skillfully it is handled and how far along in the aging process it has progressed. A fish passes through many hands from the moment it is caught and the time you buy it. Many people don't realize that fish has to age slightly—just like meat. When a fish dies, its muscles tighten up and it goes into rigor mortis, which we call "rigor." By putting their catch on ice as soon as possible, commercial fishermen use this process to their advantage. The longer the fish stays in rigor, the better it keeps. (Rigor is essentially a holding action.) Some large fish stay in rigor between two and four days, while small fish come out of rigor quickly, often in a matter of hours. Many sports fishermen might deny the existence of rigor because they don't ice down their fish immediately after they are caught. Instead, the fishermen either allow the fish to stay in the sun, which prematurely ages them, or troll the fish on lines behind their boats, which also ages them because the water is too warm. Or they don't understand the process and end up eating tough fish, just assuming that the species of fish has a tough texture.

Once a fish comes out of rigor, its muscles relax, and it is ready to cook. *At this point, the fish is at its optimum point of flavor, but also is highly perishable.* Unlike meat, fish have cold-tolerant bacteria that can continue growing even under refrigerated conditions. That's why once the fish gets into your hands you should cook it as soon as possible. Storing fish in the refrigerator can stave off spoilage only for a short while. Fish must be fresh to taste good. Although this statement sounds obvious, you'd be surprised how many people ignore it. They buy fish for dinner, then decide to eat out. A day or two later when they get around to cooking the fish, they grumble that the fish has a mushy texture and ammonia-like flavor. Not surprising. The first rule of cooking fish is to buy fresh fish and cook it the same day.

As a consumer, how can you tell if a fish is fresh or on the verge of spoiling? When I was buying fish for our restaurants, I was always checking the big three: the look, the feel, and the smell. A fresh fish looks bright: The skin is moist and bright; the eyes are clear and bright; and the gills are a bright red. As the fish ages, the flesh dulls and dehydrates, the eyes turn cloudy, and gills darken, eventually becoming a brownish color. If you're buying a whole fish, it should have a shine—almost a slimy look. (In the fish industry, this is called the "butter.") The cavity of a fresh fish has the fresh smell of the ocean; only a fish that is spoiling smells bad. If a fish has a pungent or repulsive odor, it is long past the point of eating. When you press down on the flesh, it springs back. Should the indentations from your fingers remain, the fish is old and you should not buy it.

The same principles apply for filleted fish. Remember that a fish's flesh is about 70 percent water. As a fish fillet is exposed to the air, it starts to dehydrate, loses moisture, and its flesh flakes more easily. A fresh fish fillet has a firm texture. When you buy an uncooked fish fillet that practically falls apart in your hand, you have bought old fish. You can make your life easier if you take the time to locate a good fish store known for high-quality fish. If I were new to an area, I would ask for recommendations from people who like to cook.

Don't count out the large supermarket chains, either, because many supermarkets are upgrading the quality of their fish selections. Know, however, that several large chain stores now sell fish that have been dipped in a salt and/or chemical brine to give them an extended shelf life. These fish keep longer, it's true, but also they end up with a salty, artificial, unpleasant taste.

Legal Sea Foods is all about purity. You'll never find any chemicals or additives in our fish. We never buy brined fish—nor should you. Your fish merchant should be able to tell you how the fish he sells was handled. If he is evasive, examine the fish's surface, a dead giveaway of brined fish. An almost artificially shiny appearance is one tip-off. Also, if you run your hand along the flesh, and it feels slippery, the fish may have been brined.

If you have any distance to go shopping, take along a cooler filled with ice, and store the fish in the cooler until you arrive home. Once there, immediately wrap the fish loosely in waxed paper and put it in the coldest part of the refrigerator near the back (or in the meat compartment) until you are ready to cook it. If your refrigerator tends to dry out food, cover the fish with moistened paper towels. If you live in an area where your only recourse is frozen fish, there's an easy way to check its quality. Take about one ounce of the fish, put it in the microwave, and cook it only until it starts steaming. Smell the fish. Any off odor means that you should return the fish to the market.

Safety Precautions

Legal Sea Foods always has been known for the purity of its seafood and its innovative sanitation practices. Our customers realize that they can eat any kind of shellfish or fish without niggling worries about high bacterial counts, parasites, or dangerous toxins. Not only is our preoccupation with seafood purity good health, it is also good business. Often, customers tell me that our restaurants are the only places where they dare eat raw oysters or clams. Long before the industry was concerned about sanitation and seafood-borne illnesses, we were taking steps to insure our customers' safety.

From the beginning, my father, George, a fanatic about cleanliness, practiced the most rigorous sanitation procedures in the seafood industry. We have always bought the high-priced "top of the catch," considered to be the freshest fish on the market, because it's the last fish caught before the fishing boat returns to the pier. About thirty years ago, when New England was experiencing scares about red tide and shellfish poisoning, we knew our seafood was fresh and safe, but we wanted to go further to instill consumer confidence. At the time, I was operating the Inman Square restaurant, and I arranged for a technical group to come in and spot-check our shipments and facilities. When we opened

The Early Bird

SOMETIMES THE EARLY BIRD gets the worm. When I was buying fish for the restaurants, I always had one eye on the weather, because when fishing boats don't go out in rough seas, supply dwindles and prices go up. In those days before the Weather Channel and the omnipresence of weather forecasters, I had a friend who worked for the weather service who gave me updates on the potential severity of coming storms. On February 18, 1978, he told me a storm was brewing. I had a four-wheel-drive vehicle at the time, and I got it prepared for the day. I also decided to stock up on fish.

At this point, I was the only fish buyer who knew of the potential severity of the storm. I really ended up with the lion's share of the fish coming to market. I went back to Inman Square congratulating myself—a little too soon, as it turned out. I was working and lost track of time. It started snowing, and snowing, and snowing. Pretty soon the streets were deserted. When I went out to the street, I discovered a storm in full spate. Heading home, I was the last person allowed on the Massachusetts Turnpike before it was closed. The Blizzard of '78 had arrived.

I couldn't get to the restaurant for four days. All the fish was spoiled. I was the only restaurateur in the city of Boston who had to throw out tons of fish.

Sometimes you can be too smart for your own good.

a commissary at our headquarters, one of the first things we did was establish an in-house laboratory to check for seafood purity.

Our quality-testing operation includes a state-of-the-art Quality Control Center, with testing facilities and a microbiology laboratory run by a registered sanitarian, as well as a temperature-controlled plant where our seafood is received, tested, packed, and sent to our restaurants.

Although insuring our customers' safety was our primary motivation, our seafood safety practices have become models for both the fish and restaurant industries, and have been featured in national media, such as the *New York Times, National Geographic,* and network television programs. That's why, a few years ago, we were selected for a pilot program set up by the government and industry associations to design the Hazard Analysis Critical Control Points program, known as HACCP. In 1997, this program became a mandatory requirement for all seafood processors (companies that buy and sell fish wholesale). At present, there is no mandatory HACCP plan for retail businesses. However, we have voluntarily set up a HACCP proram for all of our restaurants. We also work closely to promote shellfish safety with the Center for Science and the Public Interest.

We think that being vigilant about seafood purity is far more than common sense. It is essential. The ocean is not a sterile environment. Fish is perishable. Combine these realities with the possibility of improper harvesting or careless handling, and you have the potential for problems. We buy and handle our fish under the strictest of conditions, but, even so, our laboratory runs a wide range of microbiological analyses, including tests for histamines that can cause allergic reactions (often introduced by storing oily fish, such as bluefish or tuna, at improper temperatures); fecal bacteria levels in shellfish that could lead to hepatitis; and the presence of Listeria in cooked seafood products that Legal buys, such as cooked crabmeat and smoked salmon.

Obviously, as a home cook, you don't have our resources. But if you buy from reputable sources and handle your fish properly, the chances of getting sick from seafood are virtually nonexistent. Be cautious—and be sure to follow these suggestions:

When you're selecting seafood, do your research. Only buy from a vendor whose premises are spotless. Any seafood for sale should be iced and held in cold temperatures that will retard the growth of bacteria and the physiological breakdown of the fish. If the personnel are gutting and cutting fish, watch to make sure that they are keeping the flesh separate from the guts, because cross-contamination in the cutting process is easy. (Any knife used to gut fish, for example, should be cleaned before the fish is filleted.) Never, *ever,* buy or eat shellfish from waters of unknown origin. Always consume shellfish that your fish purveyor can prove came from inspected areas. (The government requires tagging, and any reputable fish purveyor can show you a tag of origin.) If you enter a fish market and smell a heavy "fishy" odor, leave immediately. No properly stored fish ever has an

ammonia odor or strong smell. Odorous fish indicate spoilage. Be sure that the employees are using disposable gloves and that they are wearing hats or hairnets. Whole fish should be displayed on a mound of fresh ice, preferably in a case, placed bellies angled down so that any melting ice drains away from the fish, not into them.

After you buy the seafood, handle it just as responsibly as you expect your merchant to have done. Home cooks often unwittingly instigate their own food-borne illnesses. Ice down fish at all times. Ask that the fish market put your fish in a plastic bag with ice, even if you are only traveling a short distance by car. (An inexpensive cooler filled with ice is a wise accessory for food shopping.) Once you get the seafood home, make sure that you immediately place it in the refrigerator, loosely wrapped, in the coldest spot (usually the rear of the bottom shelf). Keeping it in a tightly wrapped plastic bag allows bacteria to grow. Use the fish the same day you buy it. Refrigerate the seafood at all times. It should *never* be left at room temperature. (At our restaurants, all seafood is iced up to the moment it is cooked.) Be mindful of cross-contamination: Never have raw fish anywhere near cooked fish—or near raw vegetables or salad ingredients. If you're cutting up raw fish, be sure to soak your knife and cutting board in a diluted solution of bleach (two tablespoons of bleach mixed with one gallon of water). Also remember to wash your hands for at least twenty seconds after handling raw foods. (Twenty seconds is longer than it seems. To make sure our kitchen staff wash their hands for a long enough period, the sinks near our food-handling areas have timers that go off after twenty seconds.)

I suggest that you invest in two thermometers: an inexpensive refrigerator thermometer to insure that your food is being held at 40° to 41°F, and a quick-temp thermometer to check the internal temperature of the flesh once the fish is cooked. (Fish should be cooked to an internal temperature of 140°F to kill any parasites or bacteria.) If you plan to eat raw fish, if it hasn't been previously frozen, freeze the fish for at least a week at a temperature of minus 10°F, about the coldest temperature most home freezers are capable of maintaining. (Many states mandate that if you're shipping raw fish, with the exception of tuna, it must be frozen first.) Parasites and bacteria are destroyed by heat and extreme cold.

Taking these few precautions allows you the maximum enjoyment of one of nature's most healthful and delicious resources.

Fin Fish

WE OFFER MORE THAN FORTY KINDS OF FISH AND SHELLFISH on our Legal Sea Foods menu. Some are seasonal specialties, while others are available year-round. With few exceptions, the fish come from North Atlantic waters, where I believe the most flavorful fish in the world originate. In this book, we'll give recipes for the fish Legal offers that are readily available to you as a consumer. You will find familiar species, such as cod, and lesser-known choices, such as wolffish—or ocean catfish—one of the most delicious fish in the ocean. If you have a favorite fish I don't mention, decide what kind of texture and flavor it has, and substitute it in our recipes. Mako shark, for example, works well in the swordfish recipes, while tilefish, sea perch, and sea trout are excellent substitutes for white-fleshed fish such as cod or haddock. I'll give you a little background information about each species, and explain about their flavor and texture so that you can make an informed choice at the market.

Let's assume you're standing at the counter of the best fish market in town. The fish looks terrific. It's fresh, and the selection is excellent. You're thinking about making a fish chowder for dinner. Both the haddock and the cusk look good. The cusk has the advantage of costing far less than the haddock—but you don't know much about it. Finally you decide to buy the haddock, and vow to find out more about cusk and try it some other day.

You have just made two of the most common mistakes in cooking with fish—you have selected a familiar standby rather than trying an equally tasty, less-expensive choice, and you have overlooked the texture the finished dish should have.

Haddock is a fine choice for stew. (It's been a fish chowder ingredient for centuries.) As long as you prefer a stew where the fish flakes and disintegrates somewhat, haddock works well. However, if you are aiming for a stew with firm chunks of fish, cusk, a relative of the cod, is a better choice. Cusk has a denser texture than haddock; when it is simmered, it stays intact, rather than falling apart.

Before you shop, try to imagine the ideal flavor and texture the finished dish should have. Then, and only then, select your fish. Many fish have similar flavors and textures and are interchangeable in recipes. Should you have questions about substitutions, your fishmonger should be able to answer your questions. There's a fish to match every style of cooking. If you want a soft-textured fish to sauté and serve with a browned butter sauce, flounder works nicely. For grilling, choose a firm-textured steak such as halibut or tuna that won't fall apart on the grill. The strong flavors of mackerel or bluefish mellow when they're marinated in a tart sauce, particularly with a touch of mustard. Monkfish and cusk are good choices for braised dishes where a firm-textured fish is necessary.

If you haven't eaten much fish, start out cooking a white-fleshed variety such as cod, which has a delicate flavor, rather than a more assertively flavored fish, such as bluefish. Swordfish or tuna are good selections for novice fish eaters because their textures are more like meat than fish. (People who don't like fish will usually eat swordfish or tuna.) Once you become accustomed to the taste of mild fish, then graduate to a species with stronger fish flavors, such as salmon or mackerel. Remember that a fish's size has nothing to do with its degree of tenderness. You might assume that because a fish is larger, it's tougher, but that's incorrect. A filleted thirty-five-pound cod will be just as tender cooked as a three-pound cod.

Arctic Char

If you like salmon, you will love arctic char. (I've never met anyone who didn't like this delicious fish.) Found in cold waters as far away as Mongolia, arctic char is one of the world's premier game fish, but most of the char available at the market is farm-raised. Char is a relative of the salmon, but its orange spots give it a much more colorful appearance. Most of the arctic char found on restaurant menus comes from Iceland, where it is farm raised in huge tanks near the sea. Like salmon, it can tolerate crowded conditions while enclosed in tanks.

Char has become one of Legal's most popular fish choices, with a rich full flavor similar to that of salmon, but slightly sweeter. Its firm flesh makes it ideal for grilling or baking.

Fish and Health

EATING FISH at least twice a week contributes greatly to your health. It's as simple as that. Whether it's the zinc in shellfish, the omega-3 fatty acids in fatty fish such as salmon, or the lower fat profile of many other fish, it is apparent that eating fish or seafood is essential to a healthy lifestyle.

You feel good when you eat fish because it is so easy to digest. It contains a smaller amount of connective tissue than meat and short, rather than long, fibers. The connective tissue of fish breaks down at a relatively low temperature, becoming flaky and easily digested. In addition, fish has little fat. Haddock, for example, has less than 1 percent fat. Fish fat is mainly polyunsaturated and monounsaturated. (Saturated fats, such as those found in meat, cause the cholesterol levels in blood to rise.)

But the main reason to eat fish is their high concentrations of omega-3 fatty acids. Your body can't make omega-3. You can only obtain it from food, such as fish, flaxseed, walnuts, and some forms of soy. Consider the list of ailments that omega-3 is reputed to help: autoimmune problems, such as lupus and rheumatoid arthritis; heart disease; high blood pressure; blood clots; and breast cancer. Researchers are constantly coming up with new possibilities that link a fish (and vegetable) diet to better health.

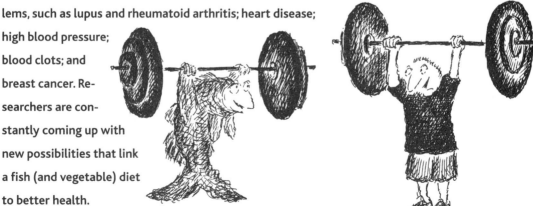

We find char so versatile that our chefs serve it in dozens of ways: over salads, in wraps, or grilled with vegetable accompaniments. The flesh color ranges from pink to dark red, and its high fat content keeps it moist.

Bass

The term bass covers many different fish, including both saltwater and freshwater types. All bass have dense, tender flesh and delicate, fresh flavors. Most of the bass we sell at Legal is saltwater, so I'll concentrate on these varieties.

Striped bass, the largest member of the saltwater bass family, is native from Maine to Louisiana. Its delicate flavor and firm flesh have made it a favorite of chefs worldwide, but for many years it was impossible to buy because of the danger of the fish retaining PCBs from pollutants. The catch is considered safe now, but commercial fishermen are regulated by the Striped Bass Conservation Act as to the quantity and size of fish they can catch. At Legal, we sell only wild striped bass, but fish farmers are raising freshwater striped bass with some success.

The most common bass is sea bass, also known as black bass or blackfish. Black bass, which is often used in Chinese cooking, is an excellent fish choice for steaming. Served with a soy ginger dip, it is a real treat.

Cook bass just about any way. Its dense texture is a little less firm than that of halibut (although halibut is flakier). Try it stuffed and baked, broiled, sautéed, steamed, or poached. You can even grill bass because its texture holds up to this method of cooking.

Bluefish

Found traveling in schools from Maine to Florida, bluefish is one of America's great game fish. Blues hit hard and keep fighting. Perhaps it's that combative energy that gives bluefish its somewhat strong flavor—people seem either to like bluefish or to hate it. One reason people can find the flavor of bluefish too pronounced is that bluefish must be filleted immediately after being caught. Otherwise, the oil-gland flavor seeps into its flesh. Filleted quickly, and properly cared for, bluefish is delicious, with a tender flesh and distinctive flavor that varies in strength depending upon its diet. (Bluefish that eat herring will have the strongest flavor.) Bluefish has the added advantage of being an excellent source of the omega-3 fatty acids that reduce the formation of blood clots and help lower cholesterol levels.

Bluefish's distinctive flavor is accentuated by curing with a hot smoking process. I don't think there's a better fish for smoking than bluefish. It's a rare treat. We use smoked bluefish for our Smoked Bluefish Pâté (page 70), for many years one of our most popular appetizers. At home, you can smoke the fish using a grill with a domed lid, or one of the ceramic smokers that uses wood chips as fuel.

We serve bluefish broiled, grilled, or baked with mustard sauce. It's also delicious oven-steamed with vegetables. When in doubt, you'll find that the savory taste of mustard or the smoky aftertaste of bacon will cut the fish's strong flavor.

Cod

New Englanders value their cod: For centuries, it was one of our region's most plentiful fish. Many a colonial fortune was garnered selling salted cod to other parts of the world. (Even today, salt cod is a staple food in the Caribbean and Africa.) Cod was so important to the Massachusetts economy that back in 1784, a carved wooden statue of the "sacred cod" was hung at the state house. (Anyone who wants to know more about the worldwide importance of cod should pick up a copy of *Cod: A Biography of the Fish That Changed the World,* by Mark Kurlansky. It's a fascinating book for anyone interested in either history or fish.)

The cod family encompasses more than fifty species of fish, which include haddock, cusk—a favorite ingredient in chowders, and fish and chips—and pollock. Cod can grow to more than 200 pounds, although the average size is less than 25 pounds. (Small cod that weigh between $1^1/_2$ and $2^1/_2$ pounds are marketed as scrod.)

Cod has a white flesh, delicate flavor, and a tender, somewhat flaky texture. It can be cooked just about any way—including broiled—but it does tend to fall apart more easily than haddock or cusk.

Flounder

Flounder is a generic term for any number of saltwater fish, including dabs, black backs, and yellowtails. Confusion reigns because there are more than 500 species of flounder, but what they have in common is that they are flatfish. (Sometimes, gray sole is sold as flounder, but it's really a different species.) Flounders have delicate flavors and textures, although their thickness varies depending upon the species. Flounder tends to be firm and meaty, and takes sauces very well. The smaller dabs are very good deep-fried. Try flounder baked and stuffed, sautéed, deep-fried, or steamed. (Be sure to read the section on sole for further information.) Remember that the recipes for flounder and sole are interchangeable.

Haddock

Haddock and cod formed the basis for Legal Sea Foods' acclaim. Haddock has always been one of our most popular choices. True Bostonians really loved their haddock. In the 1950s, it was more plentiful than cod and more popular. When Legal Sea Foods opened, haddock was an inexpensive choice, but those days are long since gone. Now, it's harder to come by than cod.

Haddock is a magnificent fish. It is deservedly popular because it has a mild, pleasant flavor, a beautiful white color, and a medium-firm texture. It's possible to fillet the fish and make it virtually boneless, an advantage for people who dislike eating bony fish. Try haddock grilled, baked, and fried. All ways are equally good, but one of our perennial favorites is broiled with a crumb butter topping (see page 286). But, there's nothing like fish and chips made with haddock—skin and all.

Halibut

Halibut is a member of the flounder family, even though it doesn't look it. Similar to flounder, when a halibut is first born its eyes are on the sides of its head, but as the halibut matures, the eyes move to the top of its head so that it can watch out for enemies as it swims along the ocean floor. It's fascinating that halibut have a dark upper body and a white lower body, which helps them blend into their environment. We buy wild halibut, but in Europe the farm-raised halibut from Iceland has become quite popular.

We've bought halibut that weigh more than 300 pounds, although they usually weigh in between 50 and 250 pounds. Because they're so large and firm-fleshed, halibut are cut into steaks, which makes them an excellent choice for grilling. Cajun-style spicy halibut is one of our best-selling dishes. Try halibut broiled or grilled. (Our Warwick, Rhode Island, restaurant even serves it in sautéed, boneless fillets.) If you're looking for a fish that holds together well, and has bones that are easy to spot, halibut is a good choice.

Mackerel

Mackerel, one of the most prolific fish in the ocean, is certainly among the most beautiful, with its glistening blue-black skin. It is a dark-fleshed fish, with a strong "fishy" flavor that marries well with an acidic sauce or marinade. Europeans know this, and often marinate mackerel in wine or tomato sauces, which temper its strong flavor. Cooked fresh mackerel has a white flesh—not as white as haddock or codfish—but much whiter than bluefish. Eat it as soon as possible after purchasing, because its high fat content makes it spoil faster than leaner fish. This same fat content makes it an excellent source of the omega-3 fatty acids that help reduce the formation of blood clots and help prevent heart attacks. However, as its strong flavor deters many people, it remains one of the least expensive fish to buy. If you eat mackerel frequently, you not only save money; you do great things for your body.

Mackerel is at its best served broiled or grilled, but I've included a recipe for marinated mackerel that has the advantage of staying in good condition for several days in the refrigerator. When you broil the fish at home, place it skin side down and top with a dot of butter before broiling.

One hint: Mackerel has a small bone in the middle of the fillets that you should ask your fish merchant to remove.

Mahi Mahi

At one point this fish was known as dolphinfish (or dorado), but there was such confusion with porpoises and dolphins that fish purveyors started calling it by its Hawaiian name, mahi mahi, which reputedly means "strong strong," referring to its strength, not its flavor. Although the fish is found in Hawaii and Florida, much of what is available on the market comes from Ecuador, where it migrates and is harvested during the winter months.

Sports fishermen prize the fish for its tenaciousness, while cooks value its mild flavor and firm texture. At our restaurants, we usually serve it grilled (often with a tropical fruit sauce), or grilled and sliced in a flour tortilla wrap with a flavored mayonnaise and lettuce and tomatoes. Its pinkish flesh turns gray-white when cooked. Be sure to remove mahi mahi from the heat the minute the flesh is done because it quickly becomes dry.

Monkfish

When I was buying fish down at the pier one day in the early 1970s, one of the vendors had a box all crated up, labeled MONKEY TAILS. "What's that?" I asked.

The vendor said, "You don't want this, but we sell it to France for big money."

Intrigued, I bought some and carted it back to our Inman Square store. Julia Child happened to come in that day, and I asked her if she'd ever seen the fish. "Lotte," she said, excitedly. "Lotte—where did you find it?"

After explaining how prized the fish was in France, she asked me to get her a whole fish. I kept calling my sources and they kept coming up with excuses. A week went by. Two weeks. Finally, I asked my vendor what was causing the delay. "Have you ever seen a whole monkfish?" he asked. He said monkfish were so ugly that the fishermen cut off their heads while at sea, and saved only the tails. I paid him extra to locate a whole fish for Julia.

When the twenty-five-pound fish arrived, it looked like a prehistoric beast. Seventy percent of a monkfish is the head, teeth, and cartilage, covered with a viscous skin. Julia ended up using the whole fish on her cooking show, *The French Chef.* It was pictured in *Time* magazine and in her cookbook, and we have sold monkfish at Legal Sea Foods to an appreciative clientele ever since. (A year ago, at a charity auction, I bought the original tape of this program for our Legal Sea Foods archives.)

That's how we came to be probably the first American restaurant to start using this underutilized fish, often called the poor man's lobster because of its similar texture and mild flavor. The French lotte has a whiter color than our North American counterpart, but the texture and flavor of both species is similar. It's what we call an incidental catch, which means that since they don't run in schools like haddock or cod, the fishermen can count on only what they're lucky enough to catch.

Monkfish is the most firm-textured of any fish, with a mild flavor that makes it adaptable for any number of recipes. You can substitute it in any lobster recipe. Thinly slice it and deep-fry the pieces, quickly sauté them with vegetables, or cube the fish for kabobs. It is also good poached or braised in fish stock. Our fish chowder always includes some monkfish.

Pollock

You've probably eaten pollock without knowing it, because it's used for fish and chips and fish cakes. Sometimes called "Boston bluefish," pollock is one of commercial fishermen's favorite fish because it's absolutely delicious when served very fresh. Otherwise, it tastes terrible because it spoils more rapidly than most fish. It's a tasty, slightly coarse-textured fish, with a dark-hued flesh that turns white when cooked. When it is fresh, the fillets are bright and shiny; when it is on the verge of spoiling, the fillets are dull and have a noxious odor. If you are on a budget, you should try out pollock because it's still one of our least expensive fish.

Fresh pollock is an excellent choice for practically any type of cooking. Just make sure it is super fresh, and I'm sure you'll discover what good eating pollock can be.

Salmon

We all know the story of the wild salmon—how it navigates against tremendous odds to return from the sea to spawn in its freshwater birthplace. The Pacific salmon, the Northwest's most famous fish, has become "endangered" in many historic rivers, and the debate on how to restore the wild stocks is a major political and environmental issue.

Fortunately, we have yet to destroy the habitat for the wild supply that flourishes in the less-populated northern regions of Alaska and British Columbia, where purveyors ship several kinds of wild salmon throughout the world. Wild salmon is famed for its full, rich flavor and its high content of omega-3 fatty acids. Connoisseurs wait for Alaska's Copper River catches, actually three kinds of salmon—king, sockeye (red), and Coho (silver)—that come into season in May. King has the highest fat content and flavor, while sockeye (favored in Japan for its deep red color) and Coho are milder. Also found in these regions are chub and pink (a small-sized salmon predominantly used for canning).

Downeast in Maine, home of the Atlantic salmon, depleted wild stocks mean no commercial harvesting—or even any recreational salmon fishing. However, the Atlantic salmon lives on commercially as the breeding choice of many producers worldwide. Both Pacific and Atlantic salmon are anadromous (fish that spawn in freshwater and also live in seawater), but Pacific salmon die after they spawn, while Atlantic salmon can spawn more than once.

Maine—and Atlantic Canada—have turned to the farming of salmon. The United States lags well behind other countries in salmon farming. Norway leads the world mar-

Wwith the exception of the Pacific Northwest, the majority of filleted salmon sold in the United States is farmed Atlantic salmon, not wild salmon. Chile, Norway, and the United Kingdom produce the majority of the world's farmed salmon, followed by Canada and the United States. It can be difficult to distinguish farmed from wild fillets, except by price. Wild salmon, such as from Alaska's Copper River run, usually command a premium price. Supermarkets often use Chilean salmon as a loss leader (at cost) as a sale item to attract customers. Right now there's a glut of farmed salmon on the world market, leading to inexpensive pricing.

The salmon's color is another indicator. Farmed salmon are fed carotene pigments to deepen their color, which gives them a deep orange hue. On the other hand, wild salmon vary tremendously in color, depending upon the species, from a light pink (pinks) to a deep red (sockeyes).

Whole salmon, on the other hand, are easy to tell apart. A whole Atlantic salmon (the farmed choice) has a sloping head, and the spots on its back resemble little X's. By contrast, wild king salmon has a somewhat squat head, a black mouth, and round spots on its skin.

---

ket, followed by Chile, the United Kingdom, Canada, and then the states of Maine and Washington. Essentially, all salmon farming follows the same pattern.

Commercial Salmon Farming

Fertilized Atlantic salmon eggs are taken to a quarantine facility, where they are kept for two weeks to make sure they are disease free and to check their DNA. Then they go to a hatchery, where they are kept in oxygenated fresh water that is purified to remove waste. They are fed a herring-based fish meal, and once they reach a certain length (about six inches), they are transferred to larger pens, either in seawater in coastal cages, or in enormous fiberglass tanks. The fish continue to get feed, and are not treated with antibiotics unless they are sick. After eighteen months, the fish are ready to harvest.

In addition to their distinctive flavor, both wild and farmed salmon are good sources of protein; omega-3 fatty acids; vitamins A, B, D, E; potassium; iodine; and selenium. In the American wild, salmon feed on herring and smelt (East Coast) or shrimp and krill (West

Coast). In captivity, salmon are fed pellets that include fishmeal and oils. The amount of omega-3 the salmon end up with varies, but most experts agree that farmed salmon that eat a high-quality feed—with plenty of fish components—have omega-3 levels comparable to those of their wild counterparts.

Fresh wild salmon is seasonal, but because farmed salmon is harvested upon demand, it is available fresh year-round.

Salmon is one of our most versatile fish, adapting well to any cooking method (even steaming, poaching, or grilling) because of its high fat content, which also makes it a forgiving choice for inexperienced cooks because it stays moist even when overcooked. You can substitute arctic char for salmon in virtually any recipe.

Scrod

There's no such fish as scrod. Scrod is a nickname given to haddock or cod that weigh less than $2^1/_2$ pounds. When it is sold at the Boston fish auction, the auctioneer calls out, "We have a trip of scrod/cod or scrod/haddock." (Trip refers to the time the boat was out. It's another word for haul.) Generally there is little difference in the taste, but the texture varies. Some of the larger fish are flakier. I prefer a thicker cut of scrod because it retains more flavor.

Both cod and haddock are mild-flavored, white-fleshed fish, which means scrod also has a pleasant, mild flavor and a somewhat flaky texture.

Scrod is delicious cooked practically any way. I like it broiled, grilled, baked, sautéed, or steamed.

Shad Roe

Shad is a coastal fish that comes into the warmer waters of rivers to spawn. It has a mild flavor but it is too bony for most people to enjoy, although you can find shad fillets in Delaware, Maryland, and other mid-Atlantic fish markets. (Oven-steaming works well with shad fillets; or you can dip them in flour, sauté quickly in butter, and serve with lemon or lime squeezed on top. More complicated cooking methods and sauces would overpower shad's delicate flavor.)

Shad, however, contributes one of the great delicacies of regional American cooking—shad roe, available fresh in gourmet shops throughout the country during the early spring. We used shad roe as an ingredient in our first Legal Sea Foods' Chefs' "Culinary Snackdown" (see page 89).

The roe are bigger than you might expect—anywhere from five to six inches long, two to three inches wide, and about one inch thick. When you buy the roe, the double sac of eggs will be covered with a membrane, also forming the connective tissue. Try to keep the membrane intact, or the eggs will splatter all over the pan while cooking.

Traditionally, roe is broiled with bacon, but this method tends to dry out the roe. An easier way is to sauté the roe slowly in bacon fat or butter, and serve with lemon. As the roe may splatter while cooking, cover it with the lid to a steamer pot, which cuts down on the grease while allowing the steam to escape.

Snapper

One of the most delicious southern fish, snapper has a host of wanna-bes, many of which are sold as the real deal. That's because the snapper family contains more than 100 species worldwide, with at least a baker's dozen caught off the Gulf of Mexico and the Atlantic coast of the American south. Cooks savor the delicate taste and the firm texture of the red snapper, which by law in Florida must be sold skin on to prevent the substitution of less-expensive varieties. (To keep fillets from curling when you're cooking them skin-on, score the skin lightly with a knife.)

You can buy snapper virtually year-round. Most of what is available on the market weighs less than ten pounds. Hog snapper (not a real snapper) is both particularly ugly—with large teeth—and particularly delicious. At our Florida restaurants, we prepare snapper in several ways. This versatile fish, which can be fried, broiled, steamed, or baked, also holds its own with hot chile peppers and other tropical ingredients.

Sole

Gray sole is my favorite fish. There's nothing better than fried sole with lemon butter or capers. It is sublime.

Many people call all flatfish sole, but that's inaccurate. The true sole is the Dover sole, a fish we frequently serve at Legal Sea Foods. It is imported into this country from England. In the United States, the members of the sole family are all flounder—regardless of what they're called. Both sole and flounder are members of the flatfish family, but the difference lies in their body shapes: Sole is deeper-bodied with a more elliptical shape, while flounder has a more rounded body. The tendency of fishmongers to lump together all members of the flatfish family under the generic label of sole generates a great deal of confusion on the part of the consumer. In general, sole has a delicate flavor and texture, although its thickness varies considerably, depending upon the species. Some days sole is half an inch thick; other days, one inch.

The most expensive "soles" are gray and lemon sole. Gray sole has the most delicate texture and flavor in the flatfish family, while the texture and flavor of lemon sole are coarser. You will pay twice as much money for either gray or lemon sole as you will for dab, yellowtail flounder, or blackjack flounder.

Sole is one of the strangest fish. It starts life with eyes on either side of its head, but as it begins to grow, the eyes move sideways to the same side of the head. As the fish swims along the bottom of the ocean, both eyes are looking up. (This is similar to flounder; see page 19.) Although sole is usually sautéed or baked, it's also delicious deep-fried, steamed, or broiled—as long as you keep basting it.

Swordfish

Swordfish shines when grilled over a wood fire, which is the usual way we serve swordfish at Legal Sea Foods. Many fish taste delicious grilled, but swordfish tastes best because the grilling process accentuates its unique flavor. The flesh is dense and reddish-colored, turning almost beige when cooked. It's a versatile fish. We grill it both as steaks and kabobs, but it's also tasty sautéed or baked.

It's usually cut into steaks, which is the easiest way to deal with this fish, which can weigh between 200 and 600 pounds. Some vendors pretend that shark is swordfish; the tip-off is that swordfish steaks always have whorls (a pattern in the flesh that resembles the rings on a cross section of a tree). Shark does not. Mako shark's skin also feels like sandpaper when you rub it against the grain.

Swordfish are great game fish, prized by sportsmen. They're speedy, and feisty when caught. Commercial fishermen in the Northeast harpoon swordfish. These are the best-quality fish, and we pay a premium price for them. The Japanese run miles of line with hooks and barbs attached to floating barrels to catch these elusive fish. We only buy mature fish, not pups, the harvesting of which is a disgrace, but fortunately is a rarity.

I've checked with all the sources I know about the consequences of ingesting mercury contained in swordfish. The experts tell me that eating swordfish (and tuna) in moderation, even if you are pregnant, is not harmful.

Tuna

Tuna is a member of the same fish family as mackerel, which means that it is dark-fleshed and oily, but it has a firmer-textured flesh. Sometimes fresh tuna can be almost too lean, so it benefits from an oil marinade, or brushing with oil before cooking. Although bluefin is the most prevalent tuna offered for sale in America, we prefer to offer yellowfin because it has a superior flavor and texture.

Its flesh should be reddish in color. As it sits in the display case, the flesh darkens, turning a brownish color, a tip-off that the fish is old and should not be purchased. When the fish is cooked, the flesh turns brown, so always offer a colorful vegetable or salad with tuna, such as broccoli, sautéed cherry tomatoes, or a marinated cucumber salad. Also, its dense flesh means that a small amount goes far.

Try tuna grilled, broiled, or baked. Leftover tuna is delicious flaked or sliced up in main-course salads. A citrus dressing lightens the flavor.

Wolffish

We should all have a diet as delicious as the wolffish's. As ugly as monkfish, with huge, caninelike teeth (hence the name), wolffish need their teeth to pulverize the sea urchins, oysters, and other mollusks that they favor. In Iceland, where wolffish is prized, it is known as ocean catfish. It can be difficult to find in the United States, but the search is well worth your time. Its firm white flesh is somewhat flaky, with a sweet mild flavor. Usually you'll find the fish for sale as fillets. Because the skin is so tough, it's used for menu covers or wallets, and the head is so ugly, it's removed before it is sent to the wholesalers.

Wolffish takes sauces well, and can be sautéed, baked, oven-steamed, or broiled.

Shellfish

SHELLFISH IS AMERICA'S FAVORITE FORM OF SEAFOOD. LEGAL SEA Foods serves more than 500,000 pounds of shrimp every year—not to mention the staggering amounts of New England lobsters, clams, mussels, oysters, scallops, crabmeat, and squid that our customers put away.

All kinds of shellfish cook in minutes, which makes them excellent choices for the busy cook. Like fish, their flesh is naturally tender. And, like fish, shellfish can be ruined by careless treatment. Cook scallops, shrimp, lobster, or squid too long and they become tough or rubbery. Mussels wizen and lose flavor. Crabmeat loses all distinction. But cook shellfish carefully and you will enjoy flavors that evoke the essence of the sea.

Customers ask me why our scallops, clams, lobsters, and crabmeat taste so much better than those found in southern waters. Northern shellfish are fresh, of course, but there's an equally valid reason why they are so tasty. New England has large areas of un-polluted water, such as Cape Cod, that are teeming with the nutrients upon which shell-fish feed. The bay scallops that come from the clean waters off Cape Cod, for example, have a sweet, almost sugary flavor that is unique in the scallop world. Farther south, pollu-tion has sullied (or destroyed) plankton, the traditional food of many shellfish. If you are what you eat, then these shellfish have been raised on a starvation diet, and their flavor has suffered as a result. (One exception is fresh Florida shrimp, particularly the "hoppers" that have a delicate, sweet flavor Florida natives relish.)

Most shellfish is available year-round, although oysters are traditionally eaten during the winter because they spawn during the warmer months. During that time they are "wa-tery" and their flavor and texture are less satisfactory.

When you're selecting shellfish, the most important factor is to find out where they originated. Everyone has heard a horror story about someone who ate raw clams and came down with hepatitis. It's foolish to take a chance with your health by eating shellfish that might have come from contaminated waters. Bivalve mollusks, such as clams, mus-sels, and oysters, retain the toxins found in their environments, so it's particularly impor-tant to determine where these shellfish originate. And toxins, unlike parasites or bacteria, are unchanged by freezing or cooking.

Only buy from a fish store with shellfish from clean waters. If you are suspicious about where the shellfish originated, ask to see the health tags attached to the packing crates, because shellfish gathered in certified clean areas are tagged by the appropriate state inspection agency. Before buying, smell the shellfish, and if they have any odor whatsoever, put them back and do your purchasing elsewhere.

Many people limit their consumption of shellfish because they have heard that all shellfish contain high amounts of cholesterol. That's not so. In the past, inaccurate testing methods measured the amount of cholesterol in shellfish. More recent testing uses gas chromatography, which has shown that about 40 percent of the sterols in filter-feeding shellfish is cholesterol and the other 60 percent is plant sterols, which are not harmful to your health. In practical terms, this means that any shellfish that eat algae, such as oysters, clams, mussels, and scallops, are low in cholesterol. Lobsters, shrimp, crabs, and squid, on the other hand, feed on other forms of animal life and have higher choles-terol levels.

Try to use shellfish the day you purchase them. As with fish, if shellfish are kept too long before cooking, they lose moisture from their flesh. A really fresh oyster, for example, is chock-full of liquid. When you open one that is dried out, you know that it either is old or has been stored on its side so that the liquid has drained away. Either way, it's an infe-rior oyster and should be discarded.

Clams

A seaside clambake is a traditional New England ritual, in which prodigious numbers of clams and lobsters are cooked in a pit dug in the sand. Preparation for a clambake starts hours before the actual cooking. The pit is lined with large stones, then filled with firewood that burns down to coals and heats the stones. Once the stones are hot enough, the pit is layered with wet seaweed, clams, lobsters, corn—and even chicken—that steam in the heat retained by the stones. Steamed clams, lobsters, and all the trimmings make the meal that generations of New Englanders have proclaimed the ideal choice for a summer day on the beach. An abbreviated, indoor version of a clambake is always a popular choice at our restaurants.

Savoring a clambake has been part of the American culinary experience ever since the Native Americans first taught the Pilgrims how to steam shellfish in seaweed. Clams were once one of the most abundant foods in the New World. Several kinds of clams are indigenous to America, the most common of which are the hard- and soft-shell types. In New England, hard-shell clams, gathered by raking or dredging below the low-tide level, are often called by their Native American name of *quahog* (pronounced co-hog). Because the texture of large quahogs is tough, they're best chopped up for chowder or stuffing. Quahogs generally range from three to six inches. Smaller clams, known as littlenecks and cherrystones, are tender enough to eat raw.

Soft-shell clams, more commonly known as steamers, burrow into mud or sand near to shore and are gathered at low tide when their airholes are visible. Clammers gather soft-shell clams by the bucket, and then steam them and dip into their cooking liquid and butter.

Fifty years ago, when my father started Legal Sea Foods, clams were a common, inexpensive commodity. But pollution and overharvesting have taken a toll. The growing scarcity of clams prompted companies to start cultivating hard-shell clams commercially in places such as the Florida coast. These businesses raise the clams in a hatchery for four to six months, and then transfer them to a protected area to complete their growing cycles. Under ideal conditions, a hard-shell clam will mature in three years, rather than the five to eight years it would take in the wild.

At the restaurants, we keep our clam offerings simple. Perhaps our best-known clam dish is our chowder, which owes its hearty flavor to generous amounts of hard-shell clams and cream, but many customers opt for our fried or steamed soft-shell clams. If you're uncertain about which type of clam to buy, remember that for frying and steaming, soft-shell clams (steamers) would be your choice, while for chowders, baked stuffed clams, stuffing, or raw clams, select hard-shells.

lams will live for days after they are dug, but they must be stored properly under
onditions. When shipped, clams should be layered flat to keep their juices from es-
. Really fresh clams have tightly closed shells. Any soft-shell clam that has its neck
g limply out of its shell should be discarded. It is dead. When in doubt, poke the end
lam's neck. A clam that is alive will move its neck slightly.

Hard-shell clams are rarely gritty, but if you are preparing steamers, you will want to clean them as thoroughly as possible before cooking. You might have read that clams will disgorge their grit if soaked in water with a sprinkling of cornmeal on top. I don't know where this old wives' tale originated; not only will the clams fail to purify themselves, but also they will die if they stay too long in the fresh water.

The best way to clean sandy steamers is to scrub their shells with a stiff kitchen brush, rinsing each one off before placing it in the steaming pot, and then, once all the clams are steamed, to take some of the clam broth and serve it along with the clams. Dip the steamed clam first into the broth to clean it, and then into melted butter. If you are frying clams, remember that the grit is found in the clams' bellies. Some fish markets sell clam strips, which are the grit-free necks. (We always fry whole clams, not the strips, because the bellies are the real delicacies.) Whatever sand whole clams contain is easily compensated for by their delicious flavor.

Crabs

We're fortunate that the blue crab is native along the coast from Maine to Florida, be-cause its sweet, delicate flavor makes blue crab one of America's most delicious seafood delicacies. The amount of "meat" in this crab varies from north to south. Northern crabs are smaller with less meat; southern crabs are packed with meat, but are less flavorful. (One reason, I suspect, for the ubiquitous crab boil used throughout the south, which masks the flavor of the crabs.) Regardless of where you live along the coast, crabs are most plentiful during the summer. Few markets sell fresh crabs, so look for refrigerated picked fresh crabmeat usually sold in eight-ounce containers. One caution—this crabmeat is ex-ceptionally perishable and should be used immediately. You can often find cooked jumbo or lump crabmeat that has been pasteurized in gourmet shops.

The soft-shell crabs of Maryland and Virginia are blue crabs in transition. During molt-ing season (the time when crabs shed their hard shells), their new shells are paper thin. At this point almost the entire crab is edible. They're delicious either deep-fried or floured and sautéed in butter. All you need to do is to cook them carefully.

Florida's stone crabs are another seasonal delicacy. Stone crabs are usually sold pre-

Most fish markets now sell cleaned soft-shell crabs. Occasionally, however, you'll run across a batch of live crabs. Be assured, however, that they have an elementary nervous system, and after the first cut, they are dead.

A pair of kitchen shears is essential for removing the eyes, mouth, and gills. Numb the crabs by placing them in the freezer spread out on a jelly-roll pan for about five minutes. (Any longer, and they'll freeze to death.) Place the crabs on a counter, and cut them across the face at an upward angle to remove the eye sockets and the lower mouth. Then, lift up the taillike apron and trim off the gills. Cut off the apron. Everything remaining is edible.

---

cooked, and are eaten either hot or cold. You eat only the legs rather than the entire crab. When the crab is caught, one leg is removed, and the crab is tossed back into the water where it will regenerate another leg.

We have always sold Alaskan king crab at the restaurants (see my recipe on page 105). When you buy this meaty, delicious crab, be sure to soak it to remove some of the brine in which it is customarily packed. Don't, by the way, confuse this with the Dungeness crab, also found in the Pacific Northwest. The Dungeness crab, which has a finer texture and flavor than the Alaskan crab, can be found occasionally at specialty fish markets.

One of the most popular "crabmeats" isn't crab at all. The imitation crabmeat sold by virtually every supermarket in America is pollock that has been processed and pressed into leglike shapes. Don't expect any real flavor, because many of the nutrients have been leached out in the processing. At first glance, this product may appear to be less expensive than the real thing, but you're really buying fiber with chemical additives. Legal Sea Foods has never sold imitation crabmeat. We don't buy it, nor should you.

Lobsters

Virtually a symbol of New England's seafood bounty, lobster is one of our most popular items. I sometimes think that every tourist who comes to the Northeast wants to sample a Maine lobster. And no wonder. Lobsters are the prime delicacy of the shellfish family.

Once so plentiful that fishermen used them as bait, the native North American lobster is prized around the world as a delicacy.

Legal sells so many lobsters that every one of our restaurants has its own lobster tank to hold the lobsters under optimum conditions. We make our own storage water, carefully formulated to match the composition of ocean water.

Next time you eat a lobster, consider the number of years it spent growing large enough for you to enjoy. It takes five to eight years, for example, for a lobster to grow to one pound in weight. Size actually is the determining factor. A lobster weighs about one pound when it measures $3^3/_{16}$ inches from its eye sockets to the end of its main body segment (known as the carapace). Most coastal states have adopted this length as the minimum legal size for a lobster. There is no restriction on selling large lobsters. I always keep a few large lobsters on hand for customers with giant-sized appetites.

Most people, however, prefer lobsters that weigh between $1^1/_2$ and 2 pounds. Lobsters are graded by weight. The grades you're most likely to see are a "chicken" lobster weighing in at 1 pound; a "quarter," $1^1/_8$ to $1^1/_4$ pounds; "select," $1^1/_4$ to $1^3/_4$ pounds; "deuces," $1^3/_4$ to 2 pounds; "small jumbo," $2^1/_4$ to $2^1/_2$ pounds; and "jumbo," more than $2^1/_2$ pounds.

Often, our customers request "chicken" lobsters, thinking that the smaller the lobster, the more tender the meat. That's not necessarily so. A lobster moves through the water by pushing its tail backward. If it flips its tail often enough, its meat can toughen. Think about it. A baby chicken lobster is moving around constantly, while an older (and larger) lobster is more likely to spend time sitting around and eating. When you eat the big chunks of meat in a five-pound lobster, you're benefiting from its indolence. However, at a certain point, lobsters age and their flesh loses consistency and becomes almost stringy in texture. That's why I don't recommend buying a lobster larger than fifteen pounds.

Buy live lobsters only. A lobster in its prime is blue-black in color and is active. Its tail should curve under its body when you pick it up, not hang flaccidly. If the lobster seems sluggish, watch out, because it's probably near death. That's really a problem, because a dead lobster spoils quickly and its meat becomes almost like sawdust as it disintegrates in texture. Also, if you're buying lobster during the summer when the lobster molts, ask for hard-shell lobsters. Often when lobsters are unusually inexpensive, it's because they're shedding their shells. At that time there is less meat—and the flesh is softer. Lobsters take about a month after shedding their shells to regain a firm texture. If in doubt, grab the lobster by the back of the shell. Then squeeze the shell with your thumb and forefinger; a hard shell stays rigid, while a soft shell will give a little.

If you don't want to serve the lobster immediately, it's possible to keep it in the refrigerator overnight. The lobster will stay in good condition for twelve to eighteen hours if placed in a paper bag with holes punched in it. Adding seaweed also helps. Under no circumstances should you put the lobster in a bucket of fresh water. It will drown.

Eating a Lobster

Eating a boiled lobster starts with standing over the sink and piercing the lobster's body to remove some of the water from its chest cavity. Otherwise, the minute you start to take the lobster apart, the water in the cavity will splash all over you. If you want to keep the lobster whole for appearance sake, just pierce the underside; otherwise, twist the tail from the chest so that the water can drain out of the chest cavity. Then put the lobster on a serving platter and go to town. Be sure to gather up plenty of dish or paper towels, and if you have a batch of aprons or bibs that's good, because eating a lobster is a messy process.

You can use a meat pounder or hammer to crack the shells, but nutcrackers work best. Lobsters' shells vary in density. Before molting, their shells may be so hard that you'll need a hammer to crack them, while immediately after molting, their shells are so soft you can tear them apart with your fingers.

Remove the large claws and crack the shells. Crack the knuckles, if necessary. Holding the lobster in one hand, grab the tail with your other hand and bend the tail until it breaks free. Then, using kitchen shears or a knife, slice through the soft shell underneath the lobster so the tail meat is easily removed. Take the meat from the tail and the claws.

Lobster connoisseurs know that some of the tastiest and most tender meat is

contained in the lobster's body. Hold the body with the eyes facing down and pull on both sides of the shell where the body cavity opens. The upper part of the shell will break off, leaving the carcass with its sweet-tasting meat that's contained between the cartilage. You'll notice a soft green substance in the carcass. That's the lobster's liver (known as tomalley), and it's delicious stirred into a dipping sauce of melted butter and lemon juice. (Some Maine lobster pounds sell the tomalley by the pound to be eaten plain with a squeeze of lemon or lime or spread on a cracker as a delicacy.) Sometimes, you'll see some red roe (lobster's eggs), which are also edible.

Discard the stomach sac in the head found right behind the eyes, and the feathery gills above the cartilage. A nutpick is the most useful tool to extract the tender meat between the cartilage. The easiest way to enjoy the meat in the little legs is to pull the pieces through your teeth to squeeze it out.

Dip the lobster meat into melted (drawn) butter or eat it plain with a squeeze of lemon or lime. If you have guests, put out bowls of warm water, halved lemons, and plenty of guest towels so that people can clean their hands.

Cook lobster any way you wish, but leave it in the spotlight. Lobster tastes best when other ingredients do not overshadow its sweet flavor.

Mussels

Mussels or moules? Call mussels by their French name, and one of America's most plentiful and inexpensive shellfish suddenly sounds chic—evoking thoughts of Paris, where a bowl of steamed Moules Marinières, a loaf of bread, and a bottle of white wine is traditional bistro fare. The French have always known what Americans are beginning to discover: Few foods can match the virtues of this humble mollusk.

A few years ago, you couldn't give mussels away. Many cooks wouldn't eat mussels, and when they did get adventurous and tried them, too often the mussels were puny and filled with grit. Cultivated mussels have changed everything. North American mussel farming began only in recent years, particularly in New England, Washington State, and Atlantic Canada. Wild mussels still constitute the majority of the harvest, but if you can find a reliable source of cultivated mussels, try them. Most grow on either posts or ropes suspended in tidal waters, or in protected coves. Depending upon how carefully they're raised, cultivated mussels grow faster, are freer from grit, and usually lack the calcified "pearls" sometimes found in their wild counterparts. Before purchasing mussels, ask to see the obligatory inspection tag—date-coded with the month and year—that guarantees that they are harvested from pollution-free waters. Once harvested, mussels have a shelf life of seven to ten days.

Knowing the water conditions is particularly critical, because mussels are stationary feeders that eat by filtering plankton and diatoms out of the water they ingest. (A mature mussel can filter between ten and fifteen gallons of water a day.) Obviously, pollutants and toxins can contaminate them—one reason mussels are off-limits during red tide season. Their flavor is best just before spawning.

In the wild, mussels most often resemble a tangled mass of barnacles, with blue-black shells and hairlike secretions. Each mussel attaches itself to a surface with its byssus—a fiberlike substance also known as a beard. (This "glue" is reputed to be twice as strong as any known epoxy.) Cultivated mussels usually come with the beards removed.

Sometimes the mussel shells are gaping open when you buy them. To insure that the mussels are alive, smell them and discard any with an off odor. Unfortunately, even one spoiled mussel can contaminate others stored nearby, so you may have to throw out a whole batch if you detect spoilage. Store mussels in a colander, so that if one is bad, its juice will drain out rather than contaminate all the mussels nearby.

We use mussels that are about two inches long in our restaurants. Smaller ones require too much manpower to extract just a small amount of meat. To clean mussels, scrub their shells with a stiff brush to dislodge any mud or barnacles. (Cultivated mussels will need less effort.) To remove the beardlike byssus, hold the mussel in one hand and the byssus in the other. Yank up with a swift motion. Or you can remove it with a knife. Rinse under cold water.

The fact that mussels are flavorful and cook in minutes is a boon to any cook. But mussels are also exceptionally healthful. They have one-third more protein than oysters, contain the highest amount of omega-3 fatty acids found in shellfish, and because their main diet is phytoplanktons, rather than other fish, they are low in cholesterol and saturated fats. New Zealanders even use Lyprinol, an extract from mussels, to treat arthritis and asthma.

I think mussels' delicate flavor is best appreciated when they are prepared simply. Steamed mussels are perennial favorites at our restaurants, as is our Mussels au Gratin appetizer. Mussels are also an excellent ingredient in seafood pastas and cold shellfish salads. Surprisingly, although mussels have a sweet delicate taste, they hold their own when juxtaposed with strong seasonings such as the hot chile peppers used by Thai cooks. Even past their prime, mussels look—and taste—all right. However, their flavor dissipates in storage. When you've savored a batch of freshly harvested mussels, you've experienced the salty taste of the sea overlaid with a touch of sweetness (created by mussels' glycogen concentrations).

Oyster Power

Y OU'VE HEARD THE OLD ADAGE "Eat fish, live longer—eat oysters, love longer," and you've probably thought to yourself: Yeah, another old wives' tale.

Not so fast. There's more to this adage than you might think.

Several years ago, a nutritionist named Neil Solomon published a study about men and prostate problems. Solomon studied two groups of men over forty. The first group was a bit lethargic, with low sex drives and little motivation. The men in this group typically ate no shellfish and subsequently had little zinc in their systems.

The second group, however, was another story. These men were highly motivated, with normal sex drives and some pretty fair athletic prowess. They also had little evidence of prostate problems. These men also were fond of consuming raw New England shellfish, which contain more zinc than any other natural food product. The study concluded that when males ingest high doses of zinc, they substantially lower their chances of prostate problems. The study also pointed out that zinc was found to react positively on the male prostate, enhancing energy output and stamina levels.

I was intrigued. Noel Solomon, a Massachusetts Institute of Technology researcher (no relation to Neil), also was interested in the study and contacted me to see if I knew any professional athletes.

So, I approached Tom Hoffman, who was in the front office of the New England Patriots football team. I explained about the study and asked if he knew of any players who might be willing to eat oysters prior to games. Tom polled the players, and asked me if I could supply oysters for the team meal prior to home games. (The Patriots were doing rather poorly at that point, so I am sure Tom felt that the oysters couldn't hurt.)

That first Saturday, I arrived with the oysters and only about six players showed any interest. Among them were John Hannah, Pete Brock, Steve Nelson, and Don Hasselback. The next day those players had great games—so good that Hoffman called me immediately to say that the players wanted more oysters the following week.

I continued to supply the team for all home games that season. Without fail, those who ate the oysters performed better than their fellow players. I'll always remember one particular game the Patriots had with the Jets. As it took place in New York, I hadn't expected to supply

them with oysters. Tom called and asked if there was any way I could pack the oysters and send them along with the team to New York.

We decided to shuck the oysters into plastic containers and dispose of the shells, as they could be messy and somewhat cumbersome. I was home that Sunday and watched the game on television. One player in particular was having a spectacular game. In fact, according to the announcer, he was having the game of his career.

The next day, I received a call from a rather concerned Hoffman. "Were those oysters all right?"

"They were fine," I replied. "Why?"

Well, Tom said, after eating the oysters, Hasselback felt a bit light-headed and queasy. "How many oysters did he eat?" I asked. Tom said he wasn't sure because the oysters were shucked. When Tom checked with Hasselback as to how many plastic containers he had gone through, I was floored by the answer. Hasselback was feeling a bit queasy because he had eaten eight dozen oysters.

The man was on a zinc high!

Oysters

A good oyster has a fresh, briny flavor. Many people prefer to savor oysters raw on the half shell, but they're also delicious dipped in batter and fried, cooked up in a simple stew, baked in a sauce, or used as a stuffing ingredient for fish or poultry.

Oysters are found in the shallow waters along the coast of the North American continent. The oysters we harvest in this region range from two to four inches long, while those from the West Coast tend to be larger, except for the tiny Olympia oysters from Puget Sound in Washington State. In season, our raw seafood bars offer a choice of oysters from both coasts. The size and taste of oysters vary depending upon the location in which they grow. I'm partial to the Cotuit oyster found on Cape Cod, one of the best-tasting oysters in the world.

For centuries, people have eaten oysters as an aphrodisiac. Similar to many a piece of folklore, this has a basis in fact. New England oysters have an unusually high content of zinc, an element that affects energy and sexual potency, among other things. (See Oyster Power, page 38.)

As with any other shellfish, make sure that you are eating oysters from protected waters. If in doubt, ask to see the tags of origin. If the oysters have an off odor—either closed or open—they are spoiled and should be discarded. Properly packed oysters will last in storage about a month, but they should be packed top side up and stored flat, the way they were packaged when they were sent halfway around the world by ship during the last century. When oysters are packed sideways, they lose their liquid and spoil faster.

Shucking Oysters

Removing oysters from their shells (shucking) is not difficult, but it does take practice. The thickness of the shell depends upon the type of oyster. Belon oysters, native to France, are difficult to shuck because they have a thin, delicate shell that breaks easily when you try to open it.

Regardless of the type of oyster, you should always protect your hands with rubber or cloth kitchen gloves, because it's easy for the oyster knife to slip or for you to cut yourself on the shell. Using an inexpensive oyster knife that you can find at fish markets or kitchen supply stores is the best way to shuck oysters. Or, failing that, you can maneuver with a table knife and then a screwdriver. Don't under any circumstances use a sharp kitchen knife.

As you might expect, the fresher the oyster, the more difficult it is to open. One trick that works is to heat the oysters in a microwave for a few seconds, just long enough to heat their shells. Or you could place the oysters in the freezer for about five minutes, which also lulls them into relaxing their muscles.

You can shuck oysters two ways. The fastest way is to hold the oyster in one hand and open it with the other, but that takes practice. If you're a beginner, learn using a towel. The technique isn't important; however, try not to cut up its (or your) flesh in the process.

Take an oyster and place the curved part of its shell in the palm of your hand. The halves of the oyster shell are tightly closed, and it can be difficult to pry them apart with a knife. Locate the seam, insert the point of the knife into it, and wriggle the knife back and forth. If you're successful, the oyster shell will open a crack and you will be able to finish the process using your hand. Be sure to hold the oyster level at all times so that you don't lose its liquid. Next, run the knife along the top shell to release the oyster into the bottom half of the shell. Pull off the top shell and discard it. Scoop out the oyster flesh with the knife.

If you're timid about this process, try the towel technique. All this means is that you use a kitchen towel to hold the oyster. Shield your hand with a kitchen towel, grasp the oyster, and hold it down on the kitchen counter. (The towel will keep it from slipping.) To find the seam, look at the back of the oyster where the hinge is. Insert the knife in the hinge and pry up the shell to separate the top from the bottom shell. Then, follow the instructions above. Or, kitchen supply stores sell a plastic protective half glove.

Raw oysters, served on the half shell with cocktail or hot sauce and a lemon wedge, are the number one oyster preparation at our restaurants. I like oysters best that way. I also think that Green Tabasco is a sensational condiment with oysters because its pickled, hot flavor brings out the oysters' briny taste. If you prefer your oysters cooked, try scalloping, stuffing, or braising them in a stew.

Scallops

Scallops have a wonderful characteristic. Cooked for just a moment, scallops always stay tender. (Unfortunately, when they're overcooked, they become rubbery.) Their tenderness is surprising, because in America we only eat the muscle. (Europeans savor the roe, which is discarded here.) The muscle become disproportionately large because of the way scallops travel through the water, moving their shells together, expelling a jet of water.

At the market you'll basically find two kinds of scallops: large sea scallops caught miles out at sea that are available year-round, and tiny bay—or Cape—scallops that live in shallow coastal waters and are available during the winter months in the north.

Bay scallops will never get as large as sea scallops because they're an entirely different kind of scallop. The famous Cape Cod scallops inhabit waters that are continually flushed with high tides, which helps keep the water clean. For some reason, the sugar content of scallops seems to be higher when they are traveling through unpolluted waters. When you cook Cape scallops, they brown quickly and taste almost sugary. As they get older, they lose that sweet flavor and take longer to brown, one way to tell how fresh they are. Scallops from other parts of the country never brown as fast, and never seem to have as much flavor.

Similar to other shellfish, bay scallops are now being grown commercially. It makes sense to grow scallops commercially because if they are not harvested after a couple of years, they die.

Many supermarkets sell Calico Bay scallops, found in Florida's waters and shipped around the country. We don't use them in our restaurants because they are already slightly cooked by the time they reach the consumer. These scallops are so tiny that in order to open them easily, the processors steam them for a few moments which causes the scallops to lose some of their juices and flavor.

Try to buy fresh scallops, which are far preferable to the frozen kind. If you live in an area where markets stock only frozen scallops, cook them while they are still partially frozen. Once they thaw out completely, the scallops have lost too much of their juices. One caution: Some purveyors soak shucked scallops in water or a phosphate solution. This increases the volume by almost a third and whitens the flesh, but diminishes the flavor.

Scallops cook almost immediately, which makes them a boon for the busy cook. But cook them barely at all, otherwise they'll become tough and rubbery. Tiny bay scallops are most at risk for poor cooking procedures.

Shrimp

Shrimp are the most popular shellfish we serve at Legal Sea Foods—and probably the most popular shellfish in America. People who won't touch any other form of seafood will devour shrimp. They're delicious, it's true, but part of the reason they're so popular is that they're so consistently available—and so familiar. Virtually no matter where you go, you can find shrimp on the menu. (Shrimp inhabit all the oceans of the world.) But the majority of shrimp you find at restaurants and at the markets are not ocean shrimp. They're most likely farm-raised in freshwater ponds thousands of miles from the United States in countries such as Thailand, which now is the leading producer of farm-raised shrimp anywhere. Many of the tiger shrimp served in America originate there. (Other major producers are Ecuador, Indonesia, the Philippines, and India.) Shipping shrimp from afar is easy because they have the advantage of freezing well. (Unlike most other shellfish, shrimp have enough body texture so that they don't deteriorate when frozen.)

There's nothing sweeter tasting than a wild fresh southern shrimp, such as the hopper, harvested off the Gulf Coast of Florida and Louisiana. I suspect that watching shrimp boats head out to sea may soon be a pleasure of the past. Freshwater shrimp farming is the fastest-growing sector of the world's aquaculture industry. Farmed shrimp are uniform in size, consistent in quality and flavor, and are available year-round. (If the farms are poorly maintained, however, wastes from the ponds pollute the environment.)

Regardless of whether they're farmed or wild, the grading of shrimp is the same. Shrimp are graded by the average number of shrimp per pound. The larger the shrimp, the higher the price. The most expensive shrimp are "jumbo," no more than ten per pound. Average-sized shrimp are about fifteen to twenty per pound, and smaller shrimp, twenty-one to twenty-five. Shrimp continue to be graded in size as they get smaller, but most retail shops don't stock the smaller-sized shrimp, often sold to restaurants as "popcorn" shrimp.

Most shrimp you buy at the market are previously frozen, unless you're lucky enough to live near one of the shrimping areas. Whether fresh or previously frozen, shrimp should have a nice, shiny sheen. When shrimp have been standing in the store case too long, they appear dull. Good-quality shrimp also should look clean, with no dark marks on their shells, a sign of deterioration. The shrimp should smell fresh. If there is any ammonia off odor, don't buy them. Any ammonia odor whatsoever means that the shrimp are on the verge of spoiling. When you store them at home, place the shrimp in a colander, layered with ice, within a larger bowl. Shrimp deteriorate standing in water. If you leave them in a plastic bag stuck into the meat compartment and the bag leaks, the shrimp odor is hard to remove. (Baking soda and elbow grease do the job.)

Shrimp are extremely versatile. Most Americans' favorite shrimp dish is still the shrimp cocktail (try a squeeze of lime juice or a soy-and-sesame-sauce mixture for a change from cocktail sauce). We serve shrimp every which way—steamed, broiled, fried, sautéed, in pasta dishes, and with rice. The simple shrimp dish I developed years ago with jasmine rice and broccoli (page 221) is still my favorite, and a favorite of our customers. You'll find several shrimp recipes in this book, reflecting its popularity with both our customers and our chefs.

Squid

Believe it or not, squid are shellfish. They have plasticlike internal shells known as quills (or pens), rather than external shells. Squid also contain ink sacs filled with a black fluid that is ejected through a siphon. The ink clouds the water, allowing them to escape from enemies. (Remember a few years ago when every upscale restaurant had its version of the Italian squid ink pasta?) Although squid move through the water using their fins, they also use their siphons to eject water and travel in the opposite direction. Their eyes dart in all directions, so they can see their enemies easily.

People in the Mediterranean countries, such as Italy, Spain, and Greece, utilize squid to the fullest, but Americans have been slow to appreciate what good-tasting and versatile shellfish they are.

I think the problem stems from the way most people prepare squid, which cook in only a minute or two (less when fried). Wait any longer and their texture is ruined. Squid have a firm texture to begin with, and when they are overcooked, their texture becomes like rubber bands.

Fresh squid is distinguished by its color, which is creamy. Don't buy pinkish-colored squid. It is old. Fresh squid tastes bland, so frying is a good cooking choice. Squid is also delicious as part of a marinated salad—or stuffed and braised in a liquid.

Cleaning Squid

Most fish purveyors will clean whole squid for you, but it's easy to do at home. All you need is a knife and a spot near a sink so you can rinse the squid and the countertop as you're working. And be sure to clean utensils and the countertop with a bleach solution once you're done (see page 13).

Lay the squid down on a counter. Holding the body with one hand, grasp the head and the tentacles firmly with the other hand, and pull outward. The head, tentacles, and pulpy intestines will detach from the body, often called the "hood." Cut off the eyes and intestines from the tentacles and toss them out. Unless you plan to use the ink sac for a sauce, discard it as well.

Examine the tentacles. At the point where they are attached to the head, you will notice a hard brown mass smaller than a fingernail. This is the mouth. If you squeeze this part of the tentacles, the mouth will pop out. Discard it. You will be left with a tubelike body cavity and the tentacles, both of which are edible.

Put your hand into the body cavity and pull out any remaining intestines as well as the transparent bone. Rinse out the body cavity. Place the squid on the countertop and scrape off the grayish skin with a knife blade. This is easy to do after the initial scrape; usually the rest of the skin peels right off.

If you wish a tubular presentation, detach the fins attached along the bottom half of the squid, making sure you do not puncture the body cavity. Otherwise, leave them on. Once you have rinsed and dried the squid, it is ready to cook.

Basic Cooking Techniques

FISH COOKED SIMPLY REMAINS THE NUMBER ONE CHOICE OF OUR customers. They realize, as we do, that when fish is truly fresh, its flavor stands alone. Fresh fish that's grilled—or baked—and served with a touch of butter or lemon juice is gourmet food in the best sense of the word. At Legal Sea Foods you can buy fish wood-grilled, broiled, steamed, baked, deep-fried, or sautéed. We use several cooking methods because the way fish is prepared is often a matter of personal preference. Many fish are so versatile that you can cook them several ways, while a few fish taste best when prepared with a specific technique. If you master the following cooking techniques, you'll be able to cook any fish or shellfish in the ocean.

Removing Fish Bones

THE BONES IN canned sardines and salmon add calcium to your diet, but when you're eating fresh fish fillets, you want them to be bone-free. Most fish markets carefully remove any bones, but if you're filleting your catch—or just want to be on the safe side—you can check for bones in just a moment.

Hold each fillet skin side down and slightly fold the outside edges skin to skin. Any bones will be quite apparent. You can easily take them out with a pair of needle-nose tweezers that you use only for removing bones from fish. Before washing and drying the tweezers, soak them in a diluted bleach solution.

However, poorly cooked, even the best fish in the world will be ruined. Cod that's baked in an oven at just the right temperature for just the right time will be moist and flavorful. The same cod, placed in the same oven and baked ten minutes too long, will come out dry and tasteless. The most important aspect of cooking fish is the care with which you treat it, not the method you use. There's no reason why you can't prepare fish that's the equal of that found at our restaurants. All you need is a source for quality fresh fish and attention to detail while cooking.

The most common mistake people make in cooking fish is to treat it like meat. Meat flesh is formed with long bundles of muscle and connective tissue that often need to be pounded or cooked for a long time with moist heat to become tender. Fish, on the other hand, is naturally tender because its connective tissue and muscles are shaped in short fibers. Fish also contains considerably less connective tissue than meat. As fish's flesh is tender before it's cooked and remains tender when it is properly prepared, it's unnecessary to cook fish for a long time to tenderize it. Cook fish only to the point when it's done. Past this critical moment, the tissue in the flesh dries out. You can *never* make fish more tender by overcooking it, but you can make it dry or tasteless. Similar to meat, fish continues to cook after it is removed from the heat.

Regardless of the method, you should cook fish just until it has lost its translucency and turned opaque—no longer. Novice cooks often test for doneness by waiting until the flesh flakes when tested with a fork. Fish cooked to this point is overcooked. (If you tend to overcook fish, buy a thicker piece of fish, such as a salmon steak, rather than salmon fillets—or a piece of cod, rather than a fillet of sole, which cooks almost immediately. Also, a fish with a high fat content, such as arctic char or bluefish, will stay moist even when slightly overcooked.) The easiest, and most accurate, way to check for doneness is to use an instant-read thermometer to check the internal temperature. It should read 140°F. When you test the fish, be sure that the thermometer does not touch either the bone (if the fish isn't filleted) or the baking dish.

Overcooked fish is a disaster. When people tell me they dislike fish, I suspect they have spent a lifetime eating overcooked fish and really don't know how delicious properly prepared fish tastes. Fish should be served the minute it is cooked. At our restaurants, the fish is rushed to the table rather than sitting under a heat lamp, losing flavor and drying up by the minute. When you're putting together a meal at home, coordinate your vegetables and other accompaniments so that they are ready to serve slightly before the fish is done.

Baking

Most fish respond well to baking. If the fish is fatty, such as salmon or bluefish, there's little need for additional fat. A leaner fish, such as cod, needs a dab of butter or oil. You'll notice that the baking recipes in this book call for an oven temperature of 400° to 450°F, which is a higher temperature than you might expect. Fish baked at a high temperature stays moist because the high heat seals in the juices.

For plain baked fish, place it in a buttered nonreactive baking dish—or a pan strewn with vegetables for flavor—and dot it with butter. If you wish, add $1/4$ to $1/2$ cup of dry white wine to baste the fish as it bakes. (If you use wine, or any acidic vegetables such as tomatoes, be sure to put the fish in an enamel, glass, or stainless-steel baking dish because the acid in the wine or vegetables reacts to aluminum, giving an off taste to the cooking juices.) Count on about ten minutes cooking time per inch thickness of fish. The fish is done when its flesh is opaque rather than translucent. Serve immediately.

Baked Scrod

Scrod, a name given to young cod or haddock that weigh less than $2^1/_2$ pounds, remains a favorite choice of New Englanders.

SERVES 4

2 pounds scrod fillets

2 tablespoons butter

Lemon wedges or a combination of lemon and lime wedges

Preheat the oven to 425°F.

Butter a large baking dish and place the fillets in the dish, skin sides down. Dot the fish with the butter, and bake for about 10 minutes. Baste occasionally with the cooking juices if you wish. (The cooking time depends upon the thickness of the fillets.)

Remove the fillets from the heat, let them sit for about 2 minutes, then serve with the pan juices and lemon wedges.

Broiling

You can broil any fish, as long as you follow a few rules: Preheat the broiler; give the fish a protective coating with oil; and cook it the proper distance from the heat. When Legal Sea Foods was in its infancy, my father devised a way of broiling fish that we use to this day. Forget anything you have ever read about broiling fish a set amount of time on each side. Broiled fish should be cooked on only one side because the radiant heat from the pan will cook the other side. Also, the only fish that can be turned successfully are steak fish such as swordfish or salmon. Most other fish will fall apart as they are turned.

Coating the fish with a flavorless oil before broiling is important because it protects the surface from burning and retains the fish's moisture. How close you place the fish to the broiling surface depends upon how hot the broiler has become. Three to four inches away from the coils is ideal.

Note: For lean fish, try a combination of dry and moist heat. Place the fish in a buttered baking pan and barely cover the bottom of the pan with white wine or fish stock to about $1/4$ inch up the sides of the pan. Broil the fish until done, basting once or twice with the liquid. Either boil the liquid down until it has a saucelike consistency or freeze it to add flavor to future fish dishes.

Broiled Arctic Char

The oils in arctic char make it an easy choice for broiling because it doesn't dry out as quickly as a leaner fish. You could also broil a thin flatfish, such as flounder, using this technique, but watch it carefully because the fish will quickly dry out. Remember to preheat the broiler at least twenty minutes before you plan to cook the fish.

SERVES 4

2 pounds arctic char fillets

2 tablespoons oil, such as grapeseed

Butter

Preheat the broiler.

Blot the fillets with kitchen or paper towels, coat them on both sides with oil, and place them in a broiler pan. Broil the fish about 3 inches below the cooking element until cooked through. Fillets 1 inch thick should be done in 8 to 10 minutes. Dot the fish with butter just before serving.

VARIATIONS

With mayonnaise
Omit the oil. Pepper the fish and spread a thin layer of mayonnaise over the surface of the fillets. Broil as above. The mayonnaise will turn brown, coating the fish and sealing in the flavor.

With cracker crumbs
When the fillets are just about cooked through, lightly sprinkle them with 2 to 4 tablespoons of crumbs, and place them back under the broiler long enough to lightly brown the crumbs.

Frying

People shy away from frying because they are leery of food dripping with fat, filled with calories, that's impossible to digest. Unfortunately, this is too often the case. But properly prepared fried food is light, virtually greaseless, and, in moderation, easily digested. Leaden fried food is usually caused by frying at too low a temperature, or using old grease as a base.

Our customers' health is of prime importance. At Legal Sea Foods, we deep-fry food in a transfat-free canola oil. We also change the oil frequently. When you try to save money by reusing fat several times, your fish will have an off flavor—and will burn more easily. If the cooking temperature is too low, the fish coating will absorb the fat and the fish will taste greasy. Conversely, if the temperature is too high, the coating will burn, and the fish may not cook through, depending upon its density. Fish should be fried in fat heated to 365°F. A deep-fat thermometer is essential for testing the temperature of the fat.

At Legal, we first dip all food to be fried in cold buttermilk and then in a special corn-flour mix, similar to the Fried Fish Coating (page 286). Of course, you could use milk, but buttermilk adds a richer flavor. We then shake off any excess mixture and deep-fry the fish in preheated oil until it is cooked through but not overdone. It's important to fry only a few pieces at a time so the pan does not get overcrowded. When it does, the oil temperature decreases and the food becomes oily, has trouble browning and cooking evenly, and will be limp, not crisp. It's best to butterfly any thick fillets.

You could also use a wet batter, as the English do with their fish and chips. We've experimented with many a wet batter, but keep coming back to soaking the fish in buttermilk and then coating the pieces with a dry mixture. We think a wet batter tends to make the fish greasy and allows the individual pieces to stick together. A dry batter keeps the fish crisp yet juicy, because the fish steams in its own juices, which the batter seals in, and the flavor is retained.

No matter how you fry the fish, serve it immediately. Otherwise the fish will become soggy. (The steam exuded from the interior softens the coating.)

Fried Haddock

When my father started Legal Sea Foods, haddock was one of the least expensive fish in the ocean. That's no longer the case, but haddock is always a great frying choice. Be sure to serve it with a good-quality tartar sauce. We take great pride in our sauce and consider it almost as important as the fish. You could also use pollock (usually what you'll receive in a restaurant if the fish isn't named on the menu), cod, or cusk.

SERVES 4

3 cups oil, such as canola or safflower or a mixture of both

1½ to 2 pounds haddock, pollock, cod, or cusk, cut into serving pieces

Buttermilk

About 1 cup Fried Fish Coating (page 286)

Salt (optional)

Tartar Sauce (page 272)

Lemon wedges

Heat the oil in a heavy, deep, nonreactive pot (or deep-fat fryer) until it reaches a temperature of 365°F. Meanwhile, dip the haddock first in buttermilk, and then in the coating mixture. Shake the pieces well to remove any excess coating, and place on a dish next to the stove.

Test the oil with a deep-fat thermometer to make sure it is hot enough, and fry the haddock, a few pieces at a time, until they are cooked through and crispy. A piece of haddock about 1 inch thick will be ready in 2 or 3 minutes. Sprinkle lightly with salt, if you wish. Serve the fish pieces the moment they are cooked, if possible, with the tartar sauce. Garnish with lemon wedges.

VARIATIONS

Spicy Fried Haddock

Add 1 teaspoon Chinese spicy chili sauce (mae ploy) to the buttermilk and use the spicy variation for the Fried Fish Coating.

Fried Clams

We use only clams with bellies at our restaurants. Either buy shucked clams or shuck the clams and follow the cooking directions above. It's essential not to crowd the pan. The clams will cook through in about 1 minute.

Fried Soft-Shell Crabs

This is by far one of the best ways to enjoy soft-shell crabs. Follow the cleaning directions (see page 33) and the directions above. The crabs will cook through in approximately 2 minutes.

Fried Oysters

Buy shucked oysters (preferably ones that have not been blown with water) or shuck them and follow the cooking directions above. The oysters will cook through in about 1 minute.

Fried Sea Scallops

Halve if desired. Follow the cooking instructions above. The scallops will cook through in 2 to 3 minutes.

Fried Shrimp

Peel the shrimp and follow the cooking instructions above. Depending upon their size, the shrimp will cook through in 45 seconds to $1^1/2$ minutes. Fried shrimp are particularly good if you marinate them in lime or orange juice for a few minutes before cooking.

Fried Smelts

Leave the skin on the smelts. Marinate in the juice of 1 lemon for 15 minutes before dipping in the buttermilk. Follow the cooking directions above. The smelts should cook through in $1^1/2$ to 2 minutes.

Fried Squid

Cut the squid into $1/4$-inch rings. Soak them in buttermilk for at least 15 minutes, then drain and follow the cooking directions above. The squid should cook through in 1 minute.

Fisherman's Platter

For each serving, use 8 ounces haddock fillets, 3 shrimp, 4 ounces sea scallops, and 3 ounces clams. Follow the cooking instructions above, frying in order of length of cooking time. Start with the haddock, then fry the scallops, the shrimp, and finish with the clams. Serve with Spicy Hushpuppies (page 78) and George's Cole Slaw (page 200) if you wish.

Grilling

Grilling is an excellent method for cooking most fish. Many home stoves now come with grilling units—or you can use outdoor grills during several months of the year. Our restaurants are equipped with huge wood-burning grills tended by grill men who can tell just by looking at a piece of fish when it is cooked through. An experienced grill man can look at the flame and decide where to place the fish. Once it is seared, he shifts it to a cooler spot to finish cooking. You can accomplish the same thing at home by moving the fish to the edge of the grill, where the temperature is lower.

Select firm-textured fish cut into steaks—or whole fish—that will hold together as they cook. (Fillets would fall apart as you try to turn them over.) If you have a thick whole fish, such as flounder, slash it twice diagonally across its body so that the heat penetrates more evenly.

Always oil the fish with a flavorless vegetable oil before you put it on the grill. Sear it on the hottest part of the grill, then move it to the edges to finish cooking. Turn the fish once. Serve immediately.

Grilled Halibut

Halibut's firm texture makes it ideal for this method because it can be
cut like a steak and doesn't fall apart when you move it.

SERVES 4

Vegetable oil

1$\frac{1}{2}$ to 2 pounds halibut steaks

Cayenne pepper

Freshly milled black pepper

1 to 2 tablespoons butter

2 tablespoons chopped sweet
marjoram or parsley (optional)

Oil the halibut steaks and season them with cayenne and
black pepper to taste. Let the halibut sit while you prepare
the grill. (If you're using a charcoal grill, make sure that the
flames have died down and the coals are glowing before you
cook the fish.) Sear the steaks on both sides, then move them
to the edge of the grill to finish cooking. Dot with the butter
and sweet marjoram, if using, before serving.

Microwaving

Essentially, all microwaved fish is steamed in its own juices, which makes microwaving a good choice for purists (or dieters). Because fish cooks through so fast regardless of the cooking method, you really don't save a lot of time microwaving fish, but it is convenient on days when you don't want to turn on the oven or heat up the grill. Before you start, check out the wattage of your microwave, because fish microwaved in a higher-wattage oven (such as 650 to 700 watts) will take a third less time to cook through than in a lower-wattage oven (400 to 500 watts). In a higher-wattage oven, four $1/2$- to $3/4$-inch fillets placed in a microwavable dish will cook through in three to five minutes. One-inch-thick steaks will take about two minutes longer. (If you are cooking smaller quantities, such as a half-pound fish for two people, it will cook through in two to three minutes.) You can also microwave frozen fish; just add a minute or two to the cooking time.

How you arrange the fish for microwave cooking is also important. Many fish fillets are thicker in the center than on the ends. If so, fold them under to create a uniform thickness. The easiest way to arrange fish fillets for four persons is to place the fish pieces fanning out from the center of the microwavable dish.

Microwaved Red Snapper

You can substitute sole, salmon, or trout for the snapper.

1 to 2 teaspoons grapeseed oil

1½ pounds red snapper fillets

2 tablespoons fresh orange juice

1 teaspoon orange zest

Dried red pepper flakes

Orange, lemon, or lime wedges

Oil the fillets, then brush with the orange juice. Place them on a microwavable dish, either folding under any thin edges, or overlapping them. (If you have a small microwave oven, you may need to microwave the fish in two batches.) Sprinkle with the orange zest and red pepper flakes. Cover with plastic wrap, making sure the wrap does not touch the food. Cook in a microwave oven at full power until the fish is cooked through but still slightly translucent, between 4 and 6 minutes. Serve with citrus wedges.

Microwaving Lobster

I STARTED MICROWAVING LOBSTERS by chance many years ago when I was operating our Boston restaurant at Park Place. During a slow day in the restaurant, I decided to cook shellfish in the microwave as an experiment. My hunch was that each shell would serve as a controlled environment, allowing the flesh to steam in its own juices. What a success! Cooked this way, the shellfish retained their briny flavors and ended up with firm yet juicy textures. The microwaving technique worked well with all of the shellfish, but lobster was particularly delicious. The meat was juicy and tender, beautifully colored, and exceptionally flavorful.

After experimenting with this method for many months, I concluded that microwaving is an ideal way to prepare lobster, particularly if you are cooking only one or two—or want lobster meat for a cold preparation where its juicy texture and briny flavor can be best appreciated. As Boston's unofficial lobster expert, I even included this technique in a video I did about shore dinners shown nationally on the Public Broadcasting System. (You can imagine how delighted I was when Julia Child started referring people to me as the expert on microwaving lobster.)

The only disadvantage to using this technique is that you can see the lobster moving slightly in the first stages of cooking. If you stick the lobster in the freezer for twenty to thirty minutes before cooking, the cold will dull the lobster's senses and it will move less. Many cooks believe that this technique relaxes the lobster, making the meat more tender. (This freezer technique also works when you're boiling—or steaming—lobsters.) I've also found that microwave ovens that utilize a carousel seem to work best.

The lobster will exude some of its juices, so I suggest placing it in a microwavable zippered freezer bag. Remove the rubber bands around the lobster's claws. If you wish, you can stick half a lemon on the head of the lobster. This flavors the meat. Add two tablespoons water. Close the bag and place it in the microwave. (If you're worrying about the bag breaking—or do not want to microwave food in plastic—put the lobster on a microwavable plate.)

Turn the microwave to the highest setting. A one-pound chicken lobster will steam in six and a half to seven minutes. (Add a minute for each additional quarter pound.) Let the lobster cool in the microwave for about ten minutes, then place on a platter and serve with drawn butter and quartered lemons or limes (as delicious as lemons when squeezed over lobster).

NOTE: The tomalley (the lobster's liver) will turn dark green and stay liquid when the lobster is microwaved, rather than the lighter hue and firmer texture it has when boiled.

Poaching

Poaching is an excellent way to preserve the fish's moisture—particularly if you are serving it cold. If you poach fish frequently, then it's worth investing in a fish poacher, but you can improvise with a large deep pan, such as a turkey roaster, and a meat rack.

Poach the fish either in salted water or in a flavored broth. Either way, preheat the liquid. Wrap the fish in cheesecloth, place it on the rack, and lower it into the liquid. The liquid should barely cover the fish and should be kept at a gentle boil.

Poach the fish about ten minutes per pound, but check after eight minutes (per pound) so that you don't overcook it. Slightly undercook the fish if you're planning to cool it in the liquid, because it will continue to cook as the liquid cools.

Poached Salmon

Poached salmon is a traditional New England July Fourth meal,

but if you prefer, substitute striped—or black—bass.

SERVES 4

One 4-pound salmon, gutted and scaled

2 tablespoons salt

2 tablespoons white vinegar

Keep the head and tail on the salmon. Cut a cheesecloth about a foot longer than the fish. Lay it on the counter, and place the fish lengthwise in the center of the cloth. Wrap the cloth around the fish and tie it securely with string at the end of the head and tail. This will leave the ends of the cheesecloth free, to either tie to the rack to keep the fish from floating to the surface, or to be used as handles to lift the fish from the water.

Place the fish on a rack and loosely tie the cheesecloth wrapping to the rack. Eyeball the amount of water you will need, add it to the poaching pan, and bring it to a boil. The water should cover the fish by 1 inch. Add the salt and vinegar. Place the fish in the poaching pan. When the water returns to a simmer, reduce the heat, and poach the fish for about 10 minutes per inch thickness of fish. Add more water, if necessary. Remove the fish from the water, drain it for about 2 minutes, then remove the strings and cheesecloth, rolling the fish out onto a platter. Using a small sharp knife, remove the skin from the gills to the tail. Serve with mayonnaise, or mayonnaise mixed with chopped hard-boiled eggs and chopped watercress.

Oven-Steaming

We initiated this method of cooking fish many years ago. It's easy to do, and is a particularly useful cooking technique for people who work because it's a meal-in-one. Virtually any kind of fish tastes good cooked this way, as do any number of vegetable combinations. Regardless of the type of vegetables, slice them no wider than $1/4$ inch thick so that they will cook as fast as the fish.

Essentially, you steam the fish along with thinly sliced vegetables in an envelope of heavy-duty aluminum foil, allowing the fish and vegetables to steam in their juices. You can add herbs, butter, or cheese—and make the recipe as fancy or plain as you wish. Using this method, the fish always comes out moist, with plenty of fish and vegetable juices to spoon over rice, pasta, or potatoes. There's a wonderful aroma when you open the packet—and the bonus is that fish cooked this way is almost as good served cold or reheated.

Oven-Steamed Cod with Vegetables

Depending upon the time of year, vary both the fish and the vegetables. Try thinly sliced string beans, tomatoes, or summer squash—or a combination of all three. Here, we're using broccoli, mushrooms, and herbs.

SERVES 4

1½ to 2 pounds cod fillets

6 ounces broccoli

4 ounces sliced mushrooms

¼ cup chopped onion (optional)

1 tablespoon minced sweet marjoram, basil, or parsley

Salt

Freshly milled black pepper

1 tablespoon butter

Preheat the oven to 400°F.

Place the fish in the middle of a piece of aluminum foil that's large enough to hold the fish and vegetables. Cover with the broccoli, mushrooms, onion, if using, and sweet marjoram. Add salt and pepper to taste, then dot with the butter.

Make an envelope out of the foil, enclosing the fish and vegetables, and place it on a cookie sheet. Bake for about 15 minutes. The fish will be cooked through, and the vegetables will retain some of their crunch. Open the foil carefully, because the steam that is released can burn you if you're not cautious.

Sautéing

Sautéing is probably the easiest way to cook thin fish fillets. As you cook them in a small amount of hot fat on top of the stove, it's important to sauté the fish in a pan that's heavy enough to distribute the heat evenly. A professional sauté pan (available at any restaurant supply store) or iron skillet is ideal.

When you sauté fish, use enough oil (or butter and oil) so that the surface of the pan is generously coated. Make sure the fat is hot before you add the coated fish or it will stick to the pan. We use a grapeseed and olive oil mixture or a combination of grapeseed oil and butter to sauté fish. Not only is grapeseed oil heart-friendly, but also it has a high flash point, which means it can be heated to higher temperatures than conventional oils. It's considerably more expensive, but I think you'll find the added expense well worth it, once you've tasted how delicious food sautéed in grapeseed oil tastes. (Most Italian grocery stores and gourmet sections of supermarkets stock grapeseed oil.)

Place the fish in the hot oil, leaving ample space between the fillets, and cook the fish uncovered. Otherwise, the fish will steam rather than fry, and the coating will be soggy rather than crisp. Sauté the fillets until they are a light golden color on each side, turning once. Serve immediately.

Sautéed Sole or Flounder

This classic dish is a staple of French and Italian cooking.

SERVES 4

3 tablespoons butter

2 tablespoons grapeseed oil

1½ to 2 pounds sole or flounder fillets

Buttermilk

Unbleached all-purpose flour

Lemon wedges

Heat the butter and oil in a large skillet until hot. Dip the fish first in buttermilk, then in flour, shaking to remove any excess flour. Sauté the fish for 2 to 3 minutes per side, depending upon the thickness of the fish. Remove from the pan, drain on paper bags, and serve with lemon wedges.

VARIATIONS

With browned butter and almonds

After the fish is cooked through, place it on a hot serving dish and keep warm. Clean out the pan and add about 3 tablespoons of butter. Cook the butter over medium heat until it is lightly browned, adding 2 tablespoons of slivered almonds just as the color of the butter is turning. Pour the browned butter and almonds over the fish.

With herbs and butter

Follow the directions above, but add chopped chives and parsley—or chopped sweet marjoram or chervil—to the butter. Sauté the herbs with the butter for 30 seconds, then pour the herb butter over the fish before serving.

The Recipes and Ingredients

THE BEST FROM LEGAL SEA FOODS is in this book. We've chosen a wide variety of recipes, ranging from many of our traditional favorites to specials developed by our chefs, all of which were selected with the home cook in mind. Some have a few ingredients, others have several. If you're pressed for time, there are dozens of meals you can prepare in under thirty minutes.

Regardless of the recipe, you'll have the best results by starting with the best ingredients you can afford. That's what we do at our restaurants. Top-quality ingredients have a cumulative effect in determining the final taste of a dish. We specify balsamic vinegar as the base for our Tomato Balsamic Vinaigrette (page 217); we could substitute less-expensive vinegar, but it would never taste the same.

I'm a proponent of transfat-free foods. Our chefs use a mixture of canola and safflower oil for deep-frying, and a grapeseed and olive oil mixture for sautéing. Although grapeseed oil is quite expensive, it can be heated to a high temperature without burning. It is also one of the most healthful oils in existence. We serve pure butter with our lobsters, rather than an oil and butter combination. In our search for prime ingredients, such as locally grown vegetables and herbs, we've even found a bounty of Massachusetts cheeses, such as a blue cheese that we have at all of our restaurants. If you haven't cooked with Parmigiano-Reggiano, the real Parmesan cheese, you're in for a treat. Substitutes never taste the same.

We also use some specialty ingredients that might be new to you, such as Chinese *mae ploy*, a sweet-and-sour chili sauce that rounds out the flavor of sauces while giving a touch of heat, or Old Bay Seasoning, a mixture developed for shrimp and crab boils that adds a spicy touch to seafood. A small amount of chopped, peeled, and seeded jalapeños will intensify flavors in a dish and stimulate your taste buds. Many people top oysters with horseradish, but a dash of Green Tabasco is my favorite accompaniment.

Although I call for salt in many recipes, frequently you can omit it because there's enough natural salt in the fish. The recipes call for fresh—rather than dried—herbs because their oils add so much flavor and aroma. Even in remote areas, most supermarkets now stock fresh herbs year-round in their produce departments, or you can buy herbs at gourmet food shops.

These recipes are a starting point for your own creativity. Feel free to substitute any fish that you can find locally for those called for in the recipes. I've featured New England's saltwater fish, but the recipes work equally well with other regional saltwater fish or freshwater fish. Just match their textures and flavors with those of the fish I suggest.

Above all, remember that fish is a wonderful convenience food. It cooks in minutes, needing few or no embellishments to taste good. I've included many easy vegetable recipes to accompany simply prepared fish, such as sautéed plum tomatoes or spinach (see the Vegetables and Side Dishes chapter). When in doubt, cook a batch of rice and toss a green salad, and you'll be all set.

Appetizers

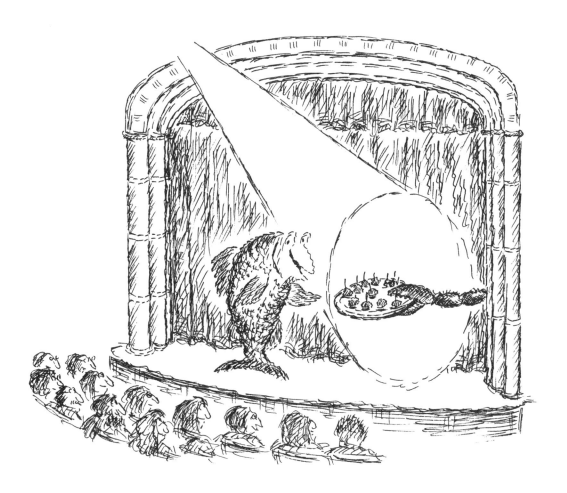

Smoked Bluefish Pâté

One of our most popular appetizers, bluefish pâté has been on the menu for many years. We serve it with Kalamata olives and commercial pickled cipollinis (bulbs of grape hyacinths that taste like pickled onions). Pickled onions are a fine substitute.

MAKES ABOUT 4 CUPS

1 pound smoked bluefish fillets

8 ounces cream cheese

$1/4$ cup butter

2 tablespoons Cognac

3 tablespoons minced onion

$1/2$ teaspoon Worcestershire sauce

2 tablespoons fresh lemon juice

Salt

Freshly milled black pepper

Chopped toasted walnuts or hazelnuts (optional)

Puree the bluefish, cream cheese, butter, and Cognac in a food processor. Add the onion, Worcestershire sauce, and lemon juice. Pulse the machine on and off until the ingredients are combined. Season with salt and pepper to taste.

Pack into a serving dish and sprinkle with the nuts, if using.

Smoky Mackerel Spread

A heavy-duty mixer or food processor makes it easier to break down the fish into a spread-like consistency, but elbow grease will work just as well.

The sweet flavors added by the roasted red pepper and hoisin sauce balance the assertive flavor of the mackerel. Garnish with strips of red pepper or chopped parsley, and serve with thinly sliced toasted rye bread. This spread freezes exceptionally well. Omit the pine nut garnish before freezing.

SERVES 4 TO 6

½ pound smoked mackerel, skin removed

1 teaspoon bottled horseradish

2 tablespoons sour cream

4 ounces cream cheese

1 tablespoon minced roasted red pepper

¼ teaspoon hoisin sauce

1 teaspoon fresh lemon juice

Salt

Freshly milled black pepper

Flake the fish into a large mixing bowl. Add the horseradish, sour cream, cream cheese, roasted red pepper, hoisin sauce, and lemon juice. Beat well until thoroughly combined, about 2 minutes with an electric mixer. Season with salt and pepper to taste. Refrigerate before serving.

VARIATIONS

With trout or bluefish
Substitute smoked trout or bluefish for the mackerel.

With garlic chives
Add 2 teaspoons minced garlic chives to the mixture.

Lower fat
Replace the sour cream and cream cheese with light versions of both. Proceed as above.

With toasted walnuts or pine nuts
Garnish with toasted nuts.

Chive and Salmon Spread

This is an ideal way to use leftover salmon. Try it for breakfast on toasted bagels, for lunch as a sandwich (see below), or in the evening as an appetizer with pita bread or crackers.

MAKES 1 CUP

$^3/_4$ **cup flaked cooked salmon**

1 tablespoon fresh lime juice

$^1/_2$ **to 1 teaspoon bottled horseradish**

$^1/_2$ **teaspoon Dijon mustard**

4 to 6 ounces cream cheese

1 to 2 tablespoons milk

2 tablespoons minced fresh chives or garlic chives

Salt

Freshly milled black pepper

Place the flaked salmon in a large mixing bowl. Add the lime juice, horseradish, Dijon mustard, and cream cheese. Beat until blended, about 30 seconds. Add 1 tablespoon of the milk and the chives, and mix again. (If you prefer a less dense consistency, add another tablespoon of milk.) Season with salt and pepper to taste.

VARIATIONS

Savory Salmon Spread

Add $^1/_4$ teaspoon Cajun seasoning and $^1/_2$ teaspoon Worcestershire sauce along with the cream cheese. Proceed as above.

Scandinavian-Style Open-Face Salmon Sandwich

For each serving, toast 1 piece of dense rye or whole wheat bread. Spread first with a thin layer of unsalted butter, and then with the salmon mixture. Top with paper-thin slices of sweet onion.

Crab Dip

This is one of our most popular appetizers. Keep in mind that it's very rich when you're planning the rest of the menu. At our restaurants, we serve this with Japanese shrimp crackers sprinkled with Old Bay Seasoning for dipping. Most Asian markets stock these colorful crackers. You can assemble the dish ahead of time, cover with plastic wrap, and refrigerate. Add five minutes to the baking time.

SERVES 4 TO 6

8 ounces whipped cream cheese with chives

2 tablespoons heavy cream

3 tablespoons minced Bermuda or sweet onion (optional)

2 teaspoons bottled horseradish

$\frac{1}{2}$ to 1 teaspoon Old Bay Seasoning

3 tablespoons sharp Cheddar cheese

1 pound fresh lump crabmeat, undrained, picked over for shells and cartilage

Preheat the oven to 400°F.

In a large mixing bowl, blend the cream cheese and cream until smooth. Mix in the onion, horseradish, Old Bay, and Cheddar cheese. Stir in the crabmeat and its juices. Place in a medium ovenproof dish, such as a 9-inch pie plate, and bake until bubbly, 10 to 12 minutes. Serve immediately.

Crab and Asparagus Roll-Ups

The whole is greater than the sum of its parts in this simple, yet elegant, appetizer. Double the portions for lunch or dinner.

SERVES 4

16 to 20 stalks pencil-thin asparagus

4 large slices ham

1 tablespoon mayonnaise

8 ounces fresh crabmeat, picked over for shells and cartilage

Fresh lime juice

1 tablespoon freshly grated Emmentaler or Swiss cheese

Preheat the oven to 400°F.

Trim the asparagus ends and place in a large bowl. Cover with boiling water, stir to separate the stalks, and let sit for 5 minutes. The asparagus should be barely cooked through. Drain, rinse with cold water to stop the cooking process, and wrap loosely in a kitchen towel. Set aside.

Place the ham slices on the countertop and spread with the mayonnaise. Arrange 4 to 5 stalks of asparagus on each slice. As you are going to fold over the ham to enclose the asparagus and crabmeat, place equal portions of crabmeat only on the portion of the asparagus that will be covered by the ham. Sprinkle with lime juice and top with grated cheese. Loosely roll up each ham slice and place on an oiled cookie sheet.

Bake for 5 to 10 minutes, or until the asparagus is warmed and the cheese has melted. Serve immediately.

Low-Fat Baked Crab Cakes

If you like the taste of crab unadulterated, try these cakes.

For southern-style cakes, see the variation.

SERVES 4

12 saltines

1/3 cup chopped fresh parsley or a mixture of parsley and chervil

2 tablespoons low-fat yogurt or sour cream

1/3 cup chopped roasted red pepper, skin and seeds removed

1 to 2 tablespoons fresh lime juice

Hot pepper sauce

Salt

1 pound fresh crabmeat, picked over for shells and cartilage

2 egg whites

Preheat the oven to 425°F.

Blend together the saltines and parsley until the saltines are pulverized. Put in a large mixing bowl. Stir in the yogurt, red pepper, 1 tablespoon water, the lime juice, 2 to 3 dashes of hot sauce, salt to taste, and the crabmeat. Lightly mix the egg whites with a fork and stir them in. It is important that the mixture be thoroughly combined.

Butter a large baking sheet. Using your hands, form 16 crab cakes and arrange them 1 inch apart on the sheet. Bake for 12 to 15 minutes, turning the crab cakes with a spatula after 10 minutes. The crab cakes are done when they are browned and cooked through.

VARIATIONS

Southern-style
Heat 1 tablespoon butter in a frying pan and add 2 to 3 tablespoons green pepper, 2 tablespoons chopped celery, and 1/3 cup chopped sweet onion. Stir constantly until the vegetables are slightly wilted. Cool them and then add along with the crabmeat. Proceed as above.

With cheese
Add 1/3 cup freshly grated Parmigiano-Reggiano cheese along with the crabmeat. Proceed as above.

With whole egg
Substitute a whole egg for the egg whites. The mixture will be softer, but the crab cakes will still hold together while baking.

Isaac Stern's Citrus Vodka

THE FAMOUS VIOLINIST Isaac Stern loved food. When he was performing in Boston, he was a regular customer at Legal's Park Square restaurant. On one of his trips in the mid-1980s, he shared with me his recipe for flavored vodka. After experimenting with the recipe, I came up with the hot chile variation that I served him the next time he was in town. Be sure to start with a smooth, Russian-style vodka such as Belvedere or Gray Goose, and try to locate organic citrus that is not waxed. Keep the vodka in the freezer and drink it like schnapps.

MAKES 1 BOTTLE

3 to 4 oranges or lemons
One 750-milliliter bottle good-quality vodka

Peel the citrus, making long strands of peel without the pith (the bitter white layer directly under the skin of citrus). Pour the vodka out of the bottle, put the peel into the bottle, and replace the vodka. (You will have a small amount that will be displaced. Drink it or use in cooking.) For the first few days, keep the vodka uncorked but cover with a clean towel. It will take about 2 weeks before the vodka is fully flavored. Serve ice-cold.

VARIATIONS

With dried chile peppers.
Substitute 1 tablespoon dried chile peppers for the citrus.

In Sangria.
Use 1 tablespoon to round out the flavor of a pitcher of red wine Sangria.

Spicy Crab Cakes

We make our crab cakes with jumbo lump crabmeat, which gives a splashy result, but you can use regular crabmeat, just as long as it's fresh. Do not drain the crabmeat—the juices add flavor.

SERVES 4

¹⁄₃ **cup plus 1 teaspoon mayonnaise**

1 teaspoon dry mustard

¹⁄₂ **teaspoon Dijon mustard**

Hot pepper sauce

¹⁄₂ **teaspoon bottled horseradish**

1 large egg, beaten

¹⁄₂ **cup finely crushed saltines**

12 ounces fresh crabmeat, picked over for shells and cartilage

Preheat the oven to 400°F.

Mix together the mayonnaise, mustards, a generous dash of hot sauce, horseradish, and egg in a large bowl. Gently stir in the saltines and crabmeat. The crab cakes may be formed immediately, but they're easier to shape if you refrigerate the mixture for an hour.

Divide the mixture into 4 to 6 large crab cakes, and place on a lightly oiled or nonstick baking sheet. Bake for 15 to 20 minutes. Serve immediately.

VARIATION

Baltimore Crab Cakes
Add a dash of Worcestershire sauce and Old Bay Seasoning to taste.

Crabmeat and Artichoke Hushpuppies

At our restaurants, we shape these in traditional hushpuppy forms (small ovals), but at home they'll cook in less oil if you form them as small patties. Vary the amount of cornmeal depending upon how dense you want the texture to be. Serve with Red Pepper Mustard Sauce (page 282).

SERVES 4

4 to 5 tablespoons finely chopped green onions (1 small bunch), both white and green parts

4 tablespoons chopped roasted red pepper, skin and seeds removed

$^1/_4$ teaspoon celery salt

$^1/_4$ to $^1/_2$ teaspoon Old Bay Seasoning

8 ounces fresh crabmeat, picked over for shells and cartilage

Hot pepper sauce

2 teaspoons ketchup or cocktail sauce

1 to 2 teaspoons bottled horseradish

1 tablespoon fresh lemon juice

1 to 1$^1/_4$ cups medium-grind cornmeal, preferably stone-ground

$^2/_3$ cup self-rising flour

$^1/_2$ cup milk

1 large egg

Grapeseed or canola oil

Salt

Freshly milled black pepper

In a large mixing bowl, toss together the onions, red pepper, celery salt, Old Bay, crabmeat, hot sauce to taste, ketchup, horseradish, and lemon juice. Stir in the cornmeal, flour, milk, and egg. Mix thoroughly. Let the mixture sit for at least 30 minutes. Add additional milk, tablespoon by tablespoon, if necessary. The mixture should be only slightly firm.

Heat the oil in a deep pot until $^1/_4$ teaspoon of the mixture cooks immediately. Take about 1 tablespoon of the crabmeat mixture, roll it between the palms of your hands to form a traditional oval shape, or form it into a patty. Fry it for 2 minutes, or until browned and cooked through. Remove the pan from the heat. Let the hushpuppy cool slightly, then taste for seasoning, and adjust as you wish, adding salt and pepper and additional spices if desired. Form the remaining mixture into patties, reheat the oil, and fry them in batches, removing with a slotted spoon and placing on paper towels to drain. Do not overcrowd the pan or they will steam slightly. Serve warm.

VARIATION

Spicy Hushpuppies

Use $^1/_2$ teaspoon Old Bay Seasoning and 2 teaspoons bottled horseradish. Add $^1/_2$ teaspoon dry mustard and $^1/_4$ teaspoon Worcestershire sauce to the ingredients listed above.

Mussels au Gratin

This has been one of our most popular recipes for many years. Be sure to use mussels that are at least two inches in diameter. If you have extra garlic butter, either freeze it or dot the mussels with extra butter before placing in the oven.

SERVES 4

4 tablespoons chopped garlic

1 cup butter

$\frac{1}{2}$ cup chopped fresh parsley

1 cup dry white wine

1 medium onion, chopped
(about 1 cup)

5 pounds cleaned mussels

$\frac{3}{4}$ to 1 cup freshly grated
Monterey Jack cheese

2 cups Cracker Crumb Mixture
(page 286)

Lemon wedges

French bread

Preheat the oven to 375°F.

Cream together 2 tablespoons of the garlic, the butter, and the parsley in a small bowl. Set aside.

Put the wine, the remaining 2 tablespoons garlic, and the onions in a large nonreactive pot. Bring the mixture to a boil, then add the mussels. Reduce the heat to medium, cover the pot, and steam the mussels until they open, about 6 minutes. Stir them occasionally to redistribute in the pot. Remove the mussels with a slotted spoon the moment their shells open, because they lose flavor if overcooked. Break off the top shell. Center each mussel in its shell, and place on a jelly-roll pan or in a large baking dish.

Reduce the mussel broth over high heat until the flavor is concentrated and pour it around the mussels in the pan. Put 1 teaspoon of the garlic butter in each mussel shell. Sprinkle with the cheese, and pat the crumb mixture over the cheese. Bake for about 10 minutes, or until the crumb topping is lightly browned. Serve the mussels immediately, garnished with lemon wedges and accompanied by French bread to mop up the pan juices.

Steamed Mussels

Wash each mussel thoroughly and pull off the "beard" along the side. Some people prefer to use dry white wine rather than water for steaming—either way tastes good. The one essential is a heavy pot. There's no need for salt, because the mussel liquor is salty.

SERVES 4

1 medium onion, chopped
(about 1 cup)

2 garlic cloves (optional)

5 pounds cleaned mussels

2 tablespoons chopped
fresh parsley

Place the onions, $^1/_2$ cup water, and the garlic, if using, in the bottom of a large, heavy pot. Add the mussels, and immediately bring the water to a boil. Cover the pot, lower the heat slightly, and steam the mussels for 5 to 8 minutes, depending upon their size. Do not overcook, or the mussel flesh will shrivel and lose flavor.

Using a slotted spoon, place the mussels in a serving bowl. Sprinkle with the parsley. Strain the broth through a coffee filter and serve with the mussels.

VARIATION

With white wine
Replace the water with white wine and omit the garlic.

Scallops with Sweet Marjoram and Scallions

Tiny Calico scallops are sold throughout the country, but remember if you use them that they are already slightly cooked, so steaming will take but a minute or two. If you use larger bay or ocean scallops, slice them into $1/2$ inch-wide pieces. Steam carefully because scallops become rubbery if overcooked. This dish tastes best prepared a day in advance. If you wait to salt until just before serving, the dish will retain its fresh flavor.

SERVES 4

1 cup whole scallion greens

2 sprigs fresh sweet marjoram

$1^{1}/_{4}$ pounds scallops

1 to 2 tablespoons fresh lemon juice

2 tablespoons thinly sliced scallions, white parts only

1 teaspoon minced fresh sweet marjoram

$1/2$ teaspoon Chinese chili sauce (mae ploy)

Sesame oil (optional)

Freshly milled black pepper

Salt (optional)

Place $1/3$ cup water, the scallion greens, and the sprigs of sweet marjoram in the bottom of a steamer. Put the scallops in the steaming container. Bring the water to a boil, add the scallops, and steam until the scallops are *just* cooked through, 2 to 3 minutes. Place them in a small, deep, heat-proof bowl.

Strain the cooking juices, return to the pot, and boil them until reduced to $1/3$ cup. Pour over the scallops. Add the lemon juice and the sliced scallions. Refrigerate overnight. Before serving, stir in the 1 teaspoon sweet marjoram. Taste and add the chili sauce, a minute quantity of sesame oil, black pepper, and salt, if desired.

Seafood Seviche

Try this fresh-tasting chef's special from Legal's Baltimore restaurant on occasions when you want something both splashy and fat free. You can vary the seafood, but be sure to buy tagged shellfish because you're serving it raw. (The lime juice slightly "cooks" the seafood.) Adding a second batch of cilantro just before serving gives an extra zing to the flavor.

SERVES 4 TO 6

8 ounces squid, cut into
$^1/_4$-inch-thick pieces

8 ounces sea scallops, quartered

8 ounces shrimp, peeled

8 ounces cubed haddock or other
white fish

$^3/_4$ to 1 cup fresh lime juice

5 to 6 tablespoons minced
fresh cilantro

8 to 10 shucked littleneck clams

Salt

Freshly milled black pepper

Boston or redleaf lettuce

$^1/_2$ cup red onions, sliced
paper-thin

Put the squid, scallops, shrimp, haddock, and lime juice into a large nonreactive bowl. Toss and add 3 tablespoons of the cilantro. Let sit for at least 3 hours, refrigerated. Before serving, add 2 to 3 tablespoons additional cilantro, the clams, and salt and pepper to taste. Arrange the lettuce on a large platter, mound the seviche in the center, and top with the thinly sliced red onion.

VARIATION

With orange or tangerine juice
Use $^1/_2$ cup lime juice and $^1/_4$ cup orange or tangerine juice.

—Chef William Garcia

Fear Not the Wine List

WHEN I WAS FIRST DATING my wife, Lynne, and wanted to impress her, I made reservations at an elegant restaurant in Boston. I asked the steward for the wine list. He plunked down a large, leather-bound volume. Let's see, I thought. I know a little about wines, there must be some names I recognize. I thumbed through the pages. "Have you decided on a selection, sir?" the sommelier intoned.

The truth of the matter was I knew far less about wine than I presumed, for there wasn't even one vaguely familiar selection. Well . . . there was one selection that was remotely familiar, but it was only available by the half bottle. "Sir?"

"Yes, well okay, let's try this one," I said, pointing to the half bottle (not trusting myself with the pronunciation).

"You want that wine!?" bellowed the sommelier somewhat incredulously.

By now, I could see every head in the place turning in my direction to observe the fool who dared to order such an obviously poor choice. Even Lynne was open-mouthed at the sommelier's response. "Yes," I announced for all to hear. "That wine. That's the wine we'd like."

When the wine arrived, I had a difficult time explaining why it was important to drink a very sweet dessert wine with prime rib of beef.

After that embarrassing incident, I resolved to learn as much as I could about wines so I could avoid ever having a similar situation. And I did. (At various stages, we owned a wine company as well as a vineyard in France.) I also wanted to make wine consumption in our restaurants as pleasant as possible by removing the intimidation factor. We have an excellent, and well-priced, wine list. Consistently, *Wine Spectator Magazine* has chosen virtually every Legal Sea Foods restaurant for its best-in-excellence awards.

For both the novice and the connoisseur, our wine flights offer a wonderful experience. For the price of one glass of wine, our customers can taste three samplings of different styles of white or red wines and decide for themselves the best choice to go with the dish they're trying. (We've even expanded this idea to have flights of other kinds of alcohol, such as ports and martinis.)

For, after all, wine is meant to be enjoyed with food. My unpleasant experience was unusual. In most restaurants, staffs are trained to make wine "user friendly." If you enjoy wine, but don't trust your knowledge of the different regions or varieties, don't worry. Select your main course. Then ask your server for a recommendation (explaining how much you'd like to spend). Or, ask which label of the variety you prefer is the most requested selection on the list.

One other piece of advice: Avoid Sauternes with prime rib.

Barbecued Shrimp

At our Copley Place, Boston, branch, we feature jumbo shrimp. Smaller-sized shrimp are equally delicious and easier to find. Use any leftover sauce with chicken or ribs—or store it in the refrigerator. When covered with a thin layer of vegetable oil, the sauce will stay in good condition for at least two weeks.

SERVES 4

1 pound shrimp, peeled

$^3/_4$ to 1 pound bacon

Add-On Barbecue Sauce (page 276)

Preheat the oven to 375°F.

Rinse the shrimp and pat dry. Halve the bacon slices crosswise. Holding a shrimp in your hand, wrap the bacon around it, leaving the end of the tail portion uncovered. Place the shrimp in a baking pan, bacon seam side down. Continue wrapping the remaining shrimp with bacon.

Bake for 10 minutes. Remove from the oven and spoon about $^1/_4$ teaspoon sauce over each shrimp. The sauce should only lightly glaze the shrimp. Return to the oven and bake another 5 minutes. Let sit for 5 minutes before serving. If you wish, serve some extra barbecue sauce on the side for dipping the shrimp.

—Chef Kevin Fisk

Baltimore "Steamed" Shrimp

Our Baltimore restaurant has a special steaming oven—but you can approximate the taste of this popular appetizer by gently boiling the shrimp in a dark beer such as Boston's Sam Adams.

SERVES 4

8 ounces dark beer

2 tablespoons malt or cider vinegar

1 teaspoon shrimp boil, such as Old Bay Seasoning

1 small onion, peeled and sliced (optional)

1 teaspoon black peppercorns

1½ to 2 pounds medium shrimp in shells

Cocktail Sauce (page 274)

Place 2 cups water, the beer, vinegar, shrimp boil, onion slices, and peppercorns in a large nonreactive pot. Bring the mixture to a boil, lower the heat, and gently boil for 10 minutes. Add the shrimp. The liquid should cover the shrimp. If not, add additional water. Raise the heat until the mixture boils, immediately lower it, and gently boil until the shrimp are pink and cooked through. The cooking time will vary depending upon the size of the shrimp, 1 to 3 minutes. Remove from the heat and drain. Serve with cocktail sauce.

Curried Shrimp Bundles

Pass big paper napkins with these splashy, yet easy to prepare, tidbits from Legal's catering department. You can double or triple the recipe for a crowd. If you're pressed for time, assemble them a day in advance. After you remove the shrimp from the refrigerator, place them in warm water to bring them to room temperature, then dry them and toss with the butter mixture. (Otherwise the butter hardens, making it difficult to coat the shrimp.) Freeze any extra phyllo dough.

SERVES 4 TO 6

3/4 cup clarified butter

2 tablespoons fresh lime juice (about 1 lime)

3 tablespoons good-quality curry powder

1 pound shrimp (about 20), peeled

6 sheets phyllo dough

1/3 cup chopped toasted hazelnuts

Preheat the oven to 400°F.

Mix together 1/3 cup of the butter, the lime juice, and the curry powder in a medium nonreactive bowl. Let sit for a few minutes to meld the flavors, then mix with the shrimp. Set the shrimp aside.

Cover the phyllo dough with a dampened towel so that it doesn't dry out. Take 1 sheet of the dough, lightly brush it with clarified butter, and sprinkle with 1 tablespoon of the chopped hazelnuts. Cover with another sheet of dough, repeat the process, and then top with a final layer of dough, butter, and nuts. Make another rectangle with the remaining dough, butter, and nuts. You should end up with 2 rectangles of 3 layers. Eyeball each rectangle and cut into 10 lengthwise strips. You will have 20 strips in total.

Place a shrimp on the bottom of each strip. Roll it up to the top, cutting off any ragged ends at the top of each piece to make a neat package. Continue rolling the shrimp until all are wrapped. Place them on a jelly-roll pan, seam side down. Brush the tops lightly with butter. Bake for 8 to 12 minutes, or until the bundles are lightly browned. Serve hot.

—Chef Siobhan Magee-Bonifacio

Shrimp Pizza

We make this as individual pizzas, but at home it's much easier to assemble one large pizza. You can vary the type of cheese, but wait to add it to the pizza until five minutes before removing from the oven. If you're planning to use a commercial crust, remember that many are made with a lot of sugar, so you might prefer to buy prepared bread dough.

SERVES 4

1 uncooked pizza crust

Olive oil

2 teaspoons minced garlic

5 Italian plum tomatoes

1 pound shrimp, peeled

$\frac{1}{4}$ cup julienned fresh basil

1$\frac{1}{3}$ cups Asiago cheese or a mixture of pizza cheeses

Freshly milled black pepper

Preheat the oven to 425°F.

Roll the crust out to fit a jelly-roll or pizza pan. Brush with olive oil, and sprinkle with the garlic. Cut the tomatoes into $\frac{1}{4}$-inch crosswise slices and arrange along with the shrimp on top. Bake for about 12 minutes. Remove the pizza from the oven. Sprinkle with the basil and then the cheese. Drizzle with 1 to 2 teaspoons olive oil. Return to the oven until the cheese is lightly browned—or melted. Sprinkle with black pepper and wait until the pizza cools slightly before serving.

VARIATIONS

With mussels
Substitute cooked mussels for the shrimp, adding them along with the cheese.

With salmon or arctic char
Cut cooked salmon or arctic char into $\frac{1}{2}$-inch strips. Arrange in alternating rows on the pizza with the tomatoes and diced mozzarella cheese. Omit the basil and sprinkle with 1 teaspoon of chopped fresh tarragon.

Stuffed Grape Leaves

This ethnic specialty from Boston's Chestnut Hill restaurant not only is delicious with shrimp but also is an excellent way to use up small amounts of leftover fish such as salmon or cod. You can find preserved grape leaves in the international foods sections of most supermarkets or at a gourmet foods store. It's important that the stuffed rolls snugly fit into a baking pan, so roll one, then select a nonreactive pan that will be the right size for sixteen leaves.

SERVES 4

1 pound preserved grape leaves in vinegar brine

2 cups cooked rice

³/₄ cup chopped raw peeled shrimp (about ¹/₂ pound)

1 tablespoon minced lemon zest (about 1 lemon)

1¹/₂ tablespoons finely chopped fresh chives

1¹/₂ tablespoons finely chopped fresh dill

2 to 3 tablespoons crumbled feta cheese

1 tablespoon fresh lemon juice, plus more for serving

Salt

Freshly milled black pepper

¹/₂ to 1 cup dry white wine

¹/₂ to 1 cup vegetable or chicken stock

Preheat the oven to 375°F.

Separate the grape leaves and soak them in cold water for 15 minutes. Wash and dry each leaf, then trim off the juncture near the stem, which can be tough. Pick out 16 of the best-looking leaves, and lay them flat on a clean countertop, stem sides at the bottom.

Mix together the rice, shrimp, lemon zest, chives, dill, feta cheese, and lemon juice in a large nonreactive bowl. Season with salt and pepper to taste. Take about 2 tablespoons of the filling and place on the lower third of each leaf. Fold over the sides and gently roll to enclose the filling. (If you've ever stuffed cabbage leaves, this is the same process.) Continue until you have finished rolling all the leaves.

Place the rolls stem side down in a single layer in a nonreactive baking pan. Pour equal amounts of white wine and stock over the rolls. The liquid should reach ¹/₂ inch up the sides of the pan. Cover the pan with aluminum foil. Bake for about 50 minutes, checking occasionally to insure that the liquid has not evaporated. Add small amounts of stock as needed to keep the rolls covered. Remove the foil, and let the leaves cool. Squeeze lemon juice over each roll before serving. Serve at room temperature.

—Chef Michael Gourgouras

Legal's "Culinary Snackdown"

I'M PROUD OF THE CALIBER of chefs that Legal Sea Foods attracts. As anyone who has ever worked in a restaurant knows, running a kitchen requires talent—but that's only the first step. Chefs also need tenacity and stamina to cope with the pressure and long hours that are implicit in the restaurant business. But we like to have fun, and we like to share ideas.

In 2001, we began an internal Chefs' Competition "Culinary Snackdown." Each restaurant picked a representative to compete for a grand prize. After several weeks of regional competitions at Legal's restaurants along the Eastern seaboard, two chefs duked it out for a week's vacation in California's Napa Valley.

At each competition, the core ingredients were either fish or shellfish, but the actual choice was a surprise until we unpacked it. Some chefs worked with lobster, others with tuna or arctic char—and one batch of chefs even got shad roe (and swordfish). To inspire the chefs, we brought in all kinds of specialty ingredients—such as morels, white anchovies, and unusual vegetables such as Peruvian purple potatoes and pea tendrils—that the chefs were required to incorporate into their presentations. We tasted some delicious—and imaginative—recipes, some of which are chef's specials at our restaurants, such as Michael Gourgouras' Stuffed Grape Leaves (page 88) or Rob Rosen's Fish Latkes (page 188).

Our chefs had the chance to showcase their talents—and to cook with some unusual ingredients—and we ended up with an increased appreciation of our chefs' abilities.

Main Courses

Arctic Char with Grilled Summer Vegetables

At Legal's Huntington, New York, restaurant, we prepare both the fish and vegetables on our commercial wood-fired grills, giving them a slightly smoky flavor. Arrange the char over the vegetables and mushrooms, letting the fish juices moisten the vegetables. The squashes should be barely cooked, with an almost crunchy texture.

SERVES 4

1½ to 2 pounds arctic char or salmon fillets

2 medium zucchini

2 medium yellow summer squash

2 beefsteak tomatoes

1 large sweet onion

2 portobello mushrooms

Grapeseed oil

⅓ cup olive oil

3 tablespoons fresh lemon juice

Zest of 1 lemon

3 tablespoons chopped fresh basil

1 teaspoon minced garlic

Dried red pepper flakes

Lightly oil the fish, vegetables, and whole mushrooms with the grapeseed oil. Place them on a preheated oiled grill. The char, which should be turned once, should be ready in about 8 minutes, the zucchini and yellow squash in 5, and the mushrooms in 2 or 3. Combine the olive oil, lemon juice, lemon zest, basil, garlic, and red pepper flakes in a small nonreactive bowl. Serve alongside the fish and vegetables.

—Chef Nelson Rothstein

Arctic Char with Pears

This is an attractive, and tasty, specialty at our 2020 K Street restaurant in Washington, D.C. You can substitute salmon for the char, and you can sauté the char, omitting the bread crumbs. However, be sure to include the walnuts for texture and flavor.

SERVES 4

3 unpeeled Bosc pears, cut into eighths

4 tablespoons fresh orange juice

2 tablespoons grapeseed oil

8 sliced shallots

2 tablespoons Grand Marnier liqueur

2 teaspoons minced fresh chives

2 to 3 teaspoons minced fresh ginger

Salt

Freshly milled black pepper

1 cup panko (Japanese bread crumbs)

2 tablespoons curry powder

2 pounds arctic char or salmon

3 tablespoons unbleached all-purpose flour

3 tablespoons melted butter

3 tablespoons chopped toasted walnuts (optional)

Toss the pears with the orange juice in a large nonreactive bowl and set aside. Heat the oil and sauté the shallots over medium-low heat for 20 to 30 minutes, until softened and slightly caramelized. Drain the pear slices and gently toss with the Grand Marnier, chives, ginger, and salt and pepper to taste. Fan out attractively on a serving platter, and top with the shallots.

Preheat the oven to 400°F.

Combine the panko with the curry powder. Dip the arctic char into the flour, shake to remove any excess, and place the fillets into a baking dish. Pat the panko onto their surfaces, and drizzle with the melted butter. Pour 2 tablespoons of water around the fillets. Bake for about 12 minutes, or until the char is cooked through and the bread crumbs are browned.

Arrange the char over the pears, so that the pear design is visible. Sprinkle with the walnuts, if desired.

—Chef Kevin Lynch

Bass with Pico de Gallo Salsa

Try this fresh-tasting salsa from Legal's Crystal City, Virginia, restaurant
with any firm-textured fish such as swordfish or halibut.

1 pound plum tomatoes, diced

⅓ cup diced red onion

⅓ cup chopped black olives

2 tablespoons chopped fresh
cilantro

2 tablespoons seeded and
chopped jalapeño

½ to 1 tablespoon fresh lime
juice

Freshly milled black pepper

Hot pepper sauce

1 teaspoon minced garlic

2 tablespoons olive oil, plus more
for the fish

2 pounds bass fillets or 1 whole
bass

Prepare a charcoal or gas grill, or preheat the oven to 425°F.

Mix together the tomatoes, onion, olives, cilantro, jalapeño,
lime juice, black pepper to taste, a dash of hot sauce, the garlic, and olive oil in a large nonreactive bowl. Taste and season
with additional lime juice and pepper if necessary.

Oil the bass fillets and either grill or bake them for 12 to 15
minutes. Cut into serving pieces and top each serving with 2
spoonfuls of the sauce.

—Chef Jose Urquilla

Striped Bass with Herbs and Garlic

Striped bass tastes best with a simple sauce. Many supermarkets now offer fresh herbs, such as sweet marjoram, in the produce section.

SERVES 4

2 pounds striped bass fillet

2 tablespoons vegetable oil

Juice of 1 lemon

3 to 4 tablespoons butter

1 tablespoon minced garlic

2 tablespoons chopped fresh sweet marjoram or parsley

½ teaspoon minced orange zest (optional)

Prepare a charcoal or gas grill or preheat the oven to 425°F.

Marinate the fish in the oil and lemon juice for about 30 minutes in a large nonreactive bowl in the refrigerator. Either grill the fish or bake it for 10 to 15 minutes, turning once. The amount of time depends upon the thickness of the fillet.

Meanwhile, heat the butter in a saucepan and sauté the garlic for about 3 minutes, stirring frequently. Do not let it brown. Add the sweet marjoram and orange zest, if using. Remove the pan from the heat.

Pour the garlic-and-herb butter over the fish just before serving.

VARIATION

With basil

Substitute basil for the sweet marjoram and add a dash of cayenne pepper.

Bluefish in a Kale and Tomato Sauce

The sharp aftertaste of the kale complements the bluefish's rich flavor. Any extra tomato sauce freezes well.

SERVES 4

2 tablespoons grapeseed or olive oil

1 cup chopped onions (about 1 medium)

28 ounces canned ground peeled tomatoes

$\frac{1}{3}$ cup roasted red peppers

$\frac{1}{4}$ cup chopped basil

1 teaspoon sugar (optional)

Salt

Freshly milled black pepper

2 pounds bluefish fillets

2 to 3 cups sliced kale

Heat 1 tablespoon of the oil in a large, nonreactive skillet. Add the onions and cook, stirring frequently, for 3 minutes. Add the tomatoes and peppers, and cook over medium heat for 10 minutes. Stir in the peppers and basil, and cook 2 minutes longer. Season with sugar (if necessary), and salt and pepper to taste. Set the mixture aside.

Preheat the oven to 425°F.

Heat 2 teaspoons of the oil in another pan and sear the bluefish on both sides. Wipe out the pan, add the remaining 1 teaspoon oil, and quickly wilt the kale. Place it in a nonreactive baking dish. Top with the bluefish, and then cover the fish with 1 cup of the sauce. Bake for about 10 minutes, or until the bluefish is cooked through.

Sautéed Bluefish with Chorizo and Potatoes

Sauté the bluefish cubes gently, because they tend to fall apart if stirred vigorously. Portuguese chorizo sausage is available in most gourmet shops. If unavailable, substitute kielbasa.

SERVES 4

1 tablespoon grapeseed or olive oil

4 to 6 ounces sliced chorizo sausage

2 to 3 cups sliced densely textured potatoes (such as Yukon Gold)

1 cup sliced onions (about 1 medium)

$1/2$ cup peeled and diced ripe pear

1 tablespoon minced garlic

2 pounds bluefish fillets, cut into $1^{1}/_{2}$-inch pieces

3 tablespoons chopped fresh parsley

Heat 1 teaspoon of the oil in a large nonreactive saucepan. Add the sausage, sauté until browned, and remove from the pan. Stir in the potatoes. Cook over medium heat for 5 minutes, turn the potato slices, and brown the other sides. Stir in the onions, pear, and garlic. Cover the pan and cook over medium heat for 3 to 4 minutes, or until the potatoes are cooked through. Remove the potato mixture from the pan and set aside. Heat the remaining oil and sauté the fish cubes until cooked through, about 4 minutes. Mound the fish in the center of a platter and surround with the potato mixture. Sprinkle with the parsley.

Bluefish with an Almond Tomato Sauce

The acid of the tomatoes goes well with the rich taste of the bluefish. Any additional sauce keeps in good condition, refrigerated, for about four days, or you can freeze it.

SERVES 4 TO 6

3 tablespoons olive oil

1 tablespoon chopped garlic

Dried red pepper flakes

1 cup sliced Spanish onions

$\frac{1}{2}$ to 1 teaspoon fresh thyme leaves, crumbled

10 plum tomatoes, peeled, seeded, and chopped

1 teaspoon sugar

$\frac{1}{3}$ to $\frac{1}{2}$ cup capers

$\frac{1}{2}$ cup coarsely chopped almonds

$\frac{1}{2}$ cup sliced fresh basil

Salt

Freshly milled black pepper

1 whole 4- to 5-pound bluefish, gutted

Preheat the oven to 400°F.

Heat the olive oil in a large nonreactive saucepan. Add the garlic and a pinch of red pepper flakes. Cook for 1 minute, stirring constantly. Stir in the onions, and cook over medium heat for about 10 minutes, or until softened. Add the thyme, tomatoes, sugar, capers, and almonds. Simmer the mixture for 10 minutes, and add the basil. Simmer an additional 5 minutes. Season with salt and pepper to taste. Cool and set aside.

Spread $\frac{3}{4}$ to 1 cup of the sauce over the bottom of an oven-proof casserole dish large enough to hold the bluefish. Lightly salt and pepper the bluefish. Place it over the sauce. Bake for 15 minutes, or until cooked through. Serve with additional sauce on the side.

—Executive Chef Rich Vellante

Bluefish with Mustard Sauce

When I was managing our downtown Boston restaurant, this was a popular specialty. Any extra sauce can be refrigerated for two to three days. It is delicious with fried oysters, squid, or as a topping for any broiled or baked fish.

SERVES 4

1 cup mayonnaise

$\frac{1}{3}$ cup Dijon mustard

$\frac{1}{4}$ cup bottled horseradish

$\frac{1}{4}$ cup minced onion

$\frac{1}{4}$ cup finely chopped fresh parsley

Worcestershire sauce

Hot pepper sauce

Grapeseed oil

2 pounds bluefish fillets

Preheat the broiler.

Combine the mayonnaise, mustard, horseradish, onion, parsley, and a generous dash of Worcestershire and hot sauces in a medium bowl. Set aside.

Lightly oil the fillets and place them in a broiler pan. Broil until almost done, about 6 minutes. Remove the fillets, spread lightly with sauce, and return to the broiler until the topping is lightly browned, 2 to 3 minutes.

Louisiana Catfish Matrimony

This perennial favorite at our restaurants gives a rich flavor to farm-raised catfish. Louisiana andouille sausage is available at many gourmet shops or supermarkets. Popcorn shrimp are available frozen in some specialty food markets. If unavailable, substitute medium shrimp cut into $^3/_4$-inch pieces.

SERVES 4

1$^1/_2$ to 2 pounds catfish fillets

Buttermilk

Fried Fish Coating (page 286)

Grapeseed oil

1 teaspoon butter

$^1/_2$ pound andouille sausage

$^1/_2$ pound popcorn shrimp (70 to 90 count) or peeled medium shrimp cut into $^3/_4$-inch pieces

$^1/_4$ to $^1/_2$ teaspoon seafood seasoning (such as Old Bay Seasoning)

1 cup heavy cream

1 tablespoon fresh lemon juice

2 tablespoons minced fresh parsley

Salt

Freshly milled black pepper

Lemon slices

Soak the catfish in buttermilk to cover for 5 minutes. Drain. Dredge in the Fried Fish Coating and shake off any excess. Place the fillets on a cake rack. Add enough grapeseed oil to come $^1/_2$ inch up the sides of a large, heavy, nonreactive skillet. Heat it until a fleck of the flour mix dropped into it sizzles. Add the catfish. Do not crowd the pan. It may be necessary to fry the fish in batches. Cook until brown, turning once, 3 to 4 minutes. Remove from the pan, and set aside.

Wipe the pan with a paper towel. Add 1 teaspoon butter and the andouille sausage. Cook the sausage over medium heat for 2 minutes, stirring constantly. Add the shrimp and the seafood seasoning, and cook 1 minute longer. Remove the sausage and the shrimp from the pan. Wipe out the pan. Add the remaining butter and the cream and cook over high heat, shaking the pan occasionally, until it is reduced by half. Add the lemon juice and parsley. Season with salt and pepper to taste. Place the catfish on a serving platter, top with the sausage and shrimp, and pour over the sauce. Garnish with lemon slices.

Baked Cod Parmesan

Try this with jasmine rice and steamed broccoli. You can substitute any white-fleshed fish, such as wolffish, halibut, haddock, or cusk for the cod.

SERVES 4

2 pounds cod fillets

1 cup fresh tomato or Marinara Sauce (page 279)

2 tablespoons chopped fresh basil

3 tablespoons freshly grated Parmigiano-Reggiano cheese

1 teaspoon olive oil

Preheat the oven to 425°F.

Place the fillets in a greased baking dish. Mix the tomato sauce with the basil and cover the fish with the sauce. Bake for about 8 minutes, or until barely cooked through. Remove the pan from the oven and sprinkle with the cheese and then dot each fillet with a few drops of olive oil. Return to the oven and bake 4 to 5 minutes longer, or until the cheese melts. Serve immediately.

VARIATION

With peppers and mushrooms
Mix 1 cup cooked mushrooms and $1/2$ cup chopped red or green bell peppers into the tomato mixture. Proceed as above.

Cod with Horseradish and Lemon

Cod's delicate flavor is enhanced by these simple ingredients. Serve with boiled baby potatoes and a simple green vegetable, such as steamed broccoli.

SERVES 4

Olive oil

One 4-pound codfish, cleaned and gutted

2 lemons, sliced

1 teaspoon bottled horseradish

Preheat the oven to 400°F.

Oil the fish and place in a baking dish just large enough to hold it. Place some of the lemon slices in the cavity. Spread the horseradish over the skin and cover with the remaining lemon slices. Bake for 20 to 30 minutes, or until cooked through.

Cod with Mushroom and Peppers

This splashy presentation of cod with a mushroom stuffing is a specialty
of Legal's Park Square restaurant in Boston.

SERVES 4

2 tablespoons butter

**2 portobello mushroom caps,
thinly sliced**

**1/2 cup stemmed shiitake
mushrooms**

**1/2 cup stemmed white button
mushrooms**

Freshly milled black pepper

1/3 cup heavy cream

Salt

1 roasted red pepper

One 2-pound cod fillet

Cornmeal

3 tablespoons grapeseed oil

Watercress or flat-leaf parsley

Heat the butter in a large nonreactive skillet. Add the mushrooms and a generous amount of pepper. Cook over medium heat for 10 minutes. Stir in the cream and cook 10 minutes longer, stirring frequently. Taste, and season with salt if necessary. Remove the pan from the heat and cover with a towel to keep warm. Peel, seed, and slice the red pepper, and set it aside.

Cut the cod in half lengthwise. Thoroughly coat both pieces with cornmeal. Heat the grapeseed oil in a fresh skillet and fry the cod until browned and cooked through, about 4 minutes per side. Put 1 slice of cod on a serving platter, cover with the mushroom mixture, and top with the roasted pepper. Top with the remaining cod. Garnish the platter with watercress or parsley.

—Chef Chris Cowen

Cod with Olive Topping

Try this assertive topping—popular at our Chestnut Hill restaurant in Boston—with any mild-flavored fish. Spoon a tablespoon of the topping on the fish, and serve any remaining sauce separately. You can chop the ingredients by hand, but using a food processor is easier. Serve with rice and a green salad.

SERVES 4

¼ cup chopped Kalamata olives

¼ cup chopped Spanish olives

2 teaspoons capers

1½ teaspoons minced anchovies (about 2)

2 to 3 teaspoons minced garlic

1½ tablespoons olive oil

1 tablespoon balsamic vinegar

⅓ cup diced tomatoes

2 tablespoons minced fresh parsley (optional)

Salt

Freshly milled black pepper

1½ to 2 pounds cod fillets

Preheat the broiler.

Mix together the olives, capers, anchovies, garlic, 1 tablespoon of the olive oil, the balsamic vinegar, tomatoes, and parsley, if using, in a medium nonreactive bowl. (Or, if you wish, pulse for 10 to 15 seconds in a food processor.) Season with salt and pepper to taste. Let sit while you prepare the cod.

Coat the cod fillets on both sides with the remaining olive oil. Place in a broiling pan, and broil for 8 to 10 minutes, or until cooked through. It is unnecessary to turn the fish—the heat of the pan will cook the bottom side. Remove from the pan and spoon the olive mixture down the center of the fillets.

—Chef Michael Gourgouras

Braised Alaskan King Crab Legs

The crab legs braise in the butter and sherry in this simple preparation I developed. Packers sometimes brine the legs, so soak them for thirty minutes before cooking, then drain thoroughly. Be sure to have a supply of large napkins or paper towels handy because crab legs are as messy as lobsters to eat.

SERVES 4

2 sticks butter (1 cup)
2 to 3 tablespoons chopped garlic
$\frac{1}{2}$ cup dry sherry
6 pounds crab legs
Lemon wedges

Preheat the oven to 425°F.

Melt the butter in a small pan over medium heat and add the garlic. Cook over low heat for 10 to 15 minutes. Remove $\frac{1}{2}$ cup of the butter and add the sherry to the remaining butter. Set both aside. Place the crab legs in a large nonreactive baking dish in a single layer. Pour over the garlic butter and sherry mixture. Place the pan on the top shelf of the oven and bake for 12 to 15 minutes, turning the legs and basting at least once during cooking. The shells will caramelize slightly. Serve with the reserved butter and lemon wedges.

Shirred Crabmeat

This richly flavored recipe takes almost no time to put together and can easily be doubled. Serve over rice alongside a green salad.

SERVES 2

8 ounces lump crabmeat, picked over for shells and cartilage

$^1/_4$ cup softened butter

1 tablespoon finely chopped garlic, green germ removed

$^1/_4$ teaspoon dry mustard

Dash of cocktail bitters, such as Angostura

$^1/_4$ teaspoon vanilla extract

Preheat the oven to 350°F.

Place the crabmeat, butter, garlic, mustard, bitters, and vanilla in a small baking dish. Gently stir together. Cover with aluminum foil, and bake for 15 minutes. Uncover and bake 15 minutes longer, or until the butter is almost completely absorbed by the crabmeat.

VARIATION

With sherry
Omit the bitters and vanilla. Add 1 tablespoon good-quality dry sherry.

Southern-Style Crabmeat

Lump crabmeat is essential for this simple preparation. Any leftovers are delicious in tortillas or crepes. Serve with rice and a sliced tomato salad.

SERVES 3 TO 4

¹⁄₂ cup fresh bread crumbs

1 tablespoon freshly grated Parmigiano-Reggiano cheese

1 to 2 tablespoons finely chopped fresh parsley, or 1 tablespoon chopped fresh sweet marjoram

1 pound lump crabmeat, drained, picked over for shells and cartilage

Dry mustard

1 tablespoon dry sherry

4 tablespoons butter

Preheat the oven to 400°F.

Mix together the bread crumbs, cheese, and parsley in a small bowl. Set aside. In a medium nonreactive baking dish, toss together the crabmeat, a pinch of dry mustard, and the sherry. Dot with 3 tablespoons of the butter. Bake for 10 minutes. Remove, stir the ingredients, and top with the reserved bread crumb mixture. Dot with the remaining butter, raise the oven heat to 450°F, and place back in the oven until the topping browns, 5 to 10 minutes. Serve immediately.

Crabmeat with Morel Mushrooms

Two luxury ingredients star in this easy company dish. If you wish, substitute white mushrooms for the morels. Save at least a few tablespoons for an omelet filling.

SERVES 4

2 tablespoons butter

2 tablespoons unbleached all-purpose flour

1 cup sliced fresh morel mushrooms

1 cup milk, heated

2 tablespoons chopped roasted red pepper

$\frac{1}{2}$ teaspoon ketchup

Dry mustard

3 tablespoons freshly grated Parmigiano-Reggiano cheese

1 pound fresh crabmeat, picked over for shells and cartilage

Hot pepper sauce (optional)

Salt (optional)

Freshly milled black pepper (optional)

3 tablespoons thinly sliced almonds

Preheat the oven to 400°F.

Heat the butter in a small nonreactive saucepan. Remove the pan from the heat and stir in the flour. Return to the heat and cook over low for 2 to 3 minutes, which will cook through the flour. Stir in the mushrooms, and cook 1 minute longer. Whisk in the milk. Add the red pepper, and cook 3 minutes longer or until the sauce is thick. Add the ketchup, a generous pinch of mustard, the cheese, and the crabmeat. Remove from the heat. Season with a dash of hot sauce and salt and pepper, if desired.

Place the mixture in a shallow, buttered baking dish, just large enough to hold the crabmeat in a layer about $1\frac{1}{2}$ inches deep. Bake for 15 minutes. Sprinkle with the almonds, and bake 5 minutes longer, or until the almonds are toasted.

Citrus Soft-Shell Crabs

This popular chef's special at Legal's West Palm Beach restaurant in Florida also uses Chipotle Sweet Potato Mash (page 264) and Grilled Tomato Salsa (page 285).

SERVES 4

$1/3$ cup fresh lime juice

2 to 3 tablespoons minced garlic

$1/4$ cup olive oil

2 teaspoons chopped fresh oregano

Salt

Freshly milled black pepper

4 soft-shell crabs

Place the lime juice, garlic, olive oil, oregano, and salt and pepper to taste in a small nonreactive bowl. Whip lightly to combine. Let sit for at least 30 minutes to allow the flavors to meld. Add the soft-shell crabs, one by one, making sure that they are coated with the marinade. Let sit for no longer than 15 minutes before grilling or broiling for 5 minutes or until cooked through. Serve immediately.

—Chef Joe Coletto

Summer Flounder in a Butter Sauce

Fluke, or summer flounders, are found in salt water from Maine to the Carolinas, and are also farmed. Either way, they have a delicate flavor that shows up best in simply prepared dishes, such as this takeoff on a classic French recipe. Treat the fish gently, and wait to flour until just before sautéing, to keep the coating from becoming gummy. Of course, if you can locate true Dover sole, you can call this recipe by its French name, *Sole à la Meunière*.

SERVES 4

2 pounds summer flounder fillets

Salt

Freshly milled black pepper

Unbleached all-purpose flour

2 tablespoons grapeseed oil

4 to 5 tablespoons butter

2 tablespoons minced fresh parsley

2 to 3 teaspoons fresh lemon juice

Pat the fillets dry and place them flat on a countertop. Generously salt and pepper both sides of each fillet. Dip them in flour, and shake to remove any excess flour. In a large nonreactive skillet, heat the oil and 2 tablespoons of the butter. Add the fish and cook quickly for 1 to 2 minutes, or until the coating is lightly browned. Turn the fillets and cook another minute. Remove from the pan to a serving dish. (You may need to do this in batches because if you crowd the pan, the fish will steam rather than fry.)

Discard the fat in the pan, and heat the remaining butter until it is lightly browned. (Watch carefully; the butter turns from an appetizing nutty-tasting brown to an unappealing bitter black in seconds.) Add the parsley and lemon juice to taste. Pour around the fish. Serve immediately.

VARIATIONS

With almonds, chopped hazelnuts, or pine nuts
Omit the chopped parsley. After the fish is fried, add the butter. Before it browns, stir in about 4 tablespoons nuts. When the nuts are barely browned, add the lemon juice. Pour the sauce over the fish.

With Mango Salsa (page 284)
Omit the butter and lemon sauce. Serve with a topping of salsa and a garnish of fresh cilantro sprigs.

Spicy Fried Grouper with Jalapeño Mayonnaise

The Fried Fish Coating (page 286) makes these fillets crispy. For best results, test the temperature of the oil with a deep-fat frying thermometer.

SERVES 4

⅓ cup mayonnaise

1 teaspoon seeded and minced jalapeño

1 to 2 teaspoons fresh lime juice

2 pounds thin grouper fillets, cut into serving pieces

⅓ cup buttermilk

1 cup Fried Fish Coating (page 286)

Grapeseed oil or a combination of grapeseed and olive oils

Mix together the mayonnaise, jalapeño, and lime juice in a small nonreactive bowl and refrigerate while you prepare the fish. Soak the fillets in the buttermilk for at least 15 minutes. Dip the fillets in the fish coating several times and then shake to remove any excess coating. Pour the oil about ¼ inch up the sides of a heavy skillet, and heat it to a temperature of 365°F. Fry the grouper, a few pieces at a time, until crispy, about 3 minutes. Remove them from the fat and drain on paper bags or kitchen towels.

VARIATIONS

With jerk seasoning

Soak the fillets in bottled jerk marinade for at least 15 minutes before placing in the buttermilk. Use the spicy variation for the Fried Fish Coating.

With curry

Mix ½ to 1 teaspoon Thai green curry paste with the buttermilk. Use the spicy variation for the Fried Fish Coating.

Grouper with Tomatoes and Corn

Buy a little extra grouper so you can make the Corn and Green Bean Chowder (page 237).

SERVES 4

One 2-pound grouper fillet

2 to 3 tablespoons fresh lime juice

2 tablespoons olive oil

1¼ cups peeled, seeded, and diced tomatoes

1¼ cups fresh corn kernels

1 cup diced onions

3 tablespoons chopped fresh cilantro

Preheat the oven to 450°F.

Marinate the grouper in the lime juice in a nonreactive bowl for about 10 minutes. Shake off any excess lime juice and place the fillets in a large nonreactive baking pan. Drizzle with 1 tablespoon of the olive oil. Top with the tomatoes, corn, and onions. Bake for 10 minutes. Remove from the oven, add the cilantro to the vegetables, and spread them around the fish. Moisten the fillet with the remaining tablespoon of oil. Bake about 10 minutes longer, or until the fish is cooked through. (Both the fish and the vegetables should be done at this point. If the vegetables look a little raw, remove the fillet to a platter and cover with a clean kitchen towel.) Stir the pan juices into the vegetables and return to the oven for another 5 minutes. Spoon the vegetables over the grouper before serving.

Easy Baked Haddock

You can make this with any fish fillets, such as cod, grouper, or salmon, and any thickness of fish. Be sure to adjust the baking time depending upon the thickness of the fish. If you live in an area where it's difficult to buy fresh fish, this works well with frozen fish, but broil the fish rather than bake it, because the moisture from the previously frozen fish softens the bread crumbs. Substitute cracker crumbs, if you wish. The quickest way to make bread crumbs is to whirl two pieces of day-old bread in a blender until the mixture is the consistency you prefer.

SERVES 4

2 pounds haddock fillets

$^1/_2$ cup freshly made bread crumbs

1 to 1$^1/_2$ teaspoons minced garlic

1$^1/_2$ tablespoons chopped fresh parsley, chives, or sweet marjoram, or 1 tablespoon chopped fresh tarragon

2 tablespoons mayonnaise

Freshly milled black pepper

Preheat the oven to 425°F.

Place the haddock fillets in a large buttered baking dish. Blend together the bread crumbs, garlic, and parsley. Spread the surface of the fish with the mayonnaise, and sprinkle with pepper to taste and the bread crumb mixture. Bake for 8 to 15 minutes, or until the fish is opaque and cooked through and the bread crumbs are lightly browned.

Haddock Escabeche with Carrots

Prepare this quick meal in the morning and enjoy it for supper on a hot day. If the fish is covered with the marinade and refrigerated, it will stay in good condition for at least four days.

SERVES 4 TO 6

Olive oil, or a combination of olive and grapeseed oils

2 pounds haddock, cod, or grouper fillets, about $3/4$ inch thick

2 large onions, peeled and thinly sliced

2 red peppers, seeded and sliced, or 1 red and 1 yellow pepper

4 medium carrots, peeled and coarsely grated

1 cup rice wine vinegar

1 tablespoon minced garlic

Salt

Freshly milled black pepper

Hot pepper sauce

$1/3$ cup minced fresh parsley

Heat about $1/4$ cup oil in a large, heavy, nonreactive skillet. Blot the fish fillets with a paper towel and fry them in the hot oil for 3 to 5 minutes per side. When they are golden brown and cooked through, place them on paper bags to drain.

Wipe out the skillet and add about 2 tablespoons oil. Reheat. Add the onions and cook, stirring, for about 3 minutes. Add the peppers and cook another 2 minutes. Stir in the carrots, vinegar, and garlic. Cook, stirring frequently, for about 5 minutes. Add salt, pepper, and hot pepper sauce to taste. Stir in the parsley.

Place half the vegetable mixture into a large glass or enameled dish. Top with the fish, then cover with the remaining vegetable marinade. Cover the dish tightly with plastic wrap and let stand in the refrigerator for at least 1 day before serving. Tip the dish and spoon the marinade over the fish occasionally to keep the oil from separating from the vinegar. Serve cold or at room temperature.

Haddock with an Herb and Bread Crumb Topping

Change the herbs to vary the flavor. This recipe works well with virtually any fish fillets.

SERVES 4

1½ to 2 pounds haddock, skin left on

Vegetable oil

½ cup bread crumbs

2 tablespoons freshly grated Parmigiano-Reggiano cheese

2 tablespoons chopped fresh parsley or sweet marjoram, or 1 tablespoon fresh tarragon

Preheat the oven to 400°F.

Dry the haddock and oil lightly. Place in a large baking dish, skin side down. Mix together the bread crumbs, cheese, and herbs. Spread over the fish. Bake for 10 to 12 minutes, or until cooked through but still slightly translucent.

VARIATIONS

With roasted red peppers

Slice about 3 tablespoons roasted red peppers into thin strips and place on the haddock. Top with the bread crumbs and proceed as above.

Salmon with Mustard and Bread Crumbs

Substitute a large fillet of salmon for the haddock. Spread with a thin coating of Dijon mustard (½ to 1 teaspoon) before topping with bread crumbs. Proceed as above.

Halibut with a Fruit Salsa

The amount of citrus juice is necessary to macerate the fruit, but pour it off before serving with the fish. We serve this with wood-grilled halibut or swordfish at our Huntington, Long Island, restaurant. The salsa makes a light, refreshing accompaniment to the halibut.

SERVES 4

⅓ cup diced red pepper

¼ cup thinly sliced scallions, both white and green parts

1 cup fresh pineapple, cut into 1-inch cubes

½ to 1 teaspoon seeded and minced jalapeño

¼ cup julienned jicama (optional)

¼ cup fresh orange juice

¼ cup fresh lime juice

1¼ to 2 cups seedless watermelon, cut into 1-inch cubes

3 to 4 tablespoons chopped fresh cilantro

Salt (optional)

Freshly milled black pepper (optional)

Vegetable oil

1½ to 2 pounds halibut or swordfish steaks

Prepare a gas or charcoal grill.

Place the red pepper, scallions, pineapple, jalapeño, jicama, if using, orange and lime juices, and watermelon in a large non-reactive bowl. Stir in 2 tablespoons of the cilantro. Taste the mixture and add more cilantro, and salt and pepper if you wish. Let sit while you grill the halibut.

Oil the halibut and place on an oiled grill. Grill for 10 to 12 minutes, or until cooked through, turning once. Place the halibut on a plate. Drain the fruit salsa, saving the liquid. Add the remaining cilantro. Moisten the fish with the reserved juices, and pass it separately.

—Chef Nelson Rothstein

Boiled Lobster

Boiling lobster is one of those cooking skills that sounds elementary, but there are a few tips you should know before dumping the lobsters in a pot and calling it quits. Be sure that the pot you are going to use is large enough to hold the lobsters with plenty of extra room.

Most lobsters cook much faster than you might expect. We've worked out a timetable for our restaurants that works well as a general rule. All timing should start from the moment the water comes to a *second* boil. Here is the timing we use:

1 to 1½ pounds	10 to 12 minutes
1½ to 2 pounds	15 to 18 minutes
2½ to 5 pounds	20 to 25 minutes
6 to 10 pounds	25 to 35 minutes

We serve our lobsters with drawn butter, which is butter melted just to the boiling point, then removed from the heat and served warm.

If you'd prefer, place the lobsters in the freezer for twenty to thirty minutes. They will be lulled and easier to handle when you put them in the pot.

SERVES 4

Four 1¼-pound lobsters
⅔ cup drawn butter

Bring a large pot of water to a boil. Immediately add the lobsters. When the water comes to a second boil, lower the heat to a gentle boil and start timing.

Remove the lobsters from the water and let them drain in the sink. Serve along with drawn butter and lots of paper towels.

Lobster Milanese

I developed this recipe for people who like their lobsters plain, yet tasty. I had just returned from Milan, Italy, and was impressed with the simplicity of great Italian cooking. There's no need for melted butter, although you can serve it with the lobster if you wish. The olive oil keeps the lobster body meat moist, while the claw meat cooks in its own juices.

SERVES 4

Four 1¼-pound lobsters
4 tablespoons olive oil
4 teaspoons finely minced garlic
Cayenne pepper
4 jumbo shrimp, peeled

Place the lobsters in the freezer for about 30 minutes.

Preheat the broiler.

Remove 1 lobster from the freezer and place it stomach side down on the counter. With a heavy knife, cut through the lobster behind the head. This kills the lobster by severing its spine, although it may continue to move after it is dead. Turn the lobster over and cut the body and tail cavities lengthwise down the center.

Gently spread open the lobster's body and brush the cavity with 1 tablespoon of the olive oil. Sprinkle with 1 teaspoon of the garlic and dust with cayenne. Stuff the tail with 1 shrimp.

Repeat this procedure with the remaining lobsters. Place them on a broiling pan and broil for 8 to 10 minutes, or until they are cooked through. Do not overcook, or the meat will dry out and toughen.

Mahi Mahi Baked with Tomatoes and Bacon

Mahi mahi's dense texture lends itself nicely to a bacon wrap.

SERVES 4

4 slices bacon

1½ cups peeled, seeded, and diced tomatoes

¼ cup diced red or green pepper

½ cup chopped onions

1 teaspoon olive oil

1½ to 2 pounds mahi mahi steaks

Freshly milled black pepper

Preheat the oven to 450°F.

Cover the bacon slices with boiling water and let sit for 5 to 10 minutes. Drain and dry the bacon.

Oil a baking pan just large enough to hold the fish. Mix together the tomatoes, pepper, onions, and olive oil. Place the fish fillets in the pan, skin side down, and sprinkle with black pepper. Top with the tomato mixture. Arrange the bacon on top. Bake for 20 minutes, or until the fish is cooked through.

Mackerel Stew

Make this one-pot meal in about twenty minutes.

SERVES 4

2 tablespoons olive oil

2 pounds skinned mackerel fillets, cut into 2-inch chunks

3 tablespoons chopped garlic

1 tablespoon seeded and chopped jalapeño

2 cups peeled, seeded, and chopped tomatoes

2 tablespoons fresh lemon juice

3 tablespoons whole green pitted olives

1 cup thickly sliced summer squash (about 1 medium)

$\frac{1}{2}$ cup chopped fresh basil or parsley

Salt

Freshly milled black pepper

Heat the olive oil in a large nonreactive skillet. Add the mackerel, sear lightly on one side, then turn and sear on the other. Add the garlic, jalapeño, tomatoes, lemon juice, olives, and summer squash. Cook uncovered for 5 minutes, then cover the pan and cook over medium heat until the fish is cooked through and the tomatoes have softened, making a light sauce, 8 to 10 minutes longer. Stir in the basil. Season with salt and pepper to taste.

Mahi Mahi with a Pear and Jalapeño Chutney

This fruit chutney works equally well with swordfish, tuna, snapper—or even pork. Any left-over chutney will keep for several days if refrigerated, and it is delicious in a cream cheese and whole wheat sandwich, either alone or with slices of smoked turkey or ham. If you're saving any extra sauce, omit the mint until just before serving.

SERVES 4

1 tablespoon grapeseed oil

⅓ cup chopped red onion

2 to 3 tablespoons fresh orange juice

2 tablespoons fresh lemon juice

2 tablespoons dry white wine

⅓ cup sugar

1 to 2 teaspoons lemon zest

5 medium-hard pears, peeled and diced (about 2 cups)

3 tablespoons chopped scallions, both white and green parts

1 jalapeño, seeded and minced

2 tablespoons diced red pepper

2 to 3 tablespoons julienned fresh mint (optional)

2 pounds mahi mahi

Heat the oil in a large nonreactive saucepan and add the onion. Cook, stirring constantly, for 1 minute. Add the orange and lemon juices, wine, sugar, and lemon zest. Cook over high heat, stirring frequently, until the juices are reduced by half. Stir in the pears. Continue cooking over medium-high heat until the pears are cooked through but still have some texture, 5 to 10 minutes. Place the mixture in a bowl, and let cool. Stir in the scallions, jalapeño, red pepper, and mint, if using.

Mahi mahi fillets can be thick, so cut them crosswise into 1-inch-thick pieces if necessary. Oil the fillets and broil or grill until done. It is unnecessary to turn the fish. Remove from the heat and top each serving with at least 1 tablespoon of the chutney.

VARIATION

With salmon and mango

Substitute salmon for the mahi mahi. Add ¼ cup diced mango along with the scallions. Substitute 1 tablespoon fresh basil or parsley for the mint if desired.

—Executive Chef Rich Vellante

Mahi Mahi Barbados

We also serve this sauce with scallops, and with shrimp that have
first been seasoned with Cajun seasoning.

SERVES 4

1¹⁄₂ to 2 pounds mahi mahi

Vegetable oil

Cajun seasoning

1 cup mango in ¹⁄₄-inch dice

1 cup diced plum tomatoes

¹⁄₃ to ¹⁄₂ cup olive oil

1 tablespoon fresh lemon or
lime juice

1 cup diced red onions

2 to 3 tablespoons seeded and
minced jalapeño

2 to 3 tablespoons julienned fresh
mint or a mixture of mint
and tarragon

Jasmine rice

Preheat the broiler

Place the mahi mahi on a broiling rack. Coat with vegetable oil, then sprinkle with Cajun seasoning to taste. Let sit for at least 15 minutes.

Meanwhile, gently toss together the mango, plum tomatoes, olive oil, lemon juice, onions, and jalapeño. Do not overmix. Broil the fish until cooked through without turning. As mahi mahi is a dense fish, this will take anywhere from 10 to 15 minutes. Just before serving the salsa, stir in the mint. Place a mound of jasmine rice in the center of a serving platter, surround with the fish, then garnish with half of the salsa. Put the remaining salsa in a bowl and pass.

Oven-Roasted Mussels

Cooking mussels this way allows them to steam in their own juices. Serve the mussel liquor as a dip, or save as a base for soup. Place the mussels flat in the baking pan so that their juices do not drain out.

SERVES 4

2 tablespoons chopped garlic

1 cup chopped onions

1 tablespoon grapeseed oil

4 pounds cleaned mussels

Preheat the oven to 400°F.

Put the garlic, onion, and oil in a large nonreactive baking dish. Top with the mussels. Roast for 10 to 12 minutes, or until the mussels open completely. Discard any that do not open. Serve immediately with the mussel liquor on the side.

VARIATION

Roasted Littleneck Clams
Proceed as above, substituting 20 littleneck clams for the mussels. Roast for 20 minutes.

Stir-Fried Monkfish with Beans and Lemongrass

Monkfish is one of the few fish that you can stir-fry. Softer-textured fish will flake and fall apart. A nonstick skillet is essential with this small amount of oil. Try to find freshly harvested lemongrass that is pliable. Otherwise, substitute cilantro.

SERVES 4

1 pound green beans, trimmed

1 tablespoon plus 1 teaspoon peanut or canola oil

2 tablespoons minced garlic

1$\frac{1}{2}$ tablespoons minced fresh ginger

1 tablespoon orange zest

1$\frac{1}{2}$ pounds monkfish fillet, cut into pieces about $\frac{1}{2}$ inch thick and 1 inch wide

3-inch-long stalk of lemongrass, sliced in half lengthwise, or 2 tablespoons chopped fresh cilantro

$\frac{1}{3}$ cup sweet onion, sliced lengthwise

1 tablespoon soy sauce

1 teaspoon sherry vinegar

$\frac{1}{4}$ teaspoon toasted sesame oil

1 teaspoon honey (optional)

1 tablespoon cornstarch

Salt (optional)

$\frac{1}{2}$ cup cashews

Lay the beans in a large shallow bowl and cover with boiling water. Let sit for 10 minutes, drain, and roll in a dish towel to dry. Cut diagonally into 1$\frac{1}{2}$-inch-long pieces and set aside.

In a large nonstick skillet, heat 1 tablespoon of the oil. Add the garlic, ginger, and orange zest. Cook over high heat, stirring constantly, for 30 seconds to 1 minute. Do not let brown. Remove from the pan with a slotted spoon and set aside. Add the fish, and cook, stirring constantly, until cooked through, about 3 minutes. Remove from the pan with a slotted spoon, and set aside.

Add the remaining teaspoon of oil if necessary. Heat the oil and add the beans, lemongrass, and onion. Cook, stirring constantly, for 2 minutes. Add the reserved garlic mixture, soy sauce, sherry vinegar, sesame oil, and honey, if using. Cook, stirring, until the sauce is heated through. Remove the pan from the heat.

Mix the cornstarch with 1$\frac{1}{2}$ tablespoons water. Stir in 2 tablespoons of the liquid from the pan, then pour the mixture over the vegetables in the pan. Return the pan to the stove, and cook, stirring constantly, until the sauce is thickened. Gently add the fish. Taste and add salt if necessary. Remove the lemongrass pieces. Serve immediately alongside white or brown rice. Top with the cashews.

With broccoli and red and yellow peppers

Omit the beans, lemongrass, and cashews. Substitute $1\frac{1}{2}$ cups blanched broccoli florets and $\frac{1}{4}$ cup each coarsely chopped red and yellow peppers. Add the peppers along with the broccoli into the heated oil. Proceed as above. Just before serving, stir in $\frac{1}{2}$ teaspoon minced fresh rosemary.

With lobster

Add 2 sliced lobster claws along with the cooked fish.

Coquilles Saint-Jacques

In the early days of Legal Sea Foods our version of this classic French dish was one of the most popular recipes on the menu. The tomatoes are Legal's addition.

SERVES 4

4 tablespoons butter

½ cup finely chopped Vidalia or other sweet onions (1 small)

⅓ cup peeled, seeded, and diced tomatoes

4 ounces baby portobello mushrooms, sliced

2 pounds sea scallops

½ cup dry white wine

2 tablespoons unbleached all-purpose flour

¾ to 1 cup cream, half-and-half, or milk

3 to 4 tablespoons freshly grated Parmigiano-Reggiano cheese

Salt

Freshly milled black pepper

Cayenne pepper

1 tablespoon chopped fresh parsley (optional)

Preheat the oven to 400°F.

Heat 1 tablespoon of the butter in a large nonreactive skillet. Add the onions and cook, stirring occasionally, for 2 minutes. Stir in the tomatoes and mushrooms and cook for 3 minutes longer. Halve the scallops, and add to the pan along with the wine. Cover the pan, lower the heat, and simmer for about 2 minutes. Remove from the heat and set aside.

In a small saucepan, heat 2 tablespoons of the butter. Remove from the heat, stir in the flour, then put back on the stove and cook over low heat for 2 minutes. Remove the pan from the heat. Heat the cream and add it to the flour mixture. Stir, return the pan to the heat, and cook over medium-low until the sauce is thickened. Stir the cream mixture into the scallops and vegetables and add 2 tablespoons of the cheese. Taste and season with salt, black pepper, and cayenne pepper.

Spoon the mixture into a buttered baking dish, sprinkle with the remaining cheese, dot with the remaining butter, and bake for 10 to 15 minutes, or until the top is browned. Or, you can brown the top under the broiler. Sprinkle with the parsley before serving.

Oyster and Mushroom Casserole

The oysters will exude a great deal of liquid as they cook, so adjust the amount of flour to fit how thick a sauce you'd like. (Three tablespoons of flour will create a thicker sauce.) This specialty of Legal's Kendall Square restaurant in Cambridge was developed for an oyster promotion. Rice—along with a mixed green salad or steamed broccoli—goes well with this dish.

SERVES 4

3 to 4 tablespoons butter

2 to 3 teaspoons minced shallots

4 ounces sliced fresh mushrooms

2 to 3 tablespoons unbleached all-puprose flour

1 tablespoon dry sherry

2 tablespoons dry white wine

1 pint shucked oysters and their juices

Cayenne pepper

Salt

Freshly milled black pepper

1/3 cup Cracker Crumb Mixture (page 286)

Preheat the oven to 400°F.

Melt the butter in a nonreactive saucepan. Add the shallots and cook for 1 minute over medium-high heat. Stir in the mushrooms and cook another 2 minutes, stirring constantly. Remove from the heat, and stir in the flour. Return to the heat and cook, stirring constantly, for 2 minutes. Add the sherry and wine. The mixture will be thick. Stir in the oysters and their juices. Season with a generous pinch of cayenne pepper, salt, and black pepper. Put the mixture into a shallow baking dish and sprinkle with the cracker crumbs. Bake for 10 to 15 minutes, or until the oysters are cooked and the top is browned.

—Chef Brian McGorry

Scalloped Oysters

This old-fashioned recipe uses shucked oysters and their juices for a simple dish that's great for a brunch or a supper with a side of corn bread and a green salad.

SERVES 3 TO 4

1 cup freshly made bread crumbs

⅓ cup crushed saltine cracker crumbs

Dry mustard

4 to 6 tablespoons melted butter

1 pint shucked oysters and their juices

3 tablespoons cream or milk

Freshly milled black pepper

Preheat the oven to 400°F.

Mix together the bread crumbs, cracker crumbs, and a generous pinch of dry mustard in a bowl. Toss with the melted butter. Spread a thin layer of bread crumbs in the bottom of a shallow ovenproof casserole. Top with half the oysters and their juices, then add half the cream and a generous grind of black pepper. Add another layer of crumbs, the remaining oysters and cream, and season again with pepper. Top with the remaining crumbs. Bake for 20 to 25 minutes, or until the crumbs are browned. Serve immediately.

Oven-Steamed Salmon

There's no fat in this easy-to-prepare meal. Using this recipe, you can also oven-steam a whole salmon, cool it, and serve with a dill mayonnaise for a buffet dinner.

SERVES 4

1½ to 2 pounds salmon steaks

½ cup chopped carrots

¼ cup chopped cucumber

3 tablespoons chopped fresh sweet marjoram, chervil, or parsley

¼ cup chopped sweet onion

Quartered lemons

Preheat the oven to 400°F.

Place the salmon steaks on a large sheet of heavy-duty aluminum foil. Scatter the carrots, cucumber, herbs, and onion over the steaks. Fold the foil over and around the salmon like an envelope so that the cooking juices don't escape. Bake the salmon for 10 to 15 minutes, depending upon the thickness of the steaks. Remember that the salmon will continue to cook slightly as it cools. Remove from the oven, loosen the foil, and spoon the cooking juices over the salmon. Cool slightly before serving. Serve with quartered lemons to squeeze over the salmon.

VARIATION

With sour cream and dill

Omit the lemons. Serve with a sauce made with 1 cup sour cream (or a mixture of sour cream and yogurt), 1 teaspoon fresh lemon juice, and 1 to 2 tablespoons chopped fresh dill. A dash of bitters deepens the flavor.

Asian Glazed Salmon

Any extra glaze will keep for weeks if refrigerated in a covered container. We serve this dish with jasmine rice and seasonal vegetables, such as sugar snap peas.

SERVES 4

½ cup brown sugar

⅓ cup soy sauce

2 tablespoons hoisin sauce

2 tablespoons peeled and sliced ginger

Dried red pepper flakes

½ teaspoon chopped garlic

1 tablespoon fresh lime juice

1½ to 2 pounds salmon fillets

Place the sugar, soy sauce, hoisin sauce, ginger, a dash of red pepper flakes, garlic, and lime juice in a medium nonreactive saucepan. Bring the mixture to a boil, reduce the heat to medium, and cook for 15 to 20 minutes, or until the sauce forms a glaze. Set aside.

Preheat the broiler.

Place the salmon fillets on a broiler pan and baste with the sauce. Let sit for 15 minutes. Broil them until cooked through, about 8 minutes, basting again with the glaze. Remove the salmon from the heat and baste once more with the glaze before serving.

—Executive Chef Rich Vellante

Salmon Milan

Popular at Boston's Long Wharf restaurant, this is a picture-pretty version of salmon and mussels. We grill the salmon, but it's equally good baked.

SERVES 4

1½ tablespoons grapeseed or olive oil

1½ to 2 pounds salmon fillets

1 to 1½ pounds cleaned mussels

1 cup thinly sliced sweet onions (about 1 large) or thinly sliced leeks

½ cup dry white wine

¼ cup diced tomatoes

¼ to ½ teaspoon balsamic vinegar

Salt

Freshly milled black pepper

4 pieces garlic toast

Preheat the broiler or prepare an outdoor grill. Oil the salmon lightly with ½ tablespoon of the oil. Place on a broiler pan, if cooking indoors, or set the fillets on the grill. If broiling, do not turn the salmon. The heat from the pan will cook the salmon through in 10 to 12 minutes. If grilling outdoors, carefully turn the salmon once.

Meanwhile, heat the remaining 1 tablespoon oil in a large nonreactive skillet. Add the mussels, onions, and white wine. Stir and cook for 2 minutes. The mussels should be opened. (If not, cover the pan, and steam over high heat for 1 minute longer.) Remove the mussels from the pan, leaving the onions and pan juices. Add the tomatoes and balsamic vinegar, and cook for 1 minute over high heat. Season with salt and pepper to taste.

Place a piece of garlic toast on each plate. Surround with the mussels, and cover the toast with the salmon. Place a tablespoon of the cooking liquid (including the onions and tomatoes) over each salmon piece. If there is any additional liquid, serve it on the side.

—Chef David Welch

Nutty Salmon

The only trick in preparing this easy—yet elegant—special of Boston's Chestnut Hill restaurant is to firmly press the sliced almonds onto the salmon. Be sure to buy thinly sliced, not slivered, almonds.

SERVES 4

1½ to 2 pounds salmon fillets, skin removed

Freshly milled black pepper

1 large egg

1 to 1½ cups sliced almonds

Grapeseed oil

Cut the salmon into serving pieces, blot dry, and sprinkle with pepper. Beat an egg and thoroughly coat the salmon pieces. Thickly sprinkle the almonds over the surface of the salmon and press down firmly on each piece to coat with the almonds. Turn the pieces and repeat the process.

Heat enough oil to cover the bottom of a large skillet ¼ inch deep, and add the salmon. Do not crowd the pan. (It may be necessary to cook the salmon in two batches.) Brown over medium-high heat on one side, turn, and brown on the other. Lower the heat, and continue cooking until desired doneness.

—Chef Michael Gourgouras

Roasted Salmon with an Avocado Sauce

Sautéing the salmon works equally well in this colorful specialty at Legal's Bethesda, Maryland, restaurant.

SERVES 4

Grapeseed oil

2 pounds salmon fillets

2 avocados

2 to 3 tablespoons fresh lime juice

1 tablespoon chopped garlic

2 to 3 tablespoons chopped red onion

Hot pepper sauce

2 tablespoons finely sliced scallion greens

1 teaspoon chopped fresh cilantro

Salt

Freshly milled black pepper (optional)

Preheat the oven to 425°F.

Lightly oil the salmon fillets and bake for 8 to 10 minutes. Remove from the oven and let cool for 2 minutes.

Meanwhile, peel and chop the avocados. Toss with the lime juice, garlic, onion, a dash of hot sauce, scallions, and cilantro. Season with salt and pepper, if desired. Place the fillets on a serving dish and spoon 2 tablespoons of the avocado mixture over each piece. Pass any extra sauce separately.

—Chef Omar Ayala

Salmon and Sole Lattice

This is an easy yet splashy way to serve fish. You weave strips of raw salmon and sole in a lattice pattern, much like making a pie crust—or the pot holders you turned out as a child. This sounds complicated, but only takes about five minutes. The fish keeps its shape while baking, and the presentation of the pink of the salmon alternating with the white of the sole is beautiful. Baby new potatoes and sautéed sugar snap or snow peas look attractive with this dish.

SERVES 4 TO 6

$1\frac{1}{4}$ **pounds salmon fillets**

$1\frac{1}{4}$ **pounds sole fillets**

$1\frac{1}{4}$ **tablespoons butter**

$\frac{1}{4}$ **cup white wine or water**

1 tablespoon minced garlic (optional)

2 tablespoons finely chopped fresh parsley

Preheat the oven to 400°F.

The salmon and sole fillets should be of equal thickness—ideally, no more than $\frac{1}{2}$ inch thick. Slice them into $\frac{3}{4}$ inch-wide strips about 5 inches long. You will have some end pieces of fish left over. Set them aside.

Line up 4 strips of the sole in parallel rows, touching each other. Take a strip of salmon at a right angle to the sole strips. Weave it over, then under, over, and under the strips of sole at one end. When you take the next strip of salmon, start it under the first strip of sole, and weave it in a similar manner. The only difference is that where you had a square of salmon in the row before, you will have a square of sole in this row. Continue weaving the salmon and sole until you have used 4 strips of salmon with the 4 strips of sole. You will end up with a square-shaped, checker form.

Continue shaping the fish into these squares. You may end up with a few extra strips. Either freeze them for a soup or salad or roll together a strip of salmon with sole into a pinwheel, anchor with a toothpick, and cook it to use as a garnish. (Or, once cooked, it's delicious cold, accompanied with yogurt or sour cream and chopped fresh dill.)

Take $\frac{1}{2}$ tablespoon of the butter and grease the bottom of a flat, nonreactive baking dish (a 9 X 12-inch glass baking dish is ideal). Using a large spatula, lift the fish squares into the pan. Make sure that each square is reassembled so that all the strips are touching and all ends are tucked under.

Add the white wine and sprinkle the garlic, if using, along the edge of the pan. Dot the fish with the remaining butter. Bake for 12 to 15 minutes, basting occasionally. Remove from the oven and sprinkle with parsley before serving.

Three Quick Glazes for Salmon

Y OU CAN PUT together an easy supper by using one of these quick glazes. Use any of them to coat salmon or arctic char before baking or broiling.

POMEGRANATE MOLASSES GLAZE

Pomegranate molasses, a concentrate of pomegranate juice, is sold at Middle Eastern specialty shops as well as at gourmet grocery stores.

1 tablespoon pomegranate molasses

$\frac{1}{2}$ teaspoon bottled horseradish

1 teaspoon grapeseed oil

$\frac{1}{2}$ teaspoon brown sugar

Mix together the molasses, horseradish, oil, and sugar.

ORANGE MARMALADE GLAZE

3 tablespoons orange marmalade

$\frac{1}{4}$ teaspoon Chinese chili sauce (mae ploy)

$\frac{1}{4}$ teaspoon bottled horseradish

1 tablespoon fresh lime juice

Mix together the orange marmalade, chili sauce, horseradish, and lime juice.

SHERRY VINEGAR GLAZE

$\frac{1}{2}$ to $\frac{3}{4}$ teaspoon sherry or balsamic vinegar

Bitters

2 to 3 tablespoons pancake or maple syrup

1 teaspoon Dijon mustard

1 tablespoon fresh lemon juice

Mix together the vinegar, a generous dash of bitters, the syrup, mustard, and lemon juice.

VARIATION

With garlic. Mix in 1 teaspoon minced garlic.

Glazed Salmon with an Herb and Tomato Salsa

Serve any extra salsa as an accompaniment. Our catering department presents the salmon hot, but it's also quite good served at room temperature. You can find the fish and chili sauces in the Asian food section of most supermarkets.

SERVES 4 TO 6

MARINADE

2 oranges

2 to 3 tablespoons sesame oil

$\frac{1}{3}$ cup soy sauce

2 tablespoons Thai fish sauce

1 tablespoon minced fresh ginger

1 tablespoon minced garlic

1 teaspoon chili paste (sambal oelek)

2 tablespoons rice wine vinegar

2$\frac{1}{2}$ pounds salmon fillets

SALSA

6 plum tomatoes, diced

1 seedless cucumber, diced

$\frac{1}{3}$ cup chopped red onion

$\frac{1}{4}$ cup chopped scallions

1 teaspoon chopped fresh cilantro

2 tablespoons chopped fresh mint

2 teaspoons black sesame seeds

2 teaspoons white sesame seeds

1 tablespoon chopped garlic

1 tablespoon chopped fresh ginger

$\frac{1}{4}$ teaspoon Chinese chili sauce (mae ploy)

1 tablespoon sesame oil

3 tablespoons soy sauce

Salt

Freshly milled black pepper (optional)

Zest both oranges and squeeze out the juice. Place the juice and zest in a large nonreactive baking dish along with the sesame oil, soy sauce, fish sauce, ginger, garlic, chili paste, and vinegar. Stir to combine, then add the salmon fillets. Spoon the sauce over the fillets, turn them, then coat again. Marinate in the refrigerator for about 30 minutes.

Meanwhile, make the salsa. Combine the plum tomatoes and half of the cucumber in a large glass bowl. Add the onion, scallions, cilantro, mint, sesame seeds, garlic, ginger, chili sauce, sesame oil, and soy sauce. Stir to combine and let sit while you bake the salmon.

Preheat the oven to 400°F.

Spoon the marinade over the salmon again and bake for 10 to 15 minutes, basting occasionally. Watch the marinade, and add a tablespoon of water if necessary. You do not want it to burn. Remove the salmon from the oven and cool slightly. Put the remaining diced cucumber in a line down the middle of a serving plate for garnish and arrange salmon around it. Taste the salsa, season with salt and pepper, if desired, then put 2 tablespoons of the salsa over each piece of salmon. Put any extra salsa in a nonreactive bowl and pass separately.

—Chef Siobhan Magee-Bonifacio

Salmon with a Jalapeño Jelly Glaze

This super-easy glaze takes but two minutes to prepare. To prevent the glaze from burning as it drips into the pan, put two tablespoons of water around the salmon. You should end up with a light glaze to top accompanying rice or couscous. Steamed broccoli with a dash of toasted sesame seeds goes nicely with the salmon.

SERVES 4

One 2-pound salmon fillet

Dry mustard

2 tablespoons jalapeño jelly

¼ teaspoon Dijon mustard

Celery salt

½ teaspoon mild curry paste
(such as Patak's original)

Preheat the oven to 450°F.

Place the salmon, skin side down, in a nonreactive baking pan. Sprinkle with the dry mustard. Mix together the jelly, Dijon mustard, a generous pinch of celery salt, and the curry paste. Spread over the salmon. Bake for about 12 minutes, or until the salmon is opaque.

VARIATION

With an apricot glaze
Substitute apricot jelly for the jalapeño jelly and add 1 to 2 teaspoons fresh orange juice. Proceed as above.

Salmon with a Mango Glaze

At Legal's Baltimore restaurant, the salmon is always garnished with thinly sliced fresh mango, which adds a splash of color to the finished dish. You can substitute virtually any fish fillets for the salmon. Puree any extra mango sauce and store it in the freezer divided into $1/4$-cup portions. It's best to prepare the sauce ahead of time, and add the chopped mangoes just before glazing the salmon. Accompany with rice or unpeeled potatoes, sliced and roasted then sprinkled with rosemary.

SERVES 4

$1/2$ **pound butter**

$1/2$ **cup brown sugar**

2 ripe mangoes

Fresh lemon or lime juice

2 pounds salmon fillets

Melt the butter in a small saucepan; add the sugar and 1 cup of water. Cook over medium heat, stirring frequently, until thick, about 30 minutes. Remove the pan from the stove. Puree one of the mangoes and pour the puree into the sauce. Halve the other mango. You're going to dice half of the mango for the sauce, and slice the other half for the garnish. (Set the sliced mango aside and squeeze with the lemon or lime juice to prevent it from browning.) Add the diced mango to the sauce, and cook it for another 30 to 45 minutes. The sauce will have a syruplike consistency.

Either grill the salmon or bake it at 425°F. Baste the salmon with the mango glaze before cooking, and once again after the salmon is cooked through, which will take about 10 minutes.

Place the salmon fillets on a serving plate, brush again with the glaze, and garnish with the mango slices placed on end.

—Chef William Garcia

Salmon with Bacon and Mustard

Contrast the rich flavor of the salmon with an acidic vegetable,
such as Spinach with Pine Nuts (page 261).

SERVES 4

Oil

One 2-pound salmon fillet

$1/2$ teaspoon soy sauce

$3/4$ teaspoon Dijon mustard

4 to 5 slices lean bacon

Preheat the oven to 400°F.

Oil the salmon and place in a large baking dish. Brush with the soy sauce and spread with the mustard. Cover with the bacon. Bake for 10 to 12 minutes, or until the salmon is cooked through.

VARIATIONS

With bluefish

Substitute bluefish for the salmon.

With mackerel fillets

Substitute mackerel fillets. Oil and place skin side down in a baking dish. Proceed as above, placing 1 slice of bacon on each fillet. Bake for 7 to 10 minutes.

Scallop and Shrimp Kabobs

You'll need the large sea scallops for this recipe. You can prepare the ingredients in advance and assemble them just before cooking. If you're using wooden skewers, soak them in water for twenty-four hours ahead of time so that they won't burn.

(2 SKEWERS PER SERVING)
SERVES 4

1 red pepper, seeded and cut into 1-inch pieces

1 pound shrimp (16 to 20 count), peeled

1 medium zucchini, cut into eight 1-inch slices

1 pound sea scallops

1 large firm tomato, cut into eighths

2 large mushrooms, cut into quarters

1 large red onion, cut into ¹⁄₂-inch wedges

Grapeseed or vegetable oil

Preheat the broiler or prepare an outdoor grill.

Thread a skewer: Start with a red pepper slice, then slide on a shrimp, zucchini, scallop, tomato wedge, shrimp, mushroom, scallop, and a piece of red onion. Continue until 8 skewers are filled. Brush with oil and broil or grill for 3 to 4 minutes, cooking no more than 4 skewers at a time. Turn the skewers once. Serve immediately.

Seafood Casserole

A perennial favorite at every Legal Sea Foods restaurant, this is an easy, yet splashy, company dish. We serve it with either a cream or a garlic and sherry sauce.

SERVES 4

1 tablespoon butter

1 tablespoon unbleached all-purpose flour

²/₃ cup fish stock or bottled clam juice

2 tablespoons heavy cream

1 pound shrimp, peeled

½ pound sea scallops, halved

½ pound haddock or cod, cut into 1-inch cubes

6 to 8 ounces lobster meat, cut into serving pieces

⅓ cup freshly grated Monterey Jack cheese

½ cup Cracker Crumb Mixture (page 286)

Preheat the oven to 400°F.

In a small nonreactive saucepan, melt the butter over low heat. Remove from the heat and whisk in the flour. Return the pan to the stove and cook for 2 minutes over moderate heat, stirring constantly, until the flour is cooked through. Remove from the heat, and pour in the fish stock. Return the pan to the stove and cook over moderate heat, whisking constantly, for 2 to 3 minutes, or until the mixture forms a light sauce. Stir in the cream and cook over medium heat, stirring frequently, until the sauce is the thickness you prefer. (This is a light, thin sauce, designed to baste the fish as it bakes.) Set the mixture aside.

Place the shrimp, scallops, and haddock in a buttered baking dish just large enough to hold them. Pour over the sauce. Bake for 8 to 10 minutes. Remove the dish from the oven, tilt, baste with the cooking juices, and add the lobster. Sprinkle with the cheese, then top with the Cracker Crumb Mixture. Return the dish to the oven and bake for 5 to 8 minutes longer, or until the crumbs are lightly browned.

VARIATION

With garlic and sherry

Omit the sauce. Toss the seafood with 2 tablespoons butter, 1 teaspoon minced garlic, and 1 to 2 tablespoons dry sherry. Proceed as above.

Shad Roe with Bacon

This is an excellent dish for a spring brunch or light supper.

SERVES 4

8 slices lean bacon

Freshly milled black pepper

2 pairs shad roe, about 1¼ pounds

Unbleached all-purpose flour

2 quartered lemons

Cook the bacon in a heavy skillet until it is crisp; remove from the pan and set aside. Grind fresh pepper over the roe, dip in the flour, and shake to remove any excess flour. Sauté the roe in the bacon fat left in the pan for 5 minutes per side. If you wish, cover with a steamer lid while cooking.

Remove the roe to a platter, and divide along the connecting membrane. Top with the bacon and serve surrounded by lemon wedges.

VARIATIONS

With bacon, mushrooms, and tomatoes
Proceed as above. Keep the roe warm while you sauté thickly sliced mushrooms and halved tomatoes in the remaining bacon fat. Serve alongside the roe.

With lemon and chives
Omit the bacon. Use 3 tablespoons butter. Sauté the roe, remove to a serving platter, and divide. Stir 3 tablespoons fresh lemon juice into the pan juices, and pour over the roe. Sprinkle with chopped chives or sweet marjoram.

Marinated Shellfish

This is a splashy main course for a party buffet. You can vary the proportions of shellfish, but it's important to steam them and save the juices for the marinade. For best flavor, add the vegetables, herbs, and dry mustard just before serving.

SERVES 8 TO 10

2 pounds cleaned mussels

2 pounds scallops

2 pounds shrimp, preferably in shells

One 1½-pound lobster (optional)

⅓ cup fresh lemon juice

Zest of 1 lemon

1 large red pepper, cut into matchstick-sized pieces (about 1½ cups)

1 cup thinly sliced scallions, both white and green parts

2 tablespoons minced fresh sweet marjoram or parsley

Place the mussels in a steamer, add ½ cup water, cover the pan, and bring the liquid to a boil. Steam the mussels just until opened, 5 to 8 minutes, depending upon their size. Remove the mussels from the pot, reserving the liquid. Set them aside.

Using the steamer, steam the scallops and shrimp in batches, adding additional water to the steaming juices as necessary. Cool the shrimp slightly and peel. Put the lobster, if using, in a large pot, cover with water, and bring to a boil. Boil gently until cooked through, 12 to 15 minutes. Drain, shell, and cut into chunks.

Remove the mussels from their shells, reserving about 6 shelled mussels for garnish. Combine the mussels, scallops, shrimp, and lobster with the steaming juices (about 1 cup), and the lemon juice and zest. Place in a covered bowl and refrigerate overnight. Just before serving, drain off most of the marinade and stir in the red pepper, scallions, and marjoram. Serve the shellfish in a large bowl and garnish with the reserved mussels in their shells.

Double-Stuffed Baked Shrimp

This delectable duo of shrimp covered with crabmeat is one of Legal's most popular items.

SERVES 4

One 4-ounce package of Ritz crackers

4 tablespoons butter

⅓ cup chopped scallions, both white and green parts

½ cup diced celery

2 to 3 teaspoons minced garlic

1 to 2 tablespoons dry white wine

⅛ teaspoon Old Bay Seasoning

1 tablespoon fresh lemon juice

1 to 2 tablespoons chopped fresh parsley

8 ounces backfin crabmeat, picked over for shells and cartilage

Salt

Freshly milled black pepper

1 large egg, beaten

16 jumbo shrimp (about 2 pounds), peeled

Preheat the oven to 400°F.

Place the crackers in a plastic bag and crumble with your hands or with a rolling pin. Put them in a large mixing bowl, and set aside. In a large skillet, melt 2 tablespoons of the butter over medium heat and cook the scallions, celery, and garlic for 5 minutes, or until cooked through but still slightly translucent. Toss with the crackers.

Stir in the wine, Old Bay Seasoning, lemon juice, parsley, and crabmeat. Season with salt and pepper to taste. Mix in the egg.

Place the shrimp in a large buttered pan, such as a jelly-roll pan. Cover each shrimp with about 3 tablespoons of the crabmeat. Dot the crabmeat with the remaining 2 tablespoons of butter. Bake for 15 minutes, or until the shrimp and crabmeat are cooked through. Serve immediately.

VARIATION

Crab Cakes

Use any leftover crabmeat topping to make crab cakes. Add chopped red peppers to taste. Form into cakes, dust with flour, and sauté in olive oil or butter until cooked through.

—Executive Chef Rich Vellante

Gulf Coast Fried Shrimp

On Florida's Gulf Coast, where fresh shrimp are harvested, fried shrimp are a staple food.
The touch of sugar and vanilla will improve the flavor of previously frozen shrimp.

SERVES 2 TO 4

1 pound shrimp, peeled
(20 to 25 count)

¼ cup buttermilk or milk

½ teaspoon sugar

¼ teaspoon vanilla extract

1 egg, beaten (optional)

Cornmeal or lightly seasoned
cornmeal-based fish fry mix

Grapeseed or canola oil

You can leave the shrimp whole, but they fry more evenly if you butterfly them. Grasp each shrimp by the tail and cut almost through the body halfway up. Open the shrimp halves to resemble a butterfly. In a glass bowl, mix together the buttermilk, sugar, vanilla, and egg, if using. Add the shrimp, making sure that they are covered with the liquid. If not, add additional buttermilk. Let the shrimp marinate in the mixture for at least 1 hour.

Place the cornmeal on a plate, shake off any excess liquid from each shrimp, and dip in the cornmeal. Place them on a rack next to the stove.

Add the oil to a skillet to a depth of 1 inch. Heat the oil and fry the shrimp a few at a time, regulating the heat so that the shrimp do not burn. They will cook through in 30 to 45 seconds. Remove the shrimp and drain on paper bags. Serve immediately.

Jerked Shrimp with a Watermelon Coulis

The watermelon is a cool contrast to the jerk seasoning in this refreshing summer dish from Legal's Warwick, Rhode Island, restaurant. You'll need to use a potato masher or a food processor to prepare the watermelon. (A blender or food mill will puree, rather than chunk, it.) To make a wet seasoning (the method used at Legal Sea Foods), add water to a commercial dry jerk seasoning mix until it is barely moistened. This will be a much more potent mixture than a bottled commercial choice.

SERVES 4

1 to 2 tablespoons wet jerk seasoning, or $1/4$ cup bottled seasoning

2 pounds medium shrimp, peeled

$2^1/2$ to 3 cups peeled watermelon in large chunks

1 teaspoon brown sugar

2 tablespoons grapeseed oil

Mix the jerk seasoning with the shrimp in a large nonreactive bowl. Let sit for at least 15 minutes. Meanwhile, seed the watermelon and either pulse for a few seconds in a food processor, or mash with a potato masher. Drain off the juices, saving the pulp. Mix with the brown sugar and set aside.

Drain the shrimp thoroughly. Heat the oil in a large nonreactive skillet and sauté the shrimp until cooked through, but still tender, about 2 minutes. Arrange on a large platter and flank with the watermelon coulis.

VARIATION

Grilled shrimp
Skewer the shrimp, cover with the jerk seasoning, and cook on an oiled grill until cooked through, 3 to 4 minutes.

—Chef Doug Ducharme

Shrimp Hash

This specialty from our Crystal City, Virginia, restaurant is our
tribute to New Orleans–style cooking.

SERVES 4

2 pounds russet potatoes, skins on

4 slices bacon

1 cup chopped onions

2 tablespoons butter

Garlic salt

Nutmeg

Paprika

Salt

Freshly milled black pepper

½ pound small shrimp, peeled

Halve the potatoes lengthwise, and cut into 1-inch slices. Put in a large pot, cover with water, and bring the potatoes to a boil. Reduce the heat, and gently boil the potatoes until they are barely cooked through, 15 to 20 minutes. Drain and set aside.

Preheat the oven to 450°F.

Slice the bacon into ½-inch pieces. Place the bacon in a heavy skillet over medium heat and fry until barely browned, about 5 minutes. Add the onions, and cook, stirring frequently, for 5 minutes. Add 1 tablespoon of the butter.

Add the drained potatoes to the pan and season to taste with garlic salt, a pinch of nutmeg, paprika, salt, and pepper. Toss to distribute the spices. Add the shrimp, toss again, and cook over medium heat until the shrimp are barely cooked through, about 2 minutes.

Mound the shrimp and potatoes in a buttered baking dish, dot with the remaining tablespoon of butter, and bake until browned, 6 to 8 minutes.

—Chef Jose Urquilla

Marinated Grilled Shrimp

I don't do a tremendous amount of barbecuing at home, but this shrimp recipe is an exception. Remember that when you're marinating seafood, it's important to watch the clock. Less than thirty minutes is best; otherwise you'll end up with fish or shellfish with a soft, mushy texture. This marinade works equally well on seafood and poultry. In a pinch, you can substitute bottled Italian dressing.

SERVES 4

$\frac{1}{2}$ **cup red wine vinegar**

2 tablespoons Dijon mustard

2 tablespoons fresh lemon juice

$\frac{1}{2}$ **cup chopped red onions**

1 tablespoon minced garlic

2 tablespoons green or black peppercorns, crushed (optional)

1 tablespoon sugar

$\frac{1}{4}$ **cup chopped fresh parsley**

$\frac{1}{2}$ **tablespoon salt**

$1\frac{1}{2}$ **cups olive oil or a blend of olive and grapeseed oils**

2 pounds jumbo shrimp, peeled

Place the vinegar, mustard, lemon juice, onion, garlic, peppercorns, if using, sugar, parsley, and salt in a food processor. Pulse on and off for 15 seconds. With the motor running, add the oil, and pulse an additional 15 seconds. Put the shrimp in a nonreactive bowl, and toss with the marinade. Let sit for 30 minutes while you prepare the grill. Skewer the shrimp, and cook on an oiled grill, turning once. The shrimp should cook through in 5 to 8 minutes.

Tropical Shrimp and Scallops

The ingredient list is lengthy, but this dish from Legal's Sawgrass Mills restaurant in Fort Lauderdale, Florida, can be put together in less than thirty minutes. You can grill the pineapple and marinate the shellfish ahead of time. The spicy marinade contrasts with the slightly sweet sauce. Many Asian grocery stores or specialty food markets sell toasted sliced coconut. At our Sawgrass Mills restaurant, we use canned cream of coconut. For a more subtle coconut flavor, use canned coconut milk. Any leftover milk freezes well, or you can make a coconut cake as the base for the Mango and Strawberry Shortcake (page 290), or make Butterscotch Coconut Sauce (page 298).

SERVES 4

1 pound shrimp, peeled

1 pound sea scallops

2 to 3 teaspoons bottled Jamaican jerk seasoning

2 tablespoons grapeseed oil

1 tablespoon minced garlic

$^2/_3$ cup chopped onions

$^1/_4$ cup sliced red pepper

1 tablespoon seeded and minced jalapeño

1$^1/_2$ to 2 cups peeled, seeded, and diced tomatoes (about 2 large)

$^2/_3$ cup canned coconut milk or cream of coconut

1 tablespoon sugar

Marinate the shrimp and scallops in the jerk seasoning for at least 15 minutes in the refrigerator. Drain, and blot dry with paper towels. Heat the oil in a large nonreactive saucepan, and sauté the shrimp and scallops until lightly seared, about 1 to 2 minutes. Remove them from the pan with a slotted spoon. Add the garlic, onions, pepper, jalapeño, and tomatoes and cook over high heat, stirring frequently, for 3 to 5 minutes, or until the vegetables are barely cooked through and are forming a sauce. Return the shrimp and scallops to the pan, add the coconut milk and sugar, lower the heat, and cook for 2 minutes longer. Stir in the cilantro, if using.

Meanwhile, either broil or grill the pineapple slices for 5 minutes or until slightly caramelized, or place in a hot skillet and press down for 15 seconds to slightly cook. Assemble by halving the pineapple slices lengthwise and arranging them in a circle on a large platter. Fill the center with jasmine rice, then

top with the shellfish mixture. Sprinkle with the diced avo-cado and the toasted sliced coconut, if using.

VARIATIONS

With red snapper
Substitute 2 pounds red snapper fillets for the shellfish.

Green Thai-style curry
For every $1\frac{1}{2}$ cups leftover fish, add 1 tablespoon green curry paste (such as Thai Kitchen brand), $\frac{1}{4}$ teaspoon nam pla (Thai fish sauce), $\frac{1}{4}$ cup sliced baby portobello mushrooms, and $\frac{1}{4}$ cup diced fresh pineapple. Reheat and simmer for 4 minutes. Just before serving, stir in 2 tablespoons julienned basil.

—Chef Mike Campbell

1 tablespoon chopped fresh cilantro (optional)

4 slices fresh pineapple, about $\frac{3}{4}$ inch thick

4 cups cooked jasmine rice

1 avocado, peeled and diced

Toasted sliced coconut (optional)

Shrimp with Lemon and Garlic

You can make this recipe with any size shrimp, but remember to adjust the cooking time. The larger the shrimp, the longer the time, but all shrimp cook faster than you might expect. The sauce is delicious mopped up with a hunk of French bread.

SERVES 3 TO 4

1½ pounds shrimp, peeled

1 tablespoon grapeseed or olive oil

2 tablespoons fresh lemon juice

3 tablespoons butter

2 tablespoons chopped scallions, green part only

1 tablespoon chopped garlic

¼ teaspoon soy sauce

Freshly milled black pepper

Preheat the oven to 400°F.

Toss the shrimp with the oil and lemon juice. Melt the butter in a baking pan in the oven and add the shrimp, scallions, garlic, and soy sauce. Bake for 3 to 5 minutes, or until just firm. Baste and season with black pepper. Serve immediately.

VARIATION

Scallops Ted Williams's style
The great Boston Red Sox slugger Ted Williams loved garlic. Triple the amount of garlic and substitute scallops for the shrimp.

Shrimp with Peppers

The color of the peppers is a beautiful foil to the shrimp. The less expensive small shrimp work well.

SERVES 4

1 tablespoon olive oil

1$^1/_2$ pounds shrimp, peeled

$^3/_4$ cup chopped scallions, both white and green parts

1 to 2 tablespoons seeded and minced jalapeño

1 red pepper, seeded and sliced into $^1/_4$-inch-wide strips

1 yellow pepper, seeded and sliced into $^1/_4$-inch-wide strips

$^2/_3$ cup fresh orange juice

1 tablespoon chopped fresh cilantro, sweet marjoram, or parsley

2 tablespoons apple jelly

1 tablespoon fresh lime juice (optional)

Salt (optional)

Freshly milled black pepper (optional)

Heat the oil in a large nonreactive skillet. Add the shrimp and sauté over medium-high heat for 1 minute, stirring constantly. Remove the pan from the heat and lift out the shrimp with a slotted spoon.

Place the pan back on the stove and add the scallions, jalapeño, and peppers. Stir for 1 minute and pour in the orange juice. Lower the heat and let the vegetables simmer in the juice for about 3 minutes. Add the cilantro and apple jelly, raise the heat to high, and boil rapidly until the sauce is reduced, about 2 minutes. Taste and add lime juice if necessary. Put the shrimp back in the pan and stir until they are coated with sauce. Season with salt and pepper if desired. Serve immediately over rice.

Shrimp with Rice and Peas

akes less than thirty minutes to prepare—and that includes chopping the vegetables. Small to medium shrimp (20 to 25 count) work best, as they cook quickly in the rice, retaining their tender texture. Remember, if you have farm-fresh squash to use less stock, as it will add its juices to the dish.

SERVES 4

2 tablespoons olive oil

1¹/₂ cups chopped onions

3 tablespoons diced ham (optional)

¹/₃ cup coarsely chopped summer squash

1¹/₂ cups white rice, such as jasmine

2 cups chicken or fish stock

Creole or Old Bay Seasoning

Worcestershire sauce

Hot pepper sauce

1¹/₂ pounds shrimp, peeled

¹/₂ to 1 cup frozen peas

Salt

Freshly milled black pepper

2 tablespoons fresh lemon juice (optional)

Heat the olive oil in a large saucepan and add the onions and ham, if using. Cook over medium heat, stirring frequently, for 5 minutes. Stir in the summer squash and rice, and cook, stirring constantly, for another minute. Pour in the chicken stock, and add a shake of Creole seasoning as well as generous dashes of both Worcestershire and hot sauces.

Bring the mixture to a boil, lower the heat, and cover the pot. Let the mixture simmer for 10 minutes, stirring occasionally. Stir in the shrimp and frozen peas. Cover the pot, and cook over medium heat until the shrimp are pink, and both the shrimp and rice are cooked through, about 5 minutes. Remove the pot from the heat and let the mixture sit for 3 minutes. Season with salt, pepper, and lemon juice to taste, if desired. Serve immediately.

Shrimp with Tomatoes and Peppers

Save a few shrimp and some sauce for Shrimp Bruschetta (page 195).

This is equally good served over rice or tossed with linguine.

SERVES 4

3 tablespoons grapeseed or olive oil

⅓ cup peeled and chopped red onion

2 teaspoons chopped garlic

2 cups peeled, seeded, and chopped plum tomatoes (about 1 pound)

⅓ cup peeled, seeded, and chopped roasted red peppers

3 tablespoons chopped fresh parsley or 2 tablespoons chopped fresh cilantro

1 pound medium shrimp, peeled (16 to 20 count)

1 teaspoon olive oil

Salt (optional)

Freshly milled black pepper (optional)

In a nonreactive saucepan, heat 2 tablespoons of the oil and sauté the onion and garlic over high heat for 2 minutes, stirring frequently. Add the tomatoes, turn down the heat to medium, and continue to cook for 5 minutes, stirring frequently. Add the red peppers and parsley, and cook 2 minutes longer. Set the mixture aside.

Wipe out the pan and heat the remaining 1 tablespoon oil. Add the shrimp and sauté them over high heat until cooked through, about 2 minutes. Pour back the tomato mixture and stir in 1 teaspoon olive oil. Season with salt and pepper if desired.

VARIATION

With dried red pepper flakes

Add 1 teaspoon dried red pepper flakes along with the tomatoes.

Snapper and Plantains

Encasing the snapper in the plantains is easier than it sounds. Use slightly underripe plantains for best results. (Or, you can fry the snapper and plantains together; see below.) Black beans and rice are a tasty, and attractive, accompaniment.

SERVES 4

1¹⁄₂ **pounds red snapper, skinned**

Sesame oil

Freshly milled black pepper

2 plantains

3 tablespoons grapeseed oil

1 lime, quartered

Preheat the oven to 400°F.

Cut the snapper into serving pieces about 4 inches long. Spread them with a minute quantity of sesame oil mixed with water. Sprinkle with pepper. Peel the plantains and with a vegetable peeler cut several lengthwise slices. Wrap the plantains around the snapper slices until they are covered. (The plantains will stick together as they cook, so this doesn't need to be perfect.)

Heat the grapeseed oil in a large skillet. Gently place the snapper in the pan. (You may need to do this in batches.) Fry for 2 minutes on one side, then turn and brown the other side. Place in a baking dish. Continue until all the snapper has been browned. Bake for 5 to 8 minutes, or until the snapper is cooked through. Garnish with quartered limes.

VARIATION

Fried Plantains and Snapper

Cut the plantains into thick slices. Omit the sesame oil. Salt and pepper the snapper and flour it. Quickly sauté the plantains in butter, and set aside. Fry the snapper in grapeseed oil, and arrange the plantains alongside.

Hog Snapper Pepe

Any delicate white-fleshed fish works well in this special from Legal's Boca Raton restaurant. Hog snapper, which is not a true snapper, is one of the south's most delicious fish, with delicately flavored white flesh. The naturally tender broccolini—a cross between broccoli and Chinese kale—is found at many gourmet vegetable markets.

SERVES 4

1 bunch broccolini (about 1½ cups)

Clarified butter

2 pounds snapper fillets

2 tablespoons capers

2 tablespoons chopped sun-dried tomatoes

4 quartered canned artichoke hearts

¼ cup dry white wine

2 teaspoons fresh lemon juice

3 tablespoons cold butter

Separate the broccolini florets and cut the stems into 2-inch lengths. Blanch them in a pot of boiling water for 1 minute. Immediately run under cold water, drain, and set aside. Film the bottom of a nonreactive skillet with butter. Heat the butter, add the fillets skin side down, and cook for 2 minutes. Turn over, and cook for 1 minute. Add the capers, the broccolini florets and stems, sun-dried tomatoes, and artichoke hearts. Let the snapper and vegetables cook together for 3 minutes longer. With a slotted spoon, remove the fish and vegetables from the pan. Add the wine and lemon juice to the pan. Cook for 1 minute, then swirl in the cold butter to form a sauce. Pour over the snapper and vegetables. Serve immediately.

—Chef Joe Coletto

Steamed Snapper with Ginger and Scallions

We cook the snapper with julienned ginger and scallions in special steaming ovens at our Chestnut Hill restaurant in Boston. You can approximate this dish at home by oven-steaming the snapper in an envelope of aluminum foil.

SERVES 4

1½ pounds snapper fillets

2 julienned scallions, both white and green parts

2 tablespoons julienned fresh ginger

1 teaspoon grapeseed oil

¼ teaspoon sesame oil

1 to 2 tablespoons soy sauce

Preheat the oven to 425°F.

Place the snapper on a large sheet of heavy-duty aluminum foil. Cover with the scallions and ginger. Fold the foil to enclose the fish and vegetables. Place on a baking sheet and bake for 10 to 15 minutes, or until the fish is opaque and cooked through. (Carefully open the foil so that you don't burn yourself.) Place the fish on a serving platter. Mix together the grapeseed oil, sesame oil, and soy sauce. Pour it over the fish. Serve immediately.

—Chef Judy Chiu

Red Snapper with Pineapple and Peppers

When you buy red snapper, make sure the skin is attached—a requirement of southern states such as Florida, because of the many fish with similar coloring that masquerade as the real thing.

SERVES 4

2 tablespoons fresh lemon juice

1 tablespoon soy sauce

2 tablespoons olive oil

1$\frac{1}{2}$ pounds red snapper fillets

1 cup slivered Vidalia or other sweet onions

$\frac{3}{4}$ cup chopped red pepper

$\frac{1}{2}$ cup fresh pineapple chunks

1 teaspoon minced fresh ginger (optional)

Combine the lemon juice, soy sauce, and 1 tablespoon of the olive oil, and marinate the fish in this mixture for at least 30 minutes in the refrigerator.

Preheat the oven to 425°F.

Remove the fish from the marinade, place it in a large, oiled, nonreactive baking dish, and brush with the remaining olive oil. Surround with the onions, pepper, pineapple, and ginger, if using. Bake for about 15 minutes, or until the fish is cooked through. Halfway through the cooking time, stir the vegetables. Serve with the vegetables mounded on the fillets.

Tomato, Pepper, and Mango Snapper

Use super-ripe tomatoes and mangoes for this colorful dish. Simmering the fish in the sauce is a flavorful—and easy—way to cook delicate fish fillets.

SERVES 4

1½ pounds snapper or flounder fillets

Fresh lime juice

1 tablespoon butter

½ orange or yellow pepper, seeded and sliced (about ¾ cup)

¼ to ½ teaspoon seeded and minced jalapeño

2 large tomatoes, peeled, seeded, and cut into large chunks

1 mango, peeled and diced (¾ to 1 cup)

Mace

Salt

Freshly milled black pepper

Place the fillets in a large, shallow nonreactive dish and squeeze lime juice over both sides. Let sit while you prepare the sauce. In a large nonreactive skillet, heat the butter. Add the orange pepper and sauté for 3 minutes, stirring frequently. Stir in the jalapeño and tomatoes. Cook over medium heat for 10 minutes, or until the tomatoes form a sauce. Add the mango and a dash of mace and cook for 1 minute.

Place the fillets in the pan, cover with some of the sauce, and simmer for 5 to 7 minutes, or until cooked through. Season with salt and pepper to taste.

Crusty Sole

The panko bread crumbs seal in the moisture and add a welcome crunch to the soft texture of the sole. This chef's special sells out every time it appears on Boston's Park Square menu.

SERVES 4

2 cups panko (Japanese bread crumbs)

$1/2$ cup freshly grated Parmigiano-Reggiano cheese

2 large eggs

$1^{1}/_{2}$ to 2 pounds sole or flounder fillets, skinned

Freshly milled black pepper

Unbleached all-purpose flour

Grapeseed oil

Mix together the bread crumbs and cheese, and spread out on a large platter. Place the eggs in a pie plate and stir thoroughly with 1 teaspoon water. Blot the fish dry, then sprinkle with pepper. Dip in flour, shake to remove any excess, and dip in the egg mixture. Put the fillets on the bread crumbs and press down. Turn, and press down again. Continue until the surface of each fillet is thoroughly coated with the crumbs.

Pour the grapeseed oil into a large skillet to a depth of $^{1}/_{4}$ inch. When it is very hot, add the fillets. Lower the heat slightly and cook without touching for about 4 minutes. Lift an edge to see if the bread crumbs are browned. If so, turn the fillets and let their other sides brown. The whole process will take about 10 minutes. Remove to a serving platter, blot with a paper towel, and serve immediately.

VARIATION

With horseradish

Lightly spread a layer of bottled horseradish over the surface of the fish before dipping in the egg. Use horseradish sparingly; more than a tissue-paper-thin coating will overpower the fish.

—Chef Yale Woodson

Easy Baked Sole

Try this recipe on nights when you have about five minutes to fix dinner.

It's also splashy enough to serve for company.

SERVES 4

4 tablespoons butter

1 teaspoon minced garlic

1 tomato, peeled, seeded, and chopped (about $^2/_3$ cup)

2 tablespoons freshly grated Parmigiano-Reggiano cheese

2 tablespoons chopped fresh basil, or 1 tablespoon chopped fresh sweet marjoram or parsley

1$^1/_2$ to 2 pounds sole fillets

Preheat the oven to 375°F.

Heat 3 tablespoons of the butter in a small saucepan until it is bubbling. Add the garlic and tomato and cook for 30 seconds, stirring. Do not let the garlic brown. Turn off the heat and stir in the cheese and basil.

Lay the sole fillets out on the counter and spread half of each fillet with the butter-cheese mixture. Fold over the other half of the fillet, as if you were folding a piece of paper. A little butter may leak out of the sides of the fish, but that's okay.

Place the fillets in a buttered baking dish. Dot with the remaining 1 tablespoon butter. Bake for 12 to 15 minutes. If you wish, before serving, pour the pan juices into a nonreactive saucepan and boil them down to make a sauce.

Sole Stuffed with Crabmeat

This delicately flavored fish dish, made with East Coast crabmeat, is festive, yet easy to prepare. Serve with rice and a green salad or steamed broccoli.

SERVES 4

3 tablespoons butter

2 to 3 tablespoons chopped scallions, white parts only

1 stalk celery, stringed and chopped

1/2 cup chopped mushrooms

8 ounces fresh crabmeat picked over for shells and cartilage

3 tablespoons mayonnaise

1/2 teaspoon dry mustard

Salt

2 to 3 tablespoons fresh lemon juice

2 pounds sole fillets

Chopped fresh parsley

Preheat the oven to 375°F.

Heat 2 tablespoons of the butter in a large skillet. Add the scallions and celery. Cook them over medium heat for about 2 minutes, stirring frequently. Add the mushrooms and cook another 2 minutes, or until the mushrooms are cooked through and have exuded their juices. Remove from the heat and set aside.

Stir together the crabmeat, mayonnaise, dry mustard, a generous pinch of salt, and about 1 teaspoon of the lemon juice. Place the sole fillets on a clean counter. Spread the crabmeat mixture over half of each piece of sole, and then score a line where you plan to fold over the other half. Do not cut all the way through the fish. Then, fold it over. You will have the equivalent of a hinged sandwich of sole with the crabmeat in the center.

Place the fillets in a buttered baking dish, and dot with the remaining butter. Pour the remaining lemon juice over the fish. Bake for 15 to 20 minutes, or until the fish are cooked through. Sprinkle with parsley before serving.

Sole with Lemons and Capers

This is one of my favorite ways of eating sole. Try it with steamed asparagus and rice.

SERVES 4

2 pounds sole fillets or whole sole

Unbleached all-purpose flour

Grapeseed oil

3 tablespoons butter

$\frac{1}{2}$ to 1 teaspoon minced garlic

3 tablespoons fresh lemon juice

2 tablespoons capers

1 to 2 tablespoons minced fresh parsley, or 2 teaspoons chopped fresh tarragon or sweet marjoram

Dip the sole fillets in the flour. Pour the grapeseed oil into a heavy nonreactive skillet to a depth of about $\frac{1}{4}$ inch. Heat the oil until very hot. Add the fillets and sauté for 2 to 3 minutes on each side, or until browned and cooked through. Watch carefully and turn the heat down if necessary. You want the fillets to brown, not burn.

Remove the fish to a platter. Wipe out the pan, add the butter, and turn the heat to medium-high. Add the garlic, stir for 30 seconds, then pour in the lemon juice and capers. Immediately pour around the sole on the platter. Sprinkle the sole with the herbs.

Sautéed Swordfish with a Citrus Scallion Sauce

Swordfish's dense texture makes it an excellent choice for stovetop cooking. For best results, sauté in grapeseed oil.

SERVES 4

Grapeseed oil

Freshly milled black pepper

1½ to 2 pounds swordfish steaks, ¾ inch thick

1 teaspoon butter

2 tablespoons finely chopped garlic

3 tablespoons thinly sliced scallions, both white and green parts

⅓ cup peeled, seeded, and chopped tomato

2 tablespoons fresh orange or tangerine juice

¼ teaspoon Dijon mustard

2 teaspoons chopped fresh parsley or basil, or 1 teaspoon chopped fresh tarragon

Coat a large nonreactive skillet with the grapeseed oil to a depth of ⅛ inch. Place over high heat. Generously pepper the swordfish and cook on both sides until cooked through, about 5 minutes. (Unless you have a super-sized pan, you will need to do this in batches.)

Put the swordfish on a serving platter. Wipe out the pan. Heat the butter, add the garlic and scallions, and cook over medium heat for 1 minute, stirring frequently. Stir in the tomato and cook, stirring constantly, until it almost dissolves in the sauce, about 1 minute. Add the orange juice and mustard. Cook another 1 to 2 minutes and stir in the herbs. Pour over the fish.

Swordfish in a Rosemary Lime Sauce

The acidity of the sauce cuts the rich flavor of the swordfish. As both tomatoes and limes vary in acidity, the amount of sugar needed will vary.

SERVES 4

Vegetable oil

2 pounds swordfish steaks, about 1 inch thick

2 tablespoons butter

1 tablespoon minced garlic

$^1/_3$ cup fresh lime juice

$^1/_4$ to $^1/_2$ teaspoon chopped fresh rosemary

1 cup peeled, seeded, and diced tomatoes

1 tablespoon chopped roasted red pepper

2 to 3 teaspoons sugar

Preheat the oven to 400°F.

Oil the swordfish lightly, place in a baking dish, and bake for 10 to 12 minutes, or until cooked through.

Meanwhile, heat the butter in a nonreactive skillet, add the garlic, and sauté over high heat, stirring constantly, for 1 minute.

Stir in the lime juice, rosemary, tomatoes, and red pepper, and cook over high heat, stirring constantly, for 2 minutes, or until the tomatoes disintegrate, forming a sauce. Taste and use only enough sugar to give a delicate sweet-sour flavor. Serve each portion of swordfish flanked by a tablespoon of the sauce.

Swordfish Stir-Fry

Try this flavorful stir-fry popular at Legal's Tyson's Corner restaurant in Virginia.
You can substitute green cabbage for the red, and arctic char for the swordfish.

SERVES 4

2 tablespoons grapeseed oil

$1\frac{1}{2}$ pounds swordfish, cut into 1-inch pieces

1 to 2 medium carrots, sliced diagonally (about $1\frac{1}{2}$ cups)

$\frac{2}{3}$ cup snow peas, sliced diagonally into $\frac{3}{4}$-inch-wide pieces

$\frac{1}{4}$ cup sliced shiitake mushrooms

3 tablespoons soy sauce

1 teaspoon sesame oil

Thai fish sauce (nam pla)

$\frac{1}{2}$ cup julienned red cabbage

4 tablespoons sliced scallions (green parts only)

Ground chili paste (sambal oelek)

Heat the oil in a large nonreactive skillet. Add the swordfish, and cook over high heat for 2 minutes, turning constantly. Remove from the pan and set aside. Add the carrots to the pan. Cook for 1 minute. Add the peas and mushrooms and cook for 1 minute longer. Return the swordfish to the pan and add the soy sauce, sesame oil, and a dash of Thai fish sauce. Cook for 1 to 2 minutes longer. Stir in the red cabbage and scallions and serve immediately over rice. Drizzle a touch of ground chili paste over the top.

—Chef Brad Downs

Catering Exploits

CATERING IS OFTEN a first choice for someone starting out in the food industry. I'm not sure why. Perhaps it's the challenge of operating a business on a shoestring, perhaps it's a love of food, or a belief that catering is lucrative. However, catering is not for dilettantes. It requires hard, often tedious, work. I learned this firsthand, thanks to our family's sporadic forays into the catering world.

Our first catering endeavor was about thirty-five years ago, when my father was operating our fish market, prior to opening our first restaurant. As his friend, Bruce Ota, was selling his Japanese food business, he and my father decided it would be interesting to establish Kyoto Caterers, providing Japanese food for Boston suburbanites. They even had a cheap source of labor: me. As a consequence, I spent my teen years as a busboy, packing and unpacking boxes, and loading station wagons with food for Kyoto Caterers.

On what was to become our last job, Bruce was driving the lead station wagon with the cooks and crew, and we were behind with the food and utensils. It was always Bruce's job to lead, as all Berkowitzes have an incredibly poor sense of direction. As fate had it, my father not only lost sight of Bruce, he became lost in the process. I've eradicated most of that journey from my mind, save for winding through street after identical street, passing by house after identical house. Let's just say that we arrived at the catering job three hours behind schedule to face some incredibly irate customers. This long, painful evening marked the demise of Kyoto Caterers.

Undeterred by the end of my father's catering business, I decided to strike out on my own. It would be different this time, I rationalized. I'd stick to a simple menu of steamed clams and lobsters; I'd only book parties of fewer than twenty-five; and I'd be the only employee. This catering concept couldn't miss. For a while, I was right on target. It seemed I had perfected an ideal formula.

Then, I booked a party for twenty at a couple's home. I got there early to begin preparations. The guests arrived, eagerly anticipating a shore dinner. About 7:30 P.M., the host came into the kitchen to see when I'd be ready. Not long, I assured him, about twenty minutes. A half hour later he checked back again. "Not too much longer," I said.

But something was amiss. The two large pots I had put on the stove almost two hours before had failed to boil. The burner was on high, but the water was still cool enough to touch. This went on almost another hour. Finally, the water began to boil. Twelve minutes later, I was serving the steamed clams. Everyone was appeased.

Next came the lobsters. As I was removing them from the water, I happened to glance at the stove. I thought my eyes were playing tricks. Could it be? The plastic control buttons on the stove had melted into one glob. I continued splitting the lobsters. At that moment, the party's hosts came back to the kitchen, complimenting me on the food and the good time their guests were having. "They've even forgotten about the delay."

"Great," I mumbled, avoiding their eyes.

"Everything's all right, isn't it?" they asked.

"Well," I began, "everything is fine—except your stove has melted."

They stared at me incredulously, as if I had spoken to them in a foreign tongue. As one, they turned and looked at the stove. The wife sat down on the floor and started to cry, while her husband went back out to the party to have another drink. I just kept plating the lobsters. That was the end of my do-it-yourself catering business.

A few years later, Legal got back into the catering field in a small way. We agreed to book a party aboard a large boat that was cruising Boston Harbor. It was a brisk, windy October night. If you've ever been on the deck of a boat in the late fall, you might guess what happened. A great gust of wind literally blew all of our plates, silverware, and glasses overboard. That was it. Finis equipment. Finis that stage of Legal's catering.

Now, once again, we're back in the catering business. But now, someone else runs the operations.

I just pay the bills.

It's easier that way.

Swordfish with Onion Jam

You can make the onion jam ahead of time and bring it to room temperature before serving. Although we serve this with swordfish, it's also an excellent choice for mahi mahi, tuna, or bluefish. It's important to use a large pan so that there's plenty of space for the onions to caramelize. Any extra jam can be frozen. Unfrozen, it will stay fresh, refrigerated, for three to four days.

SERVES 4

3 tablespoons olive oil, plus more for the fish

$2^1/_2$ pounds red onions, julienned

$^1/_2$ cup red wine vinegar

2 to 3 tablespoons extra-fine sugar

Salt

Freshly milled black pepper

$1^1/_2$ to 2 pounds swordfish steaks

Heat the oil in a large skillet. Add the onions. Cook over medium-high heat for 5 minutes. Do not stir. Lower the heat and cook for 20 minutes longer, stirring only to prevent scorching. The onions should be browned and reduced in volume. Add $^1/_2$ cup water and continue cooking for 10 minutes longer. Add the vinegar and sugar. Bring the mixture to a boil and let cook for 15 minutes, stirring often. The onions will achieve a jamlike consistency. Cool to room temperature before serving. Season with salt and pepper to taste.

Preheat the broiler.

Brush the swordfish with oil. Broil for 8 to 12 minutes, or until cooked through. Serve flanked with the onion jam.

—Executive Chef Rich Vellante

Balsamic Roasted Trout

This is a great dish to prepare when you're feeling pressed for time.

SERVES 4

Four 10-ounce dressed trout

5 tablespoons cold butter

³/₄ cup balsamic vinegar

Salt

Freshly milled black pepper

Preheat the oven to 400°F.

Fill each fish cavity with 1 tablespoon cold butter. Press the cavity sides together. Place the fish in a small, nonreactive baking dish and cover with the vinegar. Bake for 7 to 10 minutes, or until cooked through. Place the trout on a serving plate. Swirl the remaining tablespoon cold butter in the pan juices to form a sauce, and pour over the trout. Sprinkle with salt and pepper to taste.

—Executive Chef Rich Vellante

Sage-Infused Trout

At our restaurants we garnish the trout with *ogo,* a Japanese
seaweed sold by Asian grocery stores.

SERVES 4

4 stems sage with leaves
4 dressed trout
4 tablespoons cold butter
Salt
Freshly milled black pepper
³/₄ cup dry white wine
Lemon wedges
***Ogo* (optional)**

Preheat the oven to 425°F.

Put a sage stem into the cavity of each trout. Salt and pepper
the cavity. Melt 2 tablespoons of the butter and coat the surface of the trout. Place the trout into a nonreactive baking
dish. Pour the wine over the trout. Bake for 7 to 10 minutes.
Remove the trout from the oven and discard the sage from
their cavities. Place the trout on a serving dish. Add the remaining 2 tablespoons butter to the pan drippings and swirl
to create a sauce. Pour over the fish. Serve immediately, garnished with lemon wedges and *ogo,* if using.

—Executive Chef Rich Vellante

Stuffed Trout

Farm-raised rainbow trout are stuffed with crabmeat and vegetables in this popular chef's special from Legal's Bethesda, Maryland, restaurant. You can prepare the stuffing a few hours ahead of time and refrigerate it.

SERVES 4

2 tablespoons olive oil

¼ cup coarsely chopped mushrooms

2 tablespoons chopped green pepper

2 tablespoons chopped red pepper

1 teaspoon seeded and minced jalapeño

¼ cup chopped red onion

¼ cup celery (optional)

Salt

Freshly milled black pepper

4 ounces lump crabmeat

4 dressed rainbow trout

Old Bay Seasoning

Fresh lemon juice

Chopped fresh parsley

Preheat the oven to 425°F.

Heat the olive oil in a large nonreactive saucepan. Stir in the mushrooms, peppers, jalapeño, onion, and celery, if using. Cook for 2 to 3 minutes over medium-high heat, stirring frequently. Remove from the heat and cool for 15 minutes. Season with salt and pepper to taste. Stir in the crabmeat. Set the mixture aside.

Fan open the trout and sprinkle with the Old Bay Seasoning. Loosely pack the cavities of the fish with the vegetable-and-crabmeat mixture. Place in a large baking dish and bake for 12 to 15 minutes, or until cooked through. The fish will expand, displaying the stuffing. Remove the trout from the pan and squeeze a lemon into the pan juices. Pour over the fish. Garnish with chopped parsley before serving.

—Chef Omar Ayala

Rainbow Trout with Mandarin Oranges

This versatile sauce, served at our Warwick, Rhode Island, restaurant, is also good with meat, such as grilled pork chops. Cook the tomatoes only long enough to heat them through, and wait to add the mandarin segments until just before serving. You want the tomatoes to be barely cooked and the segments to stay whole. Overcooking will make both mushy.

SERVES 4

4 dressed rainbow trout

Grapeseed oil, for the trout, plus 2 tablespoons

1 tablespoon minced garlic

1 cup peeled, seeded, and chopped plum tomatoes

One 11-ounce can mandarin oranges with juice

1 to 2 tablespoons cold butter

1 tablespoon chopped fresh parsley

Oil the trout and either cook on a grill or broil in the oven until cooked through, 8 to 10 minutes. Remove from the heat and let sit for a minute before topping with the sauce.

While the trout is cooking, heat the oil in a large nonreactive saucepan. Add the garlic and cook, stirring, for 1 minute. Lower the heat and stir in the tomatoes. Reserve the mandarin segments and add the liquid in the can to the tomatoes. Bring the ingredients to a simmer, and cook for 2 to 3 minutes. The tomato segments should soften only slightly. Bring the mixture to a boil and immediately stir in the butter. Add the mandarin segments and parsley before serving.

—Chef Doug Ducharme

Tuna with a Cucumber Garnish

Unwaxed cucumbers work best in this recipe. The green color of the skin is attractive, but if you can buy only waxed cucumbers, peel them, and use chives or parsley for color.

SERVES 4

2 unwaxed cucumbers

$\frac{1}{2}$ teaspoon salt

2 to 3 tablespoons sugar

3 tablespoons cider or rice wine vinegar

One 2-pound tuna steak, about 1 inch thick

2 tablespoons vegetable oil

2 tablespoons fresh lemon juice

Hold 1 cucumber in your hand and run the tines of a fork lengthwise down its side to score it. Repeat with the second cucumber. Thinly slice both cucumbers. Place them in a bowl and toss with the salt. Mix in the sugar and vinegar. Press down upon the cucumbers with the heel of your hand or with a wooden spoon to extract some of the cucumber liquid. Marinate the cucumbers for at least 30 minutes.

Preheat the broiler.

Marinate the tuna in the oil and lemon juice for at least 15 minutes. Drain the tuna and broil it just long enough to sear the outside, about 2 minutes. Diagonally slice the tuna and arrange the pieces in a mound in the center of a serving dish. Drain the cucumbers and arrange around the perimeter.

Broiled Tuna with Tomatillos and Peppers

This recipe also works well with fresh swordfish or mahi mahi. This calls for broiling the tuna until just the surface is cooked through; if you prefer the entire steak cooked through, double the cooking time.

SERVES 4

1 pound fresh tomatillos

2 tablespoons, plus 1 teaspoon olive oil

1¼ cups chopped Vidalia or other sweet onion (about 1 medium)

2 tablespoons seeded and minced jalapeño

½ cup seeded and coarsely chopped red or yellow pepper

¼ to ⅓ cup chopped fresh cilantro

1 teaspoon cider vinegar (optional)

One 2-pound tuna steak, approximately 1 inch thick

Preheat the broiler.

Remove the husks from the tomatillos and wash under lukewarm water. Chop into chunks. Heat 2 tablespoons of oil in a heavy pan and add the tomatillos, onion, jalapeño, and pepper. Cook over high heat, stirring frequently, for 10 to 15 minutes, or until the tomatillos have softened and the vegetables have cooked through. Remove from the heat and stir in the cilantro and vinegar, if using. Set aside.

Meanwhile, oil the tuna on both sides with the remaining teaspoon of oil. Place on a broiling pan and broil for 2 to 3 minutes, or until the surface is cooked through. Do not turn. Remove from the oven and cut diagonally into slices. Serve with about ½ cup of the tomatillos alongside.

Wolffish with Peppers and Mushrooms

If you can't find this delicately flavored fish (also known as ocean catfish), substitute sole or flounder. This meal-in-one takes less than fifteen minutes to prepare. It is particularly attractive with red and green peppers and a densely textured yellow heirloom tomato.

SERVES 4

1 tablespoon grapeseed or olive oil

1½ to 2 pounds wolffish fillets

2 cups sliced mushrooms (about 4 ounces)

1 tablespoon chopped garlic (optional)

4 thin-skinned peppers (such as Cubanelle), thinly sliced

¾ cup peeled, seeded, and chopped tomato

¼ cup dry white wine

2 tablespoons chopped fresh sweet marjoram

1 tablespoon cold butter

Salt

Freshly milled black pepper

Heat the oil in a large nonreactive skillet. Brown the wolffish fillets, remove from the pan, and set aside. Add the mushrooms, garlic, if using, peppers, and tomato to the pan. Cook over medium heat for 5 minutes, or until wilted. Return the fish to the pan, cover with the pepper mixture, and cook over medium-high heat for 2 minutes. Add the wine, raise the heat, and cook for 1 minute. Stir in the marjoram. Take the pan off the heat, remove the fish, and stir in the cold butter. The sauce will thicken. Season with salt and pepper to taste. Pour the sauce over the fish and serve immediately.

Learning the French Way

A GREAT THING ABOUT being a restaurateur is the enormous number of opportunities that come along. Some of these can be very seductive, and on occasion (as we found out), even too seductive.

Conventional wisdom dictates that regardless of the business you're in, if you're successful at something, don't—under any circumstances—deviate from that path.

That kind of thinking is only for people who lack a real sense of adventure, or so I thought until I tried something completely different and regretted it. The year was 1985, and we were successfully operating five restaurants. I proposed to my family that we purchase some vineyard property in France. The dollar was strong and the franc was weak. "We should be able to strike a good deal on land," I argued. Besides, we had good luck when we had leased a vineyard in California the year before and hired a wine maker to produce a house wine for us.

We decided to purchase a vineyard in the southwest region of France just outside of Bordeaux in an up-and-coming "appellation" called the Côte de Duras. After viewing a number of properties, we couldn't believe our good fortune when we were shown a seventy-five-acre parcel, complete with its own house, as well as a storage complex and a wine-making facility. We were shocked, as the price was no more than that of a two-bedroom condominium in the Boston area. This was one deal too good to pass up.

Once we had possession, we set out to staff the vineyard and property. We were fortunate that one of our top executives at Legal Sea Foods was both European and fluent in French, and that one of our top summer waiters, John Shepard, a French major, was graduating from college right around the time we were taking possession of the vineyard. He volunteered to act as our liaison.

Now, although we understood wine, we did not pretend to know how to *make* wine. Therefore, instead of just hiring a wine maker to live on the property, I decided to hire a well-known master enologist from nearby Bergerac and also hire a manager with wine-making experience to carry out the wine maker's instructions.

I certainly did not expect my first message from John Shepard to be, "Come quick." When I arrived blurry-eyed the next day at the village of Duras, John told me that our property manager, Gilbert, was disobeying the instructions of our master wine maker. I met with Gilbert and stressed to him that it was essential to follow instructions. He said he understood fully and would comply. Three weeks later it was the same story. I gave him another chance, and then finally our European-born executive went over to bid Gilbert "adieu."

Lesson Number 1: It is not easy to terminate an employee if the employer happens to be in the United States and the employee is a French citizen living in France. Three months after Gilbert was fired, he moved off our property. In turn,

we agreed to pay a fine to the French government. How were we to know that it is almost impossible to fire someone in France?

But, there was more to come. It happened on a Sunday. John Shepard noticed a white car leaving the vineyard. As he knew the car belonged to some of Gilbert's friends, he went to check on the wine and discovered that two of the four stainless vats of wine had been emptied. The incident, of course, was reported to the police, and we were assured that the matter would be handled.

Lesson Number 2: When we bought the property, we were told that French law mandated that we purchase "sabotage insurance." We laughed. "How can they be serious—sabotage insurance?" We had never heard of such a thing. Now we understood. However, all of a sudden the police didn't. Because there were no signs of forced entry, they refused to support our claims of sabotage. "How can that be?" we argued. Seven thousand gallons of wine literally down the drain?

Yet, we still had 50 percent of our production. Ah, but that was soon to change. One of the requirements of maintaining an Appellation Controlée designation for wine is that you must periodically bring your wine in for testing. Unfortunately, Gilbert had added sugar to one of the two remaining vats of wine. The process is called chapellation, and the addition of sugar speeds up the fermentation process. Although not harmful, this practice is outlawed in France.

As a result, the French government confiscated the offending vat, and fined us a fairly significant amount of money. Finally, we decided that perhaps it was time to give up overseas ownership of a wine-making business. After virtually no discussion, we decided to sell the vineyard. In spite of ourselves, the venture wasn't a total flop because we managed to make a pretty good table wine from the remaining production. And, we also knew that from now on, we're sticking to seafood and seafood restaurants.

Leftovers

Arctic Char Burritos

You can replace arctic char with salmon or virtually any leftover fish—or shellfish, such as shrimp or mussels.

SERVES 2 TO 4

1 peeled ripe avocado

1 to 2 tablespoons fresh lime juice

Hot pepper sauce

1½ cups peeled, seeded, and diced tomatoes

½ cup chopped sweet onions

Salt

Freshly milled black pepper

4 flour tortillas

½ cup canned kidney beans, rinsed, or ½ cup canned refried beans

1 cup flaked cooked arctic char, skin removed

Lettuce leaves

4 to 6 tablespoons freshly grated Monterey Jack or Cheddar cheese

Mash the avocado and mix with the lime juice and a dash of hot sauce in a nonreactive bowl. Set aside. Combine the tomatoes and sweet onions. Season with salt and pepper. Set aside.

You can warm the tortillas by placing them in a hot skillet for 10 to 15 seconds, or in the microwave for about 5 seconds. Place them on a countertop. Spread each tortilla with the avocado mixture, and top with kidney beans, the tomato mixture, and the char. Cover with lettuce leaves and cheese. Roll the tortillas to enclose the fillings.

Chinese-American Egg Rolls

The ample amounts of vegetables and shellfish make these egg rolls substantial enough for a light meal. You can vary the seafood depending upon what's on hand. Shrimp, crabmeat, mussels—or flaked fish—go well with the other ingredients. Freeze any extra egg roll skins, then defrost them before using. There's no salt called for in this recipe because the soy sauce is salty.

MAKES 8 EGG ROLLS

Grapeseed or peanut oil

1 to 1¹⁄₂ tablespoons minced ginger

1 tablespoon chopped green pepper

¹⁄₄ to ¹⁄₃ cup chopped scallions, both white and green parts

1¹⁄₂ cups finely shredded cabbage

³⁄₄ cup chopped shrimp

2 tablespoons shredded carrot

1 to 2 teaspoons soy sauce

¹⁄₂ teaspoon sesame oil

2 teaspoons dry sherry

¹⁄₄ cup chopped cilantro

1 tablespoon unbleached all-purpose flour

8 store-bought egg roll skins

Heat 1 tablespoon oil in a heavy, nonreactive saucepan. Add the ginger, pepper, and scallions. Cook over medium-high heat, stirring frequently, for 2 minutes. Stir in the cabbage, and cook 3 minutes longer. Add the shrimp, carrot, soy sauce, sesame oil, sherry, and cilantro. Cook for 1 minute, stirring constantly. Taste and adjust the seasonings if needed. Drain in a colander over a large bowl, and let cool.

Mix together the flour and 1 tablespoon water; set aside. Place the egg roll skins on a flat surface, with a pointed end facing you. Put about 2 tablespoons filling in the middle of each roll, then fold the lower third of each roll over the filling. Fold in the two ends to enclose the filling. Moisten the top edge of each egg roll with the flour and water mixture and fold it down until it encloses each roll.

Pour about 2 cups oil into a deep pot or wok. Heat the oil until a small piece of egg roll skin dropped into the oil immediately starts to cook, about 350°F. Depending upon the size of the pot, fry a few rolls at a time for 3 to 4 minutes, or until they are lightly browned.

Drain the egg rolls on paper bags or a kitchen towel. Serve with Sweet Dipping Sauce (page 281).

VARIATIONS

With garlic

Add 1 to 2 tablespoons minced garlic along with the scallions.

With bean sprouts

Add 3 tablespoons bean sprouts after the mixture has drained.

Egg Foo Yung

This staple from the Chinese restaurants of my youth is a fine way to use leftover shellfish—or fish such as salmon. Traditionally, this omelet is covered with the sauce, but the omelet texture is better when the sauce is served alongside.

SERVES 4

OMELET

4 large eggs

1 teaspoon dry sherry

1 cup chopped cooked shrimp, shredded crabmeat, or coarsely chopped cooked fish

1 cup fresh bean sprouts

$1/3$ cup chopped celery

$1/3$ cup chopped sweet onion or scallions, white part only

Grapeseed or peanut oil

Salt

SAUCE

$1/2$ cup chicken broth

$1/2$ to 1 teaspoon ketchup

2 teaspoons light soy sauce

$1/4$ teaspoon Thai fish sauce (optional)

$1/4$ teaspoon dry sherry

1 quarter-sized piece fresh ginger

1 tablespoon cornstarch

$1/2$ cup fresh pineapple chunks

1 tablespoon scallion stems, sliced diagonally

Beat the eggs in a large nonreactive bowl. Mix in the sherry, shrimp, bean sprouts, celery, and scallions. Let sit while you prepare the sauce.

In a nonreactive saucepan, mix together the chicken broth, ketchup, soy sauce, fish sauce, if using, sherry, and ginger. Place over medium heat, and cook for 5 minutes. Meanwhile, mix the cornstarch with 1 tablespoon water. Lower the heat, remove the ginger, and stir in the cornstarch. Cook, stirring constantly, until thickened, 30 seconds to 1 minute. Remove from the heat.

Place about 3 tablespoons of oil into a large skillet, preferably nonstick. Heat it until hot. Add salt to taste to the egg mixture, then pour it into the hot oil. Let cook for 2 minutes, or until the bottom is slightly browned, but the top still is slightly runny. Cut the omelet into 4 quarters, then turn each section over. Let the other sides set. Remove to a round serving platter and arrange the sections around the outside edge. Fill in the center with the sauce. Top with the pineapple chunks and the scallions.

Zesty Fish Cakes

Make these flavorful cakes out of virtually any leftover fish with a medium-soft texture. Frequently, our chefs use panko, the Japanese bread crumbs available at most Asian markets and some supermarkets. You can serve these for breakfast—or dinner with Baked Beans (page 256) or with Sesame Seed Avocado (page 275).

MAKES 6 FISH CAKES

$3/4$ cup flaked cooked fish

$1/3$ cup crushed saltine crackers (about 8)

$1/8$ cup minced fresh basil

$1/8$ cup minced fresh parsley

Cayenne pepper

$2/3$ cup fresh mashed potato (about 1 medium)

2 tablespoons sour cream or yogurt

1 large egg

1 teaspoon bottled horseradish

Salt

Freshly milled black pepper

Panko (Japanese bread crumbs)

Grapeseed oil, olive oil, or butter

Combine the fish, crackers, herbs, a pinch of cayenne pepper, the potato, sour cream, egg, and horseradish in a medium bowl. Season with salt and pepper to taste. Divide into cakes about 2 inches in diameter. Place the bread crumbs in a bowl and dip each cake into the crumbs to coat lightly.

Pour oil into a large skillet to a depth of $1/4$ inch. Heat over medium to medium-high heat. Cook the fish cakes on both sides until heated through and the bread crumbs are browned, about 6 minutes. Drain thoroughly on paper towels before serving.

VARIATION

With salmon and dill
Use salmon for the fish, and substitute 1 to 2 tablespoons chopped fresh dill for the parsley and basil. Proceed as above.

Easy Fish Curry

Try some of the condiments to jazz up this simple curry made with leftover fish or shellfish. This recipe features the fish; the variation has a smaller amount of fish and a greater number of fresh vegetables.

SERVES 4

2 tablespoons butter

$^1/_3$ cup chopped red pepper

1 teaspoon minced fresh ginger

1 teaspoon minced lemongrass (optional)

1 to 1$^1/_2$ tablespoons mild curry paste

2 tablespoons unbleached all-purpose flour

1 cup milk, fish stock, or chicken stock (preferably heated)

$^1/_3$ cup green beans, cut crosswise into thirds

1$^1/_2$ cups flaked leftover fish

CONDIMENTS:

Sliced bananas, sprinkled with lime juice

Toasted coconut

Chopped dry-roasted peanuts

Sliced scallions, both white and green parts

Cubed fresh pineapple

Heat the butter in a medium nonreactive saucepan. Add the red pepper, ginger, lemongrass, if using, and curry paste. Cook for 1 minute, then stir in the flour. Cook, stirring frequently, for 2 minutes until the flour is cooked through. Off the heat, stir in the milk. Return to medium heat and cook for 2 minutes, stirring frequently, until the sauce thickens. Add the beans, lower the heat, and cook for 5 minutes, until the beans are slightly cooked through but very crunchy. Stir in the fish and continue cooking (and stirring) until the mixture is heated through. Serve the curry over rice with accompanying condiments.

VARIATION

With corn, cabbage, and tomatoes

Decrease the fish to 1 cup. Omit the beans. Add 1 tablespoon chopped garlic along with the ginger. When the sauce thickens, add $^1/_4$ cup fresh corn kernels, 1 cup thinly sliced cabbage, and $^1/_2$ cup diced tomato. Proceed as above.

Fried Rice

Smidgens of fish or shellfish zip up American-style fried rice. Shrimp or cooked squid work particularly well. You can add virtually any vegetable, such as cooked peppers, broccoli, or thinly sliced carrots. Use your imagination and the contents of your refrigerator.

SERVES 1 TO 2

1 teaspoon peanut, walnut, or grapeseed oil

2 teaspoons finely chopped garlic

1 tablespoon finely chopped fresh ginger

$^1/_3$ cup chopped scallions, both white and green parts

$^1/_2$ cup sliced leftover cooked shellfish or fish

1 large egg, beaten

$1^1/_2$ cups cooked rice

2 teaspoons soy sauce

$^1/_4$ cup frozen peas, or $^1/_2$ cup finely sliced cooked vegetables, such as broccoli (optional)

1 teaspoon good-quality chunky peanut butter

Heat the oil in a large skillet and add the garlic, ginger, and scallions. Cook over medium-high heat, stirring frequently, for 2 minutes. Add the shellfish or fish, and cook 30 seconds more.

Move the mixture aside and add the egg. Let it set for 1 minute, then scramble into the other ingredients. Stir in the rice, soy sauce, and peas. Cook 1 or 2 minutes longer until heated through. Just before serving, add the peanut butter.

Fish Latkes

This Middle European specialty, which the chef at Boston's Prudential restaurant made for our "Culinary Snackdown" (page 89), is a personal favorite. It's traditionally served with applesauce and sour cream. Use any mild soft-textured fish. You can find matzoh meal in the ethnic foods section of most supermarkets.

MAKES ABOUT 12 LATKES

2 pounds russet potatoes

2 large eggs

1 small onion

4 ounces cooked cod or similar-textured fish

$1/2$ cup unsalted matzoh meal

Salt

Freshly milled black pepper

1 tablespoon minced fresh chives or chopped fresh parsley (optional)

Grapeseed oil

Applesauce

Sour cream

Peel the potatoes and beat the eggs. Using a standing 4-sided grater, grate the potatoes directly into the eggs, using the largest size holes in the grater. Grate the onion into the mixture. Stir in the flaked fish and matzoh meal. Season with salt, pepper, and chives, if using.

Heat at least $1/2$ inch of oil in a large skillet. Form the potato mixture into $2^1/2$-inch cakes (latkes) about $3/4$ inch thick. Fry the cakes a few at a time over medium-high heat until thoroughly browned on both sides, about 10 minutes. Set the latkes aside on a paper towel. Continue forming and frying the cakes until all the potato mixture is cooked. Serve with bowls of applesauce and sour cream on the side.

—Chef Rob Rosen

Mushroom-and-Fish-Stuffed Crepes

French cooks have always known that crepes turn leftovers into a festive occasion. You can use virtually any fish, but soft-fleshed white fish, such as haddock, grouper, or snapper, work particularly well. Any extra crepes can be frozen separated by waxed paper so that they don't stick together. You also can buy ready-made crepes in many supermarkets.

MAKES 4 TO 6 CREPES

4 to 6 fresh or frozen crepes

$3\frac{1}{2}$ tablespoons butter

$\frac{1}{4}$ cup finely chopped onion

3 tablespoons chopped red pepper

3 to 5 ounces sliced baby portobello mushrooms

1 cup flaked leftover fish

Worcestershire sauce

Salt

Freshly milled black pepper

Dry mustard

2 tablespoons unbleached all-purpose flour

1 cup milk or a combination of cream and milk

2 teaspoons chopped fresh tarragon

1 tablespoon freshly grated Parmigiano-Reggiano cheese

Either make fresh crepes or defrost frozen ones. Set aside. In a large skillet, preferably nonstick, heat 1 tablespoon of the butter. Add the onion and red pepper. Cook, stirring frequently, for 2 minutes, or until the onion begins to soften. Add the mushrooms, and cook another 2 to 3 minutes, stirring frequently. Stir in the fish. Spoon into a large bowl and season with a dash of Worcestershire sauce, salt, pepper, and a pinch of dry mustard.

Preheat the oven to 350°F.

In a small saucepan, melt 2 tablespoons of the remaining butter. Off the heat, stir in the flour. Return to the heat and cook for 2 minutes, stirring frequently. In a small saucepan, heat the milk and, off the heat, pour it over the flour mixture. Quickly whisk to incorporate the ingredients and return once again to the heat. Cook for 2 to 3 minutes, or until the mixture has a saucelike consistency. Stir in the tarragon and cheese. Stir half of the sauce into the fish mixture.

Butter a baking dish just large enough to hold 4 to 6 crepes. Place the crepes top side down on a countertop. Take about 2 tablespoons of the filling and arrange it down the center of a crepe. Fold over the sides and place the crepe seam side down in the baking dish. Continue with the remaining crepes until the filling is used up. Pour the reserved sauce over the remaining crepes, and dot with the remaining butter. Bake the crepes for 20 to 25 minutes, or until they are heated through.

The Chinese Connection

IT HAS TO BE GENETIC—there is no other explanation. The truth is that my entire family is obsessed with Chinese food. I've traced this phenomenon back to my father's family. In the 1930s and '40s, Harry and Frances Berkowitz, my grandparents, literally ate Chinese food seven days a week, mostly in Boston's Chinatown. I'm not sure how this affected my father, George, but he ended up spending his tour of duty in the Marine Corps stationed in Beijing. When he returned to the United States, both he and my mother, Harriet, ate Chinese food at least three times a week.

From the moment I tasted my first Chinese dish, which was wonton soup, I was hooked. The Chinese food I remember eating as a child is linked in my memories with the Jewish food that my grandmother Anna cooked. She favored robust ingredients, such as lots of garlic, onion, and tomatoes, and was probably the best instinctive cook I have ever known. Everything she made was just incredible. To this day, I've never tasted better Jewish cooking. Her seasonings were perfect and her food was addictive—just like a good Chinese meal.

Going out for Chinese food was an important part of our family history. Nine times out of ten, when there was a family celebration, it ended up at a Chinese restaurant. In the mid-1960s, we developed many a strategy about opening our own seafood restaurant over a feast of Chinese specialties. Even now, at our restaurants, we always have a Chinese dish or two on the menu.

At one point, to the surprise of many of our customers, we arranged an exchange program with the province of Shandong in the People's Republic of China. Many people marveled at the

cleverness of this program . . . a well-known seafood restaurant introducing a unique type of Chinese cuisine to America. Was it cleverness? Or, instead, was it my solution to finding a more convenient way of satisfying my incurable appetite for Chinese food? To be honest, probably the latter.

My wife, Lynne, at times has a hard time comprehending how it's possible for the entire Berkowitz family—including our children—to consume as much Chinese food as we do. I keep telling her, though: It's in the genes.

Salmon and Jalapeño Nachos

You can substitute practically any leftover fish or shellfish for the salmon.
Shrimp or mussels are equally good choices.

SERVES 2 TO 4

6 ounces bite-size tortillas (³⁄₄ of an 8.5-ounce bag)

2 to 3 tablespoons seeded and minced jalapeño

1 cup flaked cooked salmon, skin removed

3 tablespoons feta cheese

²⁄₃ cup chopped sweet onions

¹⁄₂ to ³⁄₄ cup freshly grated Monterey Jack or Cheddar cheese

Preheat the oven to 400°F.

Spread a double layer of tortillas in a baking dish. Sprinkle them with the jalapeño, salmon, feta cheese, and sweet onions. Top with the grated Monterey Jack cheese. Bake for 10 minutes, or until the cheese is melted.

VARIATION

With processed American cheese

Spread 6 slices of processed American cheese with Dijon mustard and place mustard side down on top of the tortilla mixture. Proceed as above.

Salmon Frittata

Substitute just about any leftover fish for the salmon in this flat egg omelet, inspired by the frittatas of Northern Italy, where you'll find them served cold as appetizers or as sandwich fillings. It is unnecessary to add salt to this recipe because of the saltiness of the cheeses.

SERVES 2 TO 4

4 large eggs

2 tablespoons sour or regular cream

1 tablespoon cream cheese (optional)

1 tablespoon olive oil

2 tablespoons feta cheese

$^{1}/_{3}$ cup chopped roasted red pepper

$^{3}/_{4}$ cup flaked cooked salmon

3 tablespoons chopped scallions, both white and green parts

1 to 2 tablespoons freshly grated Parmigiano-Reggiano cheese

Preheat the oven to 400°F.

Stir together the eggs, 2 teaspoons water, the sour cream, and cream cheese, if using. Set aside. Put the olive oil into a shallow baking dish about 8 inches in diameter. Heat it on the stove. Add the egg mixture. Evenly sprinkle with the feta cheese, red pepper, salmon, and scallions. Bake for 15 to 20 minutes, or until the eggs are cooked through. Sprinkle with the Parmigiano-Reggiano cheese and cook about 3 minutes longer, or until the cheese is melted, forming a glaze.

VARIATIONS

With asparagus, broccoli, or spinach
Add $^{1}/_{3}$ cup peeled, blanched asparagus; $^{1}/_{3}$ cup blanched broccoli; or 3 tablespoons blanched, squeezed, and chopped spinach to the egg mixture. Proceed as above.

With zucchini and mushrooms
Omit the red pepper. Cook $^{1}/_{2}$ cup thinly sliced zucchini and $^{1}/_{4}$ cup sliced mushrooms in 1 teaspoon additional olive oil. Drain and add to egg mixture. Proceed as above.

With fresh corn kernels and green pepper
Substitute cooked green pepper for the red pepper. Remove the kernels from 1 ear of fresh corn. Break them up with your fingers and add them to the egg mixture along with the green pepper. Proceed as above.

Savory Turnovers

A cross between Cornish pasties and Mexican empanadas, these turnovers stretch a small amount of fish into another meal. You can use either piecrust dough or refrigerated commercial roll pastry.

SERVES 4

2 medium potatoes, peeled and diced

1 medium carrot, peeled and diced

1 tablespoon butter or olive oil

$^1/_3$ cup sliced celery

2 tablespoons seeded and minced jalapeño

$^3/_4$ cup chopped onions

4 ounces chopped mushrooms

2 tablespoons chopped fresh cilantro or a combination of fresh tarragon and mint

1 cup flaked leftover fish

Dough for a double-crust 9-inch pie or a container of roll dough

$^1/_3$ cup sour cream

$^1/_4$ cup mixed grated cheese (optional)

Salt (optional)

Freshly milled black pepper (optional)

Place the potatoes and carrot in a pot of water, bring to a boil, and gently boil for 12 to 15 minutes, or until barely cooked through. Drain and set aside. Heat the butter in a skillet; add the celery, jalapeño, and onions. Cook over medium-high heat, stirring frequently, for 2 minutes. Stir in the mushrooms, and cook for another 2 minutes, stirring constantly. Add the cilantro and fish, and cook 1 minute longer, stirring frequently. Scrape into a mixing bowl and set aside.

Preheat the oven to 400°F.

Roll out the dough into 8 circles. (You can form them with an upside-down saucer.) Add the sour cream and cheese, if using, to the fish mixture. Taste and season with salt and pepper, if desired.

In the center of each circle, place about 2 tablespoons filling. Fold over the dough and crimp the edges to form a turnover. Cut a small steam vent in the center surface of each turnover.

Place the turnovers on a baking sheet and bake for about 20 minutes, or until browned and cooked through.

Easy Shellfish Tart

My wife, Lynne, makes a fabulous seafood quiche. This slightly easier version is an excellent way to utilize small amounts of leftovers. If the shrimp, clams, and/or mussels are small, leave them whole; otherwise chop into bite-size pieces. Shred any crabmeat. Make this for people who cannot eat garlic or onions.

SERVES 4

One 9-inch pie shell

3 large eggs

$2^{1}/_{2}$ cups milk

1 teaspoon bottled horseradish

1 teaspoon Dijon mustard

$^{1}/_{3}$ cup freshly grated Parmigiano-Reggiano cheese

1 cup leftover shellfish, such as shrimps, mussels, clams, or crabmeat

1 tablespoon chopped fresh parsley (optional)

1 tablespoon butter

Preheat the oven to 375°F.

Place the pie shell in a pan and flute the edges. Thoroughly mix together the eggs, milk, horseradish, mustard, cheese, shellfish, and parsley, if using. Pour into the pie shell and dot with the butter.

Place the pie on the middle shelf of the oven and bake for 40 to 45 minutes. Check after 25 minutes to make sure the crust is not browning too fast. If it is, cover the edges with thin strips of aluminum foil. Test after about 40 minutes. If the tart is cooked through, a knife inserted into it will come out clean. Remove from the oven and cool on a rack before serving.

VARIATIONS

Smoked Salmon and Dill Tart
Substitute $^{1}/_{2}$ cup diced smoked salmon for the shellfish and 1 to 2 tablespoons chopped fresh dill for the parsley.

Arctic Char or Salmon and Asparagus Tart
Substitute $^{3}/_{4}$ cup arctic char or flaked salmon for the shellfish. Add $^{1}/_{3}$ cup cooked asparagus, well drained, cut into 1-inch lengths.

With artichokes
Add $^{1}/_{2}$ cup cooked, sliced artichoke hearts along with the shellfish, and add a pinch of dry mustard. If you can locate it, substitute 1 teaspoon chopped fresh chervil for the parsley.

Shrimp Bruschetta

Even a small amount of leftover shrimp and tomato sauce pr

delicious snack or light lunch.

For each serving use:

1 to 2 cooked shrimp

2 slices dense sourdough-style bread

1 to 2 teaspoons olive oil

2 tablespoons tomato or Marinara Sauce (page 279)

1 teaspoon freshly grated Parmigiano-Reggiano or Romano cheese

Preheat the broiler.

Cut the shrimp in half lengthwise. Set aside. Brush the bread with the olive oil and place under the broiler until slightly browned. Spread with the leftover sauce, top with the halved shrimp, and sprinkle with the cheese. Put under the broiler again just until the cheese melts.

Deviled Eggs with Shrimp

Virtually everyone likes deviled eggs, particularly when they are filled with morsels of shrimp. Substitute smoked or fresh salmon or arctic char for the shrimp.

SERVES 4

$^1/_3$ to $^1/_2$ cup chopped cooked shrimp

2 tablespoons fresh lemon or lime juice

8 large eggs

$^1/_4$ teaspoon dry mustard

3 tablespoons mayonnaise

$^1/_2$ teaspoon cider vinegar

Bottled horseradish

Salt

Freshly milled black pepper

Chopped fresh chives or parsley

Put the shrimp in a glass bowl, and toss with the lemon juice. Set aside. Place the eggs in a medium nonreactive saucepan, cover with water, and bring to a boil. Let boil for about 30 seconds, remove from the heat, and let sit for 15 minutes. Run the eggs under cold water, peel, and halve.

Place the cooked yolks in a bowl, and mash them with a non-reactive fork with the mustard, mayonnaise, cider vinegar, and horseradish, salt, and pepper to taste. Drain the shrimp, and mix them with the egg yolks. You may need to add additional mayonnaise. Stuff the whites, garnish with chopped chives or parsley leaves, and cover with plastic wrap. Refrigerate before serving.

Thai-Style Shrimp with Noodles

This adaptation of Thailand's pad thai is an excellent way to use a small amount of cooked shrimp. If you taste the sauce before mixing with the noodles, it may seem too strong, but it smooths out in the finished dish. Rice stick noodles are available in the ethnic foods section of many supermarkets, as well as at Asian grocery stores.

SERVES 4

8 ounces dried Thai rice sticks

1 tablespoon vegetable oil

1 tablespoon minced garlic

3 tablespoons Thai fish sauce

1 tablespoon ketchup

1 tablespoon sugar

2 to 3 tablespoons rice vinegar

1 teaspoon hoisin sauce (optional)

12 to 24 cooked medium shrimp

2 to 3 tablespoons chopped fresh cilantro

$1/3$ cup sliced scallions, both white and green parts

2 cups mung bean sprouts

$1/4$ cup finely chopped roasted peanuts

Pour boiling water over the rice sticks. Let soak until tender, anywhere from 15 to 45 minutes. Drain them well; set aside.

Meanwhile, heat the vegetable oil in a nonreactive saucepan. Add the garlic, lower the heat, and stir constantly for 2 minutes. Add the fish sauce, ketchup, sugar, rice vinegar, and hoisin sauce, if using. Cook for 1 minute until the ingredients are amalgamated. (At this point, the sauce will taste very strong and salty.) Add the shrimp, and stir to coat with the sauce.

Add the drained rice sticks, and toss to coat with the sauce. Then, top with the cilantro, scallions, mung bean sprouts, and peanuts. Serve immediately.

Shrimp and Avocado Quesadilla

...an make this either with leftover shrimp or with cooked shrimp
from the market. It comes together in minutes.

For each serving use:

1 teaspoon olive oil

2 flour tortillas

$1/3$ to $1/2$ cup diced cooked shrimp

$1/2$ cup diced avocado

3 tablespoons shredded cheese,
such as a combination of
Monterey Jack and Cheddar

1 teaspoon chopped fresh
tarragon

1 tablespoon sour cream

In a large skillet, heat the olive oil, and place 1 tortilla in the oil. Remove it quickly and set aside. Add the second tortilla to the pan, and sprinkle the shrimp, avocado, cheese, and tarragon on it. Spread the sour cream on the remaining tortilla and place it oiled side up in the pan. Press down with a spatula. Cook for 1 minute. Reverse the tortillas, press down again, and cook for 1 to 2 minutes longer, or until the cheese melts. Cut into quarters and serve immediately either plain or with a hot pepper salsa.

Salads

George's Cole Slaw

Cole slaw has been on the menu since Legal Sea Foods began.

We always serve it with our fried fish.

SERVES 4

5 cups shredded green cabbage

3 cups shredded red cabbage

$^1/_3$ to $^1/_2$ cup shredded onion (about 1 medium)

$1^1/_2$ cups shredded carrots

$^1/_4$ cup shredded green pepper

1 to $1^1/_4$ cups mayonnaise

$^3/_4$ cup sour cream or light sour cream, or $^1/_2$ cup sour cream and $^1/_3$ cup yogurt

Salt

Pour boiling water over the green cabbage and let sit for 5 minutes. Drain and press dry. Toss with the red cabbage, onion, carrots, and pepper. Add the mayonnaise and sour cream. Add salt to taste.

VARIATIONS

With fennel

Substitute 1 fennel bulb, shredded, for the red cabbage. Add celery seed or anise seed to taste.

With pineapple

Omit the red cabbage and green pepper. Add 1 cup fresh pineapple, cut into 1-inch pieces.

Tomato and Feta Salad

We use a mild Greek cheese in this salad. Add a few shrimp, some mussels—or even
a can of tuna fish—and you have a main course in minutes.

SERVES 4

3 tablespoons red wine vinegar

1 garlic clove, crushed

Dry mustard

Salt

5 leaves shredded romaine lettuce

4 large ripe tomatoes, preferably beefsteak

$^1/_3$ cup chopped green pepper

$^2/_3$ cup chopped seeded cucumber

$^1/_3$ cup crumbled feta cheese

2 tablespoons chopped fresh mint or a combination of mint, cilantro, and basil

3 to 4 tablespoons olive oil

Place the vinegar in a glass and add the garlic, along with a pinch each of dry mustard and salt. Let sit while you assemble the salad. Arrange the shredded lettuce around the perimeter of a large platter. Arrange the tomato slices in rows. Sprinkle with the pepper and cucumber, then scatter the cheese over the top. Sprinkle with the herbs. Add the olive oil to the vinegar and stir until combined. Remove the garlic, and pour over the salad. Press down gently on the tomatoes so that the vinegar starts to meld with the tomato juices.

VARIATION

With olives and lemon zest

Add $^1/_2$ cup coarsely chopped Kalamata olives and 1 teaspoon lemon zest.

Potato Salad

Potato salad can be as simple or as complicated as you wish. Serve it as an accompaniment to grilled fish, such as salmon or bluefish, or add smidgens of shellfish or smoked fish—and some ripe tomatoes—and you have a light lunch. If you wait to add the salt until just before serving, any leftovers will taste fresh for at least two days. Be sure to use a waxy-textured potato such as Yukon Gold. This is a New England–style potato salad—for a southern version see the variations below.

MAKES ABOUT 5 CUPS

4 large waxy-textured potatoes

1 tablespoon cider vinegar

$^3/_4$ cup chopped onion

1 hard-boiled egg, chopped

$^2/_3$ cup diced celery (about 1 large stalk)

$^2/_3$ cup mayonnaise

2 to 3 teaspoons fresh lime or lemon juice

Salt

Gently boil the potatoes in a large pot of water until cooked through when tested with a knife point. Drain and peel them. Put the potatoes in a bowl of ice water until they're cool enough to cut into $^1/_2$- to $^3/_4$-inch cubes. While still warm, toss with the cider vinegar. Stir in the onion, egg, and celery. Toss with the mayonnaise and citrus juice. Season with salt to taste. Refrigerate for at least 30 minutes before serving to let the flavors meld.

VARIATIONS

With shrimp or mussels

Add 1 to 2 cups cooked whole mussels or chopped cooked shrimp to the basic mixture, or toss with lime juice and mound in the center of a platter and surround with the potato salad and quartered tomatoes.

With olives or diced dill pickles

Add 2 tablespoons diced olives or dill pickles to the basic mixture.

With cucumbers and dill

Just before serving, add $\frac{1}{3}$ cup diced cucumber and 2 tablespoons chopped fresh dill to the mixture. If you add the cucumbers before this point, they will soften.

Southern style

Add 1 to 2 tablespoons spicy brown mustard and 2 to 3 tablespoons sweet pickle relish to the basic mixture.

With beets and anchovies

Add $1\frac{1}{2}$ cups diced cooked beets, 2 to 3 teaspoons minced anchovies, and 2 tablespoons yogurt to the mixture.

With herbs

Add 2 tablespoons chopped fresh parsley or lovage, or 1 to 2 tablespoons chopped fresh tarragon, chervil, or basil, just before serving.

Turkish Salad

Try this with grilled bluefish or mackerel. It's best made with farmers' market vegetables that have not been waxed and do not require peeling.

SERVES 4

1 cucumber, halved, seeded, and cut into 1-inch pieces

3 cups Italian plum tomatoes, quartered

$^{1}/_{4}$ cup chopped red onion

3 tablespoons chopped fresh parsley or cilantro

1 tablespoon finely chopped green pepper

$^{1}/_{4}$ cup fresh lemon juice

3 tablespoons olive oil

Salt (optional)

Mix together the cucumber, tomatoes, onion, parsley, and pepper. Toss with the lemon juice and olive oil. Let sit for a while to meld the flavors before serving. Add salt to taste, if desired.

Tortilla Goat Cheese Salad

We make our fried tortilla strips out of both blue and white corn tortillas. Be ___ ___ ___ toss with the salad just before serving or they will become limp. (Or, you can arrange them on top.) Leave the skin on the apples if they are not waxed.

SERVES 4

2 corn tortillas

Vegetable oil

Salt

1 head romaine lettuce

1 avocado

1 to 2 apples, such as Cortland or Granny Smith

1 cup roasted red pepper, cut into $1/2$-inch dice

$1/3$ to $1/2$ cup Salad Dressing (page 217)

One 3.5-ounce package fresh goat cheese

Cut the tortillas into $1/4$-inch-wide strips. Put enough oil in a small but deep pot to submerge the strips. Deep-fry, a few pieces at a time, until lightly browned. This should take about 20 seconds per batch. Drain the strips on paper bags, and sprinkle them with salt while still hot. Set them aside to cool.

Slice the lettuce into 1-inch strips. Peel and cut both the avocado and apples into $1/2$-inch chunks. Combine the lettuce, avocado, apples, red pepper, and tortilla strips in a large bowl. Toss with the dressing. Mound on a serving plate, and crumble the goat cheese over the top. Serve immediately.

VARIATION

With grilled scallops or shrimp
Grill 1 pound of scallops or peeled shrimp and arrange over the tossed salad.

Crabmeat and Mango Salad

With only the natural fat from the avocados, this is a light, yet exceptionally tasty, meal for a hot summer night. Look for ripe, but not soft, mangoes.

SERVES 4

2 small avocados

2 to 3 tablespoons combined lemon and lime juices

2 ripe mangoes

1 pound fresh crabmeat, picked over for shells and cartilage

½ cantaloupe

4 lemon slices

Peel the avocados and dice into ½-inch pieces. Place in a large nonreactive bowl, and toss with 2 tablespoons of the citrus juice. Peel the mangoes and dice them into ½-inch pieces over the bowl. (You want to save the mango juices that will drip into the bowl.) Thoroughly toss with the crabmeat. Taste and season with additional citrus juice if needed.

Peel the cantaloupe and slice it into 12 pieces. Arrange the cantaloupe pieces in groups of three on a large platter, leaving a space between each grouping for a slice of lemon. Add the lemon and mound the crabmeat mixture in the center of the platter. Chill for about 30 minutes before serving.

Crab Louis

This nearly century-old recipe is not only a beautiful way to highlight fresh crabmeat but also a snap to make. The lemon juice keeps the avocado slices from darkening. Garnish with Scallion Fans (page 225) and quartered tomatoes if you wish.

SERVES 4

$^1/_2$ to $^3/_4$ cup mayonnaise

2 tablespoons ketchup

$^1/_4$ teaspoon bottled horseradish

$^1/_8$ teaspoon Dijon mustard

1 tablespoon minced onion

1 tablespoon finely chopped fresh parsley, or $^1/_2$ tablespoon chopped fresh sweet marjoram

One 10-ounce bag of mixed romaine lettuce and radicchio

1 pound fresh crabmeat, picked over for shells and cartilage

Fresh lemon juice

1 avocado, peeled and sliced

2 hard-boiled eggs, sliced

Mix together the mayonnaise, ketchup, horseradish, mustard, onion, and parsley. Let sit for at least 20 minutes to let the flavors meld. On a large circular platter, arrange the greens in a circle around the edge, leaving the center open. Place the crabmeat in the center. Drizzle the mayonnaise sauce over the crabmeat. Squeeze lemon juice to taste over the avocado slices and use as a garnish along with the hard-boiled eggs.

Lobster and Israeli Couscous Salad

from Legal's Paramus, New Jersey, restaurant uses precooked lobster meat for an elegant—yet easy—salad. Israeli couscous is available in the specialty food section of most supermarkets.

SERVES 3 TO 4

1^1/$_2$ to 2 cups cooked lobster meat

^{2}/$_3$ cup fresh lemon juice

4 to 5 cups cooked Israeli couscous

1 cup quartered, cooked artichoke hearts

^{1}/$_2$ cup chopped Kalamata olives

^{3}/$_4$ cup olive oil

Salt

Freshly milled black pepper

Romaine or Boston lettuce leaves

Toss the lobster with ^{1}/$_3$ cup of the lemon juice in a large nonreactive bowl. Let sit while you assemble the remaining ingredients. Mix together the couscous, artichoke hearts, olives, olive oil, and remaining lemon juice in another nonreactive bowl. Season with salt and pepper to taste. Cover a platter with the lettuce leaves. Mound the salad in the center of the platter. Place the lobster meat around the couscous, or arrange it on top.

—Chef Stephen Calise

Lobster Vinaigrette

This vinaigrette is equally good with cooked mussels or shrimp. Try it over greens or on a mound of fresh grapefruit or tangerine slices. At Legal's West Palm Beach restaurant, the chef uses champagne vinegar, but a good-quality white wine vinegar is also a fine choice. You can also make this as a topping for baked or grilled halibut (see below).

SERVES 4

Meat from two cooked 1-pound lobsters

1 teaspoon chopped shallot

$1/2$ teaspoon lemon zest

$1/2$ teaspoon fresh thyme leaves or chopped fresh chervil

1 tablespoon olive oil

1 tablespoon grapeseed oil

1 to 2 tablespoons champagne vinegar

Salt

Freshly milled black pepper

Diagonally slice the lobster meat into large pieces. In a nonreactive bowl, whisk together the shallot, lemon zest, thyme, oils, and vinegar. Toss in the lobster meat, and let sit for 15 minutes. Season with salt and pepper to taste.

—Chef Dave Salzano

VARIATIONS

With halibut
Marinate the lobster in the vinaigrette, drain, and serve over grilled or baked halibut or flounder.

With asparagus
Serve over a mound of blanched and cooled asparagus stems.

With tomatoes and green beans
Alternate yellow and red beefsteak tomatoes around the edge of a round serving dish. Fill in the center with blanched and cooled green beans. Top with the lobster vinaigrette.

With hard-boiled eggs and black olives
Mound the lobster on a small serving plate and surround with slices of hard-boiled eggs, cut crosswise, and small niçoise olives.

With slivered fennel
Cut a bulb of fennel into slivers. Place on a serving plate and cover with the lobster vinaigrette.

Marinated Shrimp and Cucumbers

The longer this sits, the better the flavor. Marinate in a large, shallow, nonreactive pan so that the dressing covers the ingredients. Depending upon the size of the shrimp, you may need to double the marinade. Be sure to drain the mixture before serving.

SERVES 4

1 medium sweet onion, thinly sliced

1 large cucumber, peeled, scored, and thinly sliced

1½ pounds cooked shrimp

¼ teaspoon seeded and minced jalapeño (optional)

2 tablespoons minced red pepper

1 recipe Sweet Dipping Sauce (page 281), made with ½ cup fresh lime juice rather than the vinegar

1 tablespoon minced fresh tarragon

1 tablespoon minced fresh basil

Separate the onion slices into rings and toss with the cucumber slices, shrimp, and red pepper. Pour over the dipping sauce. Let sit, refrigerated, for at least 2 hours. Toss with the herbs, and drain the marinade before serving. (If you wish, you can serve the marinade on the side as a dipping sauce.)

Curried Mussel Salad

Try this also with leftover mussels or shrimp.

SERVES 4

1⅓ cups long-grain or jasmine rice

2 pounds cleaned mussels

2 tablespoons fresh lime juice

2 tablespoons olive oil

1 tablespoon minced garlic

1½ teaspoons minced fresh ginger

2 tablespoons mild curry paste, such as Patak's

3 to 4 tablespoons canned unsweetened coconut milk

1 teaspoon Chinese chili sauce (mae ploy)

1 teaspoon honey

3 tablespoons chopped roasted red pepper

1 cup cooked peas

¾ cup sliced celery

2 tablespoons minced fresh basil or mild mint

Salt

Freshly milled black pepper

Bring a pot of water to a boil, add the rice, and boil gently until the rice is cooked through, but still firm. Pour into a colander and rinse under cold water. Set the rice aside. Steam the mussels just until they open. Cool slightly, then remove from their shells, saving any liquid they exude along with the steaming liquid. Sprinkle the mussels with the lime juice and set aside.

In a nonreactive skillet, heat the olive oil, add the garlic and ginger, and cook over high heat, stirring constantly, for 1 minute, or until cooked through. Do not let the garlic brown. Stir in the curry paste and ¼ cup of the mussel liquid. Cook over medium heat, stirring, for 2 minutes. Add 3 tablespoons of the coconut milk, the chili sauce, and the honey, and cook 1 minute longer until thoroughly incorporated.

Mix in the rice along with the red pepper, peas, celery, and basil. Taste and add the remaining coconut milk, if necessary, then season with salt and pepper to taste. Mound in a nonreactive bowl and top with the mussels and lime juice.

VARIATIONS

Mild curry
Omit the ginger. Replace the curry paste with 2 tablespoons good-quality curry powder, such as Spice Islands.

With cilantro and cumin
Add ⅛ to ¼ teaspoon ground cumin along with the curry paste. Omit the basil and substitute ¼ cup chopped fresh cilantro.

With shrimp
Stir in ½ cup cooked shrimp. Top with the mussels.

Steeped Shrimp with Fruit

On a hot summer night when you don't want to cook, try this simple combination of shrimp and tropical fruit. Steeping the shrimp means that there are no shrimp odors in the house—and no work for the cook. Use this technique with smaller-sized shrimp (large shrimp should be boiled). Of course, you can start with purchased cooked shrimp, if you wish.

SERVES 4

1½ pounds shrimp

1 recipe Sweet Dipping Sauce (page 281)

½ casaba melon

2 mangoes

½ fresh pineapple, cored, sliced, and cut into cubes

1 tablespoon fresh lime juice

1 cup purple grapes (optional)

Place the shrimp in a single layer in a shallow pan. Boil enough water to completely cover the shrimp with at least 1 inch to spare. While the water is briskly boiling, pour it over the shrimp. Stir and let the shrimp sit for 5 to 10 minutes. The boiling water will cook the shrimp, while leaving them tender. Drain in a colander and cover with ice. Let sit while you prepare the dressing and fruit.

Prepare the dipping sauce, and set aside. Peel and slice the melon and arrange down the center of a large platter. Peel and dice the mangoes and toss with the pineapple and lime juice. Flank the melon with the mango and pineapple chunks. Peel the shrimp and moisten with a tablespoon of the dipping sauce. Arrange the shrimp over the melon, and garnish with the grapes, if using. Serve with the remaining sauce on the side.

VARIATION

With lobster or mussels

Reduce the amount of shrimp to 1 pound. Add ½ pound of cooked lobster cut into large pieces or 1 cup cooked mussels. (If you have any mussel liquid, use some of it to moisten the shrimp.)

Shrimp Tabbouleh

If you can find it, apple mint has a particularly delicate flavor.

SERVES 4

1 cup bulgur wheat

1 sweet onion

5 ripe tomatoes

1 large cucumber

¹/₂ cup finely chopped fresh mint

¹/₄ cup finely chopped fresh parsley

¹/₄ cup fresh lemon juice

1 teaspoon lemon zest (optional)

¹/₃ to ¹/₂ cup olive oil

Freshly milled black pepper

1 pound chopped cooked shrimp or whole cooked mussels

Salt (optional)

Mint leaves for garnish

Cover the bulgur wheat with water, and let stand for at least 1 hour until it has softened. The wheat will swell, so check and add more water as necessary.

Meanwhile, chop the onion, tomatoes, and cucumber. Set them aside. Taste the bulgur. You want the wheat to be chewy, yet softened. Drain the bulgur, place in a clean dish towel, and squeeze dry. Place it in a nonreactive bowl. Add the onion, tomatoes, cucumber, chopped mint, parsley, lemon juice, lemon zest, if using, oil, and pepper. Just before serving, add the shrimp. Add salt to taste, if desired. Garnish with mint leaves.

Shrimp, Arugula, and Chicory Salad

This light salad, ideal for hot summer nights, takes less than ten minutes to prepare once you have washed and dried the greens. The dressing in the shrimp mixture wilts the greens slightly, so assemble the salad just before serving.

SERVES 4

3 tablespoons olive oil

1 tablespoon minced garlic

$1/2$ cup chopped scallions, including some of the green stem

$3/4$ pound cooked peeled shrimp

3 tablespoons chopped fresh parsley or sweet marjoram

1 tablespoon chopped fresh cilantro

3 tablespoons fresh lemon juice

$1/2$ cup arugula

1 bunch chicory, washed, stemmed, and dried (about 2 cups)

Heat the olive oil in a large nonreactive saucepan. Stir in the garlic and scallions, and cook over medium heat for about 3 minutes, stirring frequently. Add the shrimp, parsley, and cilantro and cook for another 1 to 2 minutes until the shrimp is heated through. Remove from the heat and add the lemon juice. Taste and correct the seasonings if necessary.

Arrange the arugula and chicory on a serving platter, pour the shrimp mixture over the greens, and toss lightly.

Shrimp-Stuffed Tomatoes

Serve these at room temperature as an appetizer for a special dinner,
or for a light summer lunch.

4 firm, large tomatoes
(about 2½ to 3 inches
in diameter)

Brown sugar

2 tablespoons olive oil

1 teaspoon chopped lemon zest

2 teaspoons chopped garlic, green
germ removed

2 slices firm white bread

2 tablespoons coarsely chopped
celery leaves

1 cup chopped peeled shrimp

1 to 2 tablespoons pine nuts
(optional)

Halve the tomatoes and squeeze gently to remove some of the seeds and juices. Drain on a paper towel. Lightly dust each tomato with brown sugar. (This should be a trace element—do not use more than a pinch for each cut surface.) Heat the olive oil in a large nonreactive skillet. Put the tomatoes, cut sides down, into the pan and lower the heat to medium-low. Cook for 10 minutes.

Meanwhile, place the lemon zest, garlic, bread slices, and celery leaves in a blender or food processor. Blend (or pulse) until the bread is in coarse crumbs and all the ingredients are combined.

Preheat the oven to 400°F.

Remove the tomatoes from the pan (leaving the fat and cooking juices) and place, glazed sides up, in a lightly oiled baking dish. Place the pan back on the stove, add the shrimp, and stir until just cooked through. Stir in the bread crumbs. Arrange the shrimp in the tomatoes and top with the bread crumbs. Sprinkle with pine nuts if you wish. Bake for 10 to 15 minutes, or until lightly browned. Cool to room temperature before serving.

Soba Noodle Salad

A Japanese mandoline creates the long cucumber, daikon, and carrot strands that mimic the soba noodles in this popular salad that often accompanies shrimp or lobster at Legal's West Palm Beach restaurant. Or, you can slice them with a vegetable peeler. You can find the sambal oelek and mae ploy sauces in the gourmet section of many supermarkets or at Asian grocery stores.

SERVES 4

3 cups cooked Japanese soba noodles

$^1/_2$ to 1 cup daikon radish strands

$^1/_2$ to 1 cup carrot strands

$^1/_2$ cup cucumber strands

$^1/_4$ cup chopped scallions, both white and green parts

$^1/_4$ cup chopped cabbage (preferably savoy)

$^1/_4$ cup coarsely chopped watercress (optional)

1 tablespoon chopped fresh cilantro

3 to 4 tablespoons rice wine vinegar

$^1/_2$ to 1 teaspoon sesame oil

1 teaspoon Chinese ground chili paste (sambal oelek)

2 teaspoons Chinese chili sauce (mae ploy)

1 tablespoon grapeseed or olive oil

Salt

Toss together the noodles, radish, carrot, cucumber, scallions, cabbage, watercress, and cilantro in a large nonreactive bowl. In another nonreactive bowl, thoroughly mix 3 tablespoons of the vinegar, the sesame oil, chili paste, chili sauce, and oil. Taste and add the additional tablespoon of vinegar and salt, if necessary. Pour over the noodle and vegetable mixture, and gently toss. Let sit for at least 15 minutes before serving.

—Chef Dave Salzano

Salad Dressing

You can vary the dressing by using different vinegars. Our chefs frequently prefer a balsamic dressing tossed with fresh tomatoes (see the variation).

MAKES ABOUT ²/₃ CUP

1 garlic clove

Dry mustard

Salt

¹/₄ cup cider or rice wine vinegar

¹/₃ cup olive oil or a mixture of olive and grapeseed oils

Slice the garlic, and put into a glass along with generous pinches of dry mustard and salt. Cover with the vinegar. Let the mixture sit for at least 1 hour. Stir in the oil. Remove the garlic clove before using.

VARIATION

Tomato Balsamic Vinaigrette

Use a combination of half balsamic and half rice wine vinegar. Add ¹/₂ cup peeled, seeded, and diced tomatoes and 1 tablespoon minced fresh parsley or sweet marjoram.

Pasta and Rice Dishes with Seafood

Crabmeat with Penne

This pasta dish needs color, so serve it with blanched broccoli or a tomato salad. Or you can toss the penne with roasted red pepper (see the variation).

SERVES 4

8 ounces penne

$\frac{1}{3}$ cup cream cheese

8 ounces crabmeat, picked over for shells and cartilage

$\frac{1}{4}$ teaspoon Worcestershire sauce

1 tablespoon fresh lemon or lime juice

2 teaspoons lemon zest

2 tablespoons chopped fresh parsley or chervil, or 1 tablespoon chopped fresh tarragon

Bring a large pot of water to a boil, salt it, add the pasta and gently boil until cooked through but still slightly firm, 12 to 15 minutes. Meanwhile, mix together the cream cheese, crabmeat, Worcestershire sauce, lemon juice, and lemon zest in a large nonreactive bowl. Drain the pasta and toss with the crabmeat mixture. Sprinkle with the parsley and serve immediately.

VARIATION

With roasted red pepper

Add 2 to 3 tablespoons roasted red pepper to the crabmeat mixture.

Jasmine Special

When I was managing Boston's Park Plaza Legal Sea Foods, I develop
customers who wanted a simple preparation. I named it after the j
At Legal, everything is steamed in our commercial steamers. At home, unless you have a
large steamer, you'll need to precook the rice, broccoli, and shrimp and assemble at the
last moment.

SERVES 4

1 cup jasmine rice

1 pound broccoli

1½ pounds shrimp (21 to 25 count), peeled

⅓ cup Salad Dressing (page 217)

1⅓ to 2 cups shredded Monterey Jack or Cheddar cheese

Preheat the oven to 400°F.

Bring a large pot of water to a boil, salt it, add the rice, and boil until just cooked through. Drain. Meanwhile, trim the florets from the broccoli, saving the stems for another use. Bring a second large pot of water to a boil, add the broccoli, and gently boil until cooked through, about 4 minutes. Drain. Steam or boil the shrimp, cool, and set aside.

Place the rice in the center of a large baking dish. Surround with the broccoli florets. Arrange the shrimp in rows over the rice and bake for 2 to 5 minutes, or until the ingredients are warmed. Remove from the oven, sprinkle first with the dressing, then with the cheese. Place back in the oven just until the cheese melts.

Linguine with Littlenecks

Most clam sauces for pasta are heavy on the olive oil and garlic and light on the vegetables. This low-fat version is teeming with flavor from the reduced clam stock and vegetables.

SERVES 4

1 pound cherry tomatoes (about 2 cups)

2 to 3 tablespoons olive oil

1 cup chopped sweet onions

3 teaspoons chopped garlic, green germ removed

$\frac{1}{4}$ to $\frac{1}{2}$ teaspoon dried red pepper flakes (optional)

2 tablespoons chopped fresh parsley, basil, or sweet marjoram

1 pound linguine, preferably made with durum wheat

36 littleneck clams

Salt

Wash and quarter the cherry tomatoes. Place them in a 4-cup measure and press down several times. Pour off the seeds and tomato liquid. Heat the olive oil in a medium nonreactive saucepan and add the onions and garlic. Cook over medium-high heat for 2 to 3 minutes, stirring constantly. Remove the mixture from the heat and stir in the tomatoes. Cook for 3 minutes over medium-high heat, stirring frequently. Stir in the red pepper flakes and herbs. Cover the pan and put it aside.

Bring a large pot of water to a boil, salt it, and add the pasta. Gently boil until the linguine is cooked through but still firm (al dente), 10 to 15 minutes. The cooking time will vary depending upon how long the pasta has been sitting around at the grocer.

Meanwhile, put the clams in a large, shallow, nonreactive saucepan, add 2 to 3 tablespoons water, cover the pan, and cook over high heat for 3 to 5 minutes. After 3 minutes, remove any clams that have opened. Continue steaming until virtually all the clams have opened. Discard any that are still closed. Pour off the clam juice. You should have about $1\frac{1}{2}$ cups. Put the juice in a sauce pan and rapidly boil until it is reduced to $\frac{1}{3}$ to $\frac{1}{2}$ cup. Add to the tomato sauce. Take most of the clams out of their shells and add to the tomato sauce. Add salt to taste.

Drain the pasta and serve with the sauce. Garnish with the remaining clams in their shells.

VARIATION

Portuguese-style clams

Take $\frac{1}{4}$ pound boneless pork, cut it into 1-inch cubes, and brown in oil until cooked through, about 5 to 7 minutes. Drain on paper bags. Add the pork to the sauce along with the clams.

Lobster Edgardo

This flavorful recipe is a special-occasion treat at Boston's suburban Braintree restaurant.

SERVES 4

2 tablespoons grapeseed oil

1 tablespoon chopped garlic

1 cup corn kernels

1 cup chopped roasted red pepper

2 ounces dry white wine

$3/4$ cup heavy cream

Meat from one $1^{1}/_{2}$-pound cooked lobster, including the tomalley

$^{1}/_{2}$ pound cooked sea scallops

Salt

1 pound linguine

2 tablespoons butter

1 to 2 tablespoons chopped fresh chives

Bring a large pot of water to a boil. While the water is heating, heat the oil in a large pan. Add the garlic, swirl, and cook for 30 seconds. Add the corn and pepper, and cook 2 minutes longer. Stir in the wine and cream. Raise the heat to medium-high and cook for 3 minutes, until reduced by one-quarter. Stir in the lobster and scallops. Simmer for 4 minutes so that the seafood is coated with the sauce. Season with salt to taste.

Add the linguine to the big pot of boiling water. When the linguine is cooked through, drain thoroughly and mix first with the lobster sauce and then with the butter. Place on a serving platter and sprinkle with chopped chives.

—Chef German Garcia

Garnishes

Y OU CAN TAKE THE BEST ingredients in the world, but if you present them in a sloppy, unappetizing way, half the pleasure of eating is lost. We experience food with our senses of sight and smell as well as taste. At Legal, our chefs—and kitchen staff—understand that making food look appealing is of prime importance. Our prep staff puts together the garnishes as well as the prepared raw ingredients for the chefs. Of course, at home you lack a staff to slice the scallions, mince the lemon zest, or core the pineapple, but you can copy some of our easy ways of garnishing food.

- Add color: Watercress stems grouped on the side of the serving plate add a touch of color and texture. If you have a garden, flowering chive blossoms are an attractive, edible garnish.

- Sprinkle with lemon or orange zest.

- Arrange toasted sesame seeds around the perimeter of a serving plate.

- Make a wasabi cream: Reconstitute wasabi powder with water. Put into a squeeze bottle and use to make designs on a serving platter.

- Create a balsamic glaze: Pour a bottle of balsamic vinegar into a nonreactive saucepan. Bring to a boil, and boil it rapidly until it reduces to a glazelike consistency, about 20 percent of the original volume. This process will take anywhere from 30 to 50 minutes. Remember that the glaze will harden as it cools. Our chefs put the glaze in a squeeze bottle and use it to make designs on the plate or to give a touch of acidity to a finished dish. Restaurant-supply stores sell plastic squeeze bottles or, at home, you can recycle mustard squeeze bottles. When refrigerated, the glaze will keep in good condition for several months.

- Make scallion fans: Trim scallions and cut off most of the green stems, leaving about $1\frac{1}{2}$ inches. With a sharp knife, cut down through the stems to the bulb several times. You want about 8 parallel cuts. Place the scallions in a bowl of ice water and refrigerate for several hours. The stems will curl slightly, giving an attractive appearance. Be sure to drain them thoroughly before serving.

- Mound lemon, lime, and orange wedges in the center of a platter. Place sliced fish fillets in a spokelike pattern fanning out from the wedges.

- Use sprigs of herbs, preferably herbs that are ingredients of the main dish. Tuck a handful of sweet marjoram or thyme fanning out under a fish fillet, sprinkle it with chopped parsley, or top with fresh mint.

Mussels Marinara

The deep blue-black of the mussels contrasts beautifully with the rich, red color of the marinara sauce. Either kielbasa or chorizo sausage works well, depending upon whether you'd prefer a smoky or a spicy taste.

SERVES 4

2 tablespoons olive oil

$^1/_2$ pound kielbasa or chorizo sausage, sliced into $^1/_2$-inch rounds

1 large onion, chopped

4 cups Marinara Sauce (page 279)

3 pounds cleaned mussels

1 pound pasta shells

Salt

Freshly milled black pepper

Heat the olive oil in a large nonreactive saucepan. Add the sausage and onion. Cook for 10 minutes, stirring frequently, until the sausage and onion are browned. Tip the pan and spoon out any excess fat. Add the marinara sauce and the mussels. Cover the pan and cook for 5 minutes longer. Set the mixture aside.

Meanwhile, cook the pasta in a large pot of salted boiling water according to the package directions until cooked through but still firm (al dente). Drain the pasta thoroughly. Toss with the mussels and sauce. Season with salt and pepper to taste.

Salmon with Asparagus and Ravioli

This is an excellent way to use up leftover cooked salmon or arctic char.

SERVES 4

2 tablespoons butter

1 cup raw asparagus, cut into
1-inch lengths

1 to 2 tablespoons sliced scallions,
both white and green parts

1 tablespoon chopped
fresh cilantro

1 cup flaked cooked salmon

¼ cup cream

Freshly milled black pepper

1 tablespoon creamy cheese, such
as St. Andre, or cream cheese

4 ounces cheese ravioli

Bring a large pot of water to a boil. Meanwhile, heat 1 tablespoon of the butter in a large skillet. Add the asparagus. Cook over medium-high heat for 2 minutes, stirring constantly. Lower the heat and stir in the scallions, cilantro, and salmon. Cook another 2 minutes, stirring frequently. Add the cream, a generous amount of pepper, and the cheese. Cook just long enough for the ingredients to form a light sauce.

Add the ravioli and salt to the boiling water. Drain, toss with the remaining tablespoon butter, and then the sauce.

Scallops and Mushroom Bowtie Pasta

This is one of Legal's most popular pasta dishes. We prepare the mushroom cream sauce ahead of time. With the sauce on hand, the final preparation takes but minutes. (The sauce will keep for two or three days, refrigerated.) Be sure to dry the scallops before cooking, and do not crowd the pan or they will steam rather than sauté—and fail to develop the sweet, caramelized flavor sautéing creates. To add color, serve with Bi-Colored Plum Tomatoes (page 265), omitting the garlic.

SERVES 4

4 to 6 ounces portobello mushrooms

1 cup heavy cream

$\frac{1}{3}$ cup dry white wine

8 ounces bowtie pasta

Grapeseed oil

$1\frac{1}{2}$ to 2 pounds sea scallops

1 cup chopped scallions (white part only) or sweet onions

1 tablespoon minced garlic

4 tablespoons chopped fresh parsley, or 2 tablespoons chopped fresh chervil, or an equal mixture of parsley and basil

Salt

Freshly milled black pepper

Remove the stems from the mushrooms and coarsely chop them. Slice the caps and set aside.

Place the mushroom stems and the cream in a small nonreactive saucepan. Bring the cream to a boil, and gently boil for at least 10 minutes, or until the cream is reduced by half. Pour in the wine and boil for 2 to 3 minutes longer. Set the mixture aside. Bring a large pot of water to a boil, add the pasta and salt, and cook until cooked through but still firm, 10 to 15 minutes.

Meanwhile, put enough grapeseed oil in a hot pan to film it lightly. Add the scallops and sear them for 30 seconds, tossing constantly. The scallops' surfaces should turn a light, nutty brown. Add the mushroom caps, scallions, and garlic. Cook over medium heat for about 2 minutes, or until the mushrooms are barely cooked through. Stir in the reserved mushroom sauce and reheat gently.

Drain the pasta thoroughly, and mix with the scallop mixture. Sprinkle with the parsley. Season with salt and pepper to taste.

—Executive Chef Rich Vellante

Shellfish and Herb Pasta

This subtle sauce is great for people who don't eat onion or garlic. There should be sufficient salt in the shellfish to make additional salt unnecessary.

SERVES 4

1 tablespoon olive oil

⅓ to ½ pound Italian sausage, crumbled

1 large pepper, seeded and thinly sliced

1½ pounds Italian plum tomatoes, peeled, seeded, and chopped

1 teaspoon chopped lemongrass (optional)

3 tablespoons chopped fresh basil

3 tablespoons chopped fresh parsley

16 littleneck clams

16 cleaned mussels

1 pound linguine

Heat the olive oil in a large pot, add the sausage, and cook, stirring frequently, for about 5 minutes. Add the pepper and tomatoes. Cook, stirring frequently, for about 10 minutes, or until the tomatoes soften and form a sauce. Stir in the lemongrass, if using, basil, parsley, clams, and mussels. Cover the pan and cook for 3 to 5 minutes, or until the shellfish open. Remove them from the pan and set aside. Check the sauce to see if it is the consistency you wish. If not, boil it down, stirring constantly, and combine with the shellfish.

While the sauce is cooking, bring a large pot of water to a boil and add the pasta and salt. When it is cooked through but still firm (al dente), drain it and immediately toss with the shell-fish sauce.

Shrimp and Oyster Jambalaya

There are many versions of this Creole classic, said to be named for the French (or Spanish) word for ham. Vary the amount of seasonings and shellfish to suit your taste.

SERVES 4 TO 6

2 tablespoons olive oil

$^2/_3$ cup chopped scallions, both white and green parts

1 teaspoon seeded and chopped jalapeño

1 cup chopped green pepper

1 cup sliced celery

$^1/_2$ teaspoon Creole seasoning

$^1/_2$ cup diced ham or smoked sausage, such as andouille

One 14.5-ounce can whole tomatoes

$^1/_2$ to 1 teaspoon Worcestershire sauce

2 cups extra-long-grain rice

8 to 16 ounces shucked oysters

$^1/_2$ to 1 pound shrimp, peeled

Freshly milled black pepper

1 tablespoon fresh lemon juice

3 tablespoons chopped fresh parsley (optional)

Salt

Heat the olive oil in a large nonreactive saucepan. Add the scallions, jalapeño, pepper, celery, Creole seasoning, and ham. Sauté over medium-high heat for 5 minutes, stirring frequently. Mash the tomatoes slightly and add them with their juices. Add the Worcestershire sauce, $1^1/_3$ cups water, and the rice. Bring to a boil, stir, and cover the pan. Cook over medium heat for 10 minutes, stirring occasionally.

Stir in the oysters with their liquor, the shrimp, and a generous amount of black pepper. Cover the pan and cook another 10 minutes, or until the rice is cooked through. You may need to add additional water. Stir in the lemon juice and parsley, if using. Season with salt to taste.

WHEN I WAS A KID, Americans didn't have the interest in fish that they have today. My father worked exceedingly hard, but for many years in the 1950s and 1960s, Legal Sea Foods operated in and out of the red. (When the Pope decreed that it was no longer necessary for Catholics to eat fish on Fridays, my father even started taking classes to become an insurance broker.) We didn't go on vacations; working together at Legal Sea Foods was our family's connective tissue.

My grandfather, Harry Berkowitz, was semiretired, so he worked with my father. He was a great role model. During the Depression, my grandfather, who genuinely loved people, gave his meat market customers credit—and never kept records. He said they'd be good for it eventually. Years later, my father was flabbergasted by the number of people who would come into the market, cash in hand, saying to my grandfather, "You took care of our family. We always said we'd pay you back."

My grandfather's favorite saying was, "It's just as easy to be nice." This phrase has always stuck with me, as did the lessons I learned helping out at Legal Sea Foods. I have always thought that my background in working retail at an early age gave me a head start in life. Dealing with customers forces you to learn how to communicate—and, if you are younger—how to communicate with adults. It is a great confidence builder for any kid. (I believe this so completely that all my children worked in Legal's fish market.) At an early age, you learn that there are no free rides, and that the best way to achieve a goal is to roll up your sleeves and dig in.

And, of course, that it's just as easy to be nice.

Mediterranean Shrimp

Ideal with bowtie pasta, this shrimp dish is a favorite at Boston's Chestnut Hill restaurant. Taste the feta cheese and Kalamata olives to gauge their saltiness, and season accordingly. You probably won't need to use salt.

SERVES 4

3 tablespoons olive oil

1½ to 2 tablespoons minced garlic

1 cup chopped red onions

1 cup scallions, diagonally sliced into ½-inch pieces, both white and green parts

1½ to 2 cups peeled, seeded, and diced tomatoes

3 tablespoons dry white wine

½ to ⅔ cup feta cheese

8 to 10 ounces bowtie pasta

1½ pounds medium shrimp, peeled

⅓ cup chopped Kalamata olives, plus 2 tablespoons whole olives for garnish

1 tablespoon butter

Freshly milled black pepper

Heat 2 tablespoons of the olive oil in a large nonreactive skillet. Add the garlic, onions, and scallions, and sauté over medium heat for 2 minutes, stirring frequently. Stir in the tomatoes, raise the heat, and cook over high heat for 5 minutes. Stir in the wine and cook 1 minute longer. Remove from the heat and scrape into a large bowl. Stir in half of the feta cheese; set aside.

Meanwhile, bring a large pot of water to boil, add the bowtie pasta and salt, and gently boil until the pasta is cooked through but still firm (al dente). Remove from the heat and drain.

In the same pan in which the sauce was cooked, heat the remaining tablespoon of olive oil. Add the shrimp, and sauté over medium-high heat until cooked through, about 2 minutes. Add the chopped olives and the sauce. Lower the heat and cook for 1 minute. Stir in the remaining feta cheese, the butter, and the pepper. Toss the sauce with the pasta. Garnish with the remaining whole olives.

—Chef Michael Gourgouras

Pasta with Pancetta and Shrimp

This recipe, inspired by the Italian spaghetti carbonara, adds shrimp to the traditional pancetta version for an easy dish that comes together quickly. Bowtie pasta is attractive with the halved shrimp, which curl slightly when cooked.

SERVES 4

¹/₂ cup pancetta, cut into ¹/₂-inch pieces

1 tablespoon olive oil

¹/₂ cup chopped scallions or sweet onions

³/₄ pound shrimp, peeled and halved lengthwise

2 large eggs

¹/₂ cup plus 2 tablespoons freshly grated Parmigiano-Reggiano cheese

8 ounces bowtie pasta or spaghetti

Freshly milled black pepper

2 tablespoons sour cream or heavy cream (optional)

Slowly cook the pancetta in a skillet for about 20 minutes. It should be very lightly browned. While the pancetta cooks, bring a large pot of water to a boil. Remove the pancetta from the pan with a slotted spoon, and set aside. Discard all but 1 tablespoon of the fat. Add the olive oil, return the pan to the heat, and add the scallions. Cook for 1 minute, or until slightly wilted. Stir in the shrimp, raise the heat, and, stirring constantly, cook the shrimp for 30 seconds to 1 minute. Do not overcook. When done, the shrimp will be pink. Set aside 5 shrimp to use as a garnish. Mix together the eggs and cheese in a large bowl, and set aside.

Meanwhile, add the pasta and salt to the boiling water. Drain thoroughly. While still hot, mix the pasta with the eggs and cheese. Stir in the sour cream, if using, reserved pancetta, and shrimp and scallions. Add black pepper to taste. Garnish with the reserved shrimp. Serve immediately.

VARIATIONS

With dill or basil
Add 1 to 2 tablespoons minced fresh dill or julienned basil to the mixture just before serving.

With anchovies
Stir in 3 chopped anchovies along with the shrimp.

Risotto with Shrimp, Celery, and Peppers

This is a delicate version of the classic Northern Italian rice dish, risotto. A top-quality cheese, such as freshly grated Parmigiano-Reggiano, is key to the flavor of the dish (although Italians would not use the cheese with the shrimp as we do). Arborio rice is available in the international foods section of most large supermarkets.

SERVES 4

1 tablespoon olive oil

1 tablespoon butter

$^2/_3$ cup finely chopped sweet onions

$^1/_2$ cup coarsely chopped celery

1 cup Arborio rice

$2^1/_2$ to 3 cups fish or chicken stock

2 tablespoons roasted red pepper, finely chopped

$^3/_4$ to 1 pound medium shrimp, peeled

1 tablespoon chopped celery leaves, or $^1/_2$ teaspoon chopped fresh sweet marjoram or tarragon

$^1/_2$ cup finely grated Parmigiano-Reggiano cheese

Salt

Freshly milled black pepper

In a large nonreactive saucepan, heat the olive oil and butter. Add the onions and celery. Cook over low heat for 10 minutes, stirring frequently. Stir in the rice and cook for 3 to 4 minutes, stirring frequently. The rice will change color, turning milky or chalky.

Meanwhile, heat the stock in a small saucepan or in the microwave. Stir half the stock into the rice mixture, and stir occasionally until it is absorbed, 5 to 8 minutes. Then add the red pepper and the remaining stock. After the stock is almost absorbed, but the rice mixture is still slightly soupy, stir in the shrimp. Continue cooking for another 5 minutes, stirring frequently, or until the rice is tender but still firm. You may need to add additional stock or water. Stir in the celery leaves and cheese. Season with salt and pepper to taste.

VARIATIONS

With pesto and peas
Add 2 to 3 tablespoons pesto and $^1/_2$ cup cooked peas along with the cheese.

With asparagus and rosemary
Cover 8 stalks of trimmed asparagus with boiling water and let sit for 6 to 8 minutes, or until cooked through but still crisp. Run under cold water to stop the cooking process. Drain, and cut into $^1/_2$-inch pieces. Add to the rice mixture just before you add the cheese. Stir in $^1/_2$ teaspoon minced fresh rosemary if you wish.

Soups and Sandwiches

Clam Chowder

I think our clam chowder is the best in the business—and the public certainly agrees. We sell it at all of our restaurants as well as at some airport concessions throughout the country. The reason for its popularity is simple: We use only the best ingredients and plenty of them. Don't try and economize by cutting back on the amount of clams or cream because the chowder will not taste as flavorful as it should.

SERVES 8

4 quarts littleneck clams

1 garlic clove, chopped

2 ounces salt pork, finely chopped

2 large onions, chopped (about 2 cups)

3 tablespoons unbleached all-purpose flour

$4^1/_2$ cups clam broth

3 cups fish stock

$1^1/_2$ pounds potatoes, peeled and diced into $^1/_2$-inch cubes

2 cups light cream

Oyster crackers (optional)

Clean the clams and place them in a large pot along with the garlic and 1 cup water. Steam the clams just until they open, 6 to 8 minutes, depending upon their size. Drain the clams, reserving the broth. Let cool slightly. Mince the clam flesh and set aside. You should have about $1^2/_3$ cups chopped clams. Filter the clam broth through either coffee filters or cheesecloth; set aside.

In a large, heavy pot, slowly render the salt pork. Remove the cracklings with a slotted spoon and set them aside. Slowly cook the onions in the fat for about 10 minutes, stirring frequently, or until cooked through but not browned. Stir in the flour and cook, stirring, for 3 minutes. Add the reserved clam broth and the fish stock, and whisk to remove any flour lumps. Bring the liquid to a boil, add the potatoes, lower the heat, and simmer until the potatoes are cooked through, about 15 minutes.

Stir in the reserved clams, salt pork cracklings, and light cream. Heat the chowder until it is the temperature you prefer. Serve in large soup bowls with oyster crackers on the side, if desired.

Corn and Green Bean Chowder

You can substitute fish, chicken, or vegetable stock for the milk. We use pancetta (a cured Italian pork product) frequently at Legal Sea Foods, but you can substitute ham or salt pork if you wish. This soup is particularly nice with Corn Bread (page 268).

½ cup pancetta, cut into ½-inch pieces

1 cup fresh green beans, halved crosswise

¾ cup diced onions

¾ cup diced celery

⅓ cup fresh corn kernels

1 cup flaked cooked grouper, haddock, or similar fish

1 tablespoon chopped fresh tarragon, or 2 tablespoons chopped fresh cilantro or parsley

2 cups milk

Place the pancetta in a large nonreactive saucepan. Slowly cook it to render the fat, turning occasionally. After 10 minutes, stir in the green beans, onions, and celery. Cook, stirring frequently, for 5 minutes. Cover with about 1 cup of water, cook for 10 minutes, and add the corn, fish, and tarragon. Cook just long enough so the corn is barely cooked through, 3 to 5 minutes. Stir in the milk. Heat slowly so that the milk doesn't boil, and serve immediately.

Fish and Vegetable Soup

This flavorful soup uses virtually any kind of leftover flaked fish. Any leftovers freeze well.

SERVES 4 TO 6

8 cups Fish Stock (page 247)

1 cup chopped carrots

1 cup peeled and chopped potatoes

2 cups peeled, seeded, and chopped tomatoes

2 cups trimmed okra, cut into thirds

1 cup chopped scallions, both white and green parts

1 cup chopped green or red pepper

2 cups flaked cooked fish (such as cod, arctic char, or haddock)

Salt

Freshly milled black pepper

Heat the fish stock in a large nonreactive pot. Add the carrots, potatoes, tomatoes, okra, scallions, and pepper. Simmer over medium-low heat for 40 minutes. Add the fish. Remove from the heat and cover. Let sit for a few minutes to let the flavors meld. Season with salt and pepper to taste.

Fish Chowder

Our customers say they have never had chowder as flavorful as ours. Its special taste derives from a concentrated fish stock made from the fish frames remaining from the white-fleshed fish we fillet, as well as a generous mixture of white-fleshed fish such as cod and monkfish. This chowder recipe certainly is delicious, but it will never taste quite the same as Legal's because it is impossible to approximate the concentrated fish base at home. The chowder tastes best if you prepare it a few hours in advance to allow the flavors to meld. Freeze any extra chowder in four-cup portions.

MAKES 3 QUARTS

½ cup butter

3 cups diced onions

¼ cup finely grated carrot

2 teaspoons minced garlic

½ cup unbleached all-purpose flour

12 cups concentrated fish stock

4 pounds fish fillets, such as 2 pounds cod, 1 pound monkfish, and 1 pound cusk

2 cups light cream

½ cup finely grated Monterey Jack cheese

Salt

Freshly milled black pepper

Heat the butter in a large saucepan until softened. Sauté the onions, carrot, and garlic, stirring frequently, for about 5 minutes. Remove the mixture from the heat and slowly stir in the flour. Return the pot to the stove and cook, stirring, for about 4 minutes. Meanwhile, begin heating the stock in a large pot. Whisk the stock into the flour mixture. Bring the stock to a boil, whisking constantly, then reduce the heat, and simmer for 10 minutes.

Add the fish and simmer about 10 minutes longer. Stir in the cream and cheese, and simmer until the cheese melts, 5 to 8 minutes. Season with salt and pepper. Reheat the chowder slowly so that the cream doesn't boil.

Haddock and Vegetable Stew

You'll need to start with a good fish stock and fish removed from the frames for this hearty soup.

SERVES 4

1 tablespoon olive oil

1 teaspoon minced garlic

1 large onion, diced (about 1¼ cups)

1 large carrot, coarsely chopped

½ to 1 teaspoon chili paste with garlic (optional)

2 to 3 cups Fish Stock (page 247)

One 15-ounce can white beans, drained

1½ to 2 cups chopped tomatoes

1 to 2 tablespoons sliced fresh basil, cilantro, or parsley

1 to 3 cups flaked cooked fish

Salt

Freshly milled black pepper

Heat the olive oil in a large nonreactive pot. Stir in the garlic, onion, and carrot. Cook over medium heat for 5 minutes, stirring frequently, or until the onion is golden and the carrot has begun to cook. Stir in the chili paste, if using, and cook 1 minute longer. Add the fish stock, the beans, and the tomatoes. (It is unnecessary to peel them.) Simmer the mixture for 15 minutes, or until the vegetables are cooked through but still retain their texture. Add the basil. Stir in the fish, turn off the heat, and let sit for at least 10 minutes. Season with additional herbs and/or salt and pepper to taste.

VARIATION

With peppers

Add 1 large green pepper, seeded and cut into chunks, along with the carrots.

Three-Way Mussels

By reducing the liquid, you can have a stew, pasta sauce, or a topping for fish. Saffron threads can be found in gourmet food shops. The threads are water or acid soluble, so let the saffron steep for at least 20 minutes before you cook the mussels.

SERVES 4

1/3 cup dry white wine

1/4 teaspoon saffron threads

3 pounds cleaned mussels

1 tablespoon butter

2/3 cup chopped Bermuda onions

1 cup finely diced fennel

1/2 cup heavy cream

1/4 teaspoon chili paste with garlic (optional)

Heat the wine in a small nonreactive saucepan. Add the saffron. Let steep while you cook the mussels. Place the mussels in a large pot, add 1/4 cup water, bring the water to a boil, and cover the pot. Lower the heat and let the mussels steam for about 5 minutes, or until they have opened. Remove the mussels immediately from the pot, saving any liquid, and discarding any mussels that have not opened.

Melt the butter in a large nonreactive pot. Stir in the onions and cook for 2 minutes, stirring frequently. Add the mussel and the saffron/wine liquids. Gently boil over medium-high heat for 2 minutes. Stir in the fennel and cook for 5 minutes. Add the cream and the mussels in their shells. Taste and add chili paste if the flavors need deepening.

VARIATIONS

Mussel and Saffron Pasta Sauce

Prepare the sauce as above, adding 3/4 cup chopped tomato. Slowly simmer until the tomato is slightly cooked through, about 10 minutes. In a large pot of boiling water, cook linguine or bowties. While the pasta is cooking, remove the mussels from their shells and just before tossing with the pasta, add them to the cream mixture.

Striped Bass with Saffron Mussels

Make a topping for a white-fleshed fish, such as striped bass. Reduce the pasta sauce until it has thickened and coats a spoon. Set aside. Bake or grill a 1 1/2-pound fillet of bass. Remove about 1/2 cup of mussels from the shells and add to the sauce. Pour it over the bass and garnish with the mussels. Sprinkle with chopped fresh parsley.

Oyster and Scallop Stew

The jalapeño deepens the flavor. If you are using large sea scallops, quarter them. This is an excellent meal-in-one for a cool fall evening.

SERVES 4

1 tablespoon butter

²/₃ cup thinly sliced scallions, both white and green parts

½ cup diced celery

1 pound scallops

2 pints shucked oysters with liquid (about 2½ pounds)

1 cup frozen corn kernels

⅓ cup peeled, seeded, and diced tomato

1 to 1½ cups milk

1 teaspoon peeled, seeded, and minced jalapeño

Sesame oil

1 to 2 tablespoons chopped fresh cilantro

Melt the butter in a large nonreactive pot. Add the scallions and celery, cover the pan, and let sweat over medium heat for 2 minutes, stirring once. Uncover the pan, add the scallops and oysters and their liquids, and cook over medium-high heat, stirring frequently, for 5 minutes, or until the seafood is barely cooked through.

Stir in the corn, tomato, 1 cup of the milk, the jalapeño, a dash of sesame oil, and the cilantro. Cover the pan and let sit for 10 minutes to let the flavors meld. Just before serving, season with salt and pepper to taste. Add the additional ½ cup milk if you prefer a thinner stew.

VARIATIONS

Scallop Stew

If you live in an area where oysters are uncommon, omit the oysters and increase the amount of scallops. Be sure to barely cook the scallops or they will become rubbery.

With prosciutto or country ham

Add 1 to 2 tablespoons minced prosciutto or country ham along with the scallions.

Shellfish Gumbo

This is an easy-to-make company dish. Remember that gumbo is a peasant dish with dozens of variations. You can add leftover chicken, sliced Louisiana sausage, ham, bacon—or leave it just all shellfish. Use okra, however, as well as tomatoes and celery for texture. If you roast the flour in the oven as I suggest (see Note), you can avoid the tediousness of standing over a stove browning the flour in the fat to make a roux. Many people who cannot digest onions can enjoy sweet onions, so they're a wise choice for guests.

SERVES 6 TO 8

3 tablespoons vegetable oil (preferably grapeseed)

2 tablespoons toasted unbleached, all-purpose flour

$1^{1}/_{2}$ cups peeled and chopped sweet onions

$^{3}/_{4}$ cup chopped celery

1 pound okra, cut into $^{1}/_{4}$-inch slices (frozen is okay)

$1^{1}/_{2}$ cups peeled, seeded, and chopped tomatoes

6 cups hot fish, shrimp, or chicken stock

1 to 2 teaspoons minced garlic, green germ removed (optional)

1 to $1^{1}/_{2}$ pounds shrimp, peeled

8 ounces fresh crabmeat, picked over for shells and cartilage

1 pint fresh shucked oysters

Hot pepper sauce

Salt (optional)

Heat the oil in a large nonreactive pot and stir in the flour. Stir over medium-high heat until the flour is absorbed. Add the onions and celery. The flour will stick to the vegetables. Continue cooking, stirring constantly, until the vegetables wilt slightly. Add the okra, tomatoes, and stock. Stir until the stock comes to a boil, lower the heat, and simmer for at least 45 minutes, uncovered. Stir in the garlic, if using. (At this point the gumbo may be refrigerated for 1 to 2 days.)

Check the consistency and thin the gumbo with water or additional stock if necessary. Before serving, bring to a boil and add the shrimp, crabmeat, and shucked oysters. Cook the mixture no longer than 1 to 2 minutes, depending upon the size of the shrimp and oysters. *Do not overcook.* Season with hot sauce and salt to taste, if desired. Ladle over rice.

VARIATION

With ham

Add $^{1}/_{2}$ cup chopped country ham along with the tomatoes. Proceed as above.

NOTE: To make toasted flour, spread out $^{3}/_{4}$ cup unbleached all-purpose flour in a baking dish. Roast it in a preheated 350°F oven for 20 to 30 minutes, or until it is a light beige color. (It will darken when mixed with fat.) Cool and whirl in a blender to remove any lumps, if you wish. Store in a covered jar in the refrigerator and use as needed.

Shellfish Gazpacho

This soup is served ice-cold, so prepare it in the morning and come home to a refreshing supper for a muggy summer night. Vary the shellfish as you wish. Shrimp, crabmeat, and lobster are equally good. To save time, blend whole tomatoes, then pour the mixture through a colander. Pass the chopped vegetable garnishes separately.

SERVES 4

$3/4$ to 1 cup fresh bread crumbs

1 tablespoon minced garlic

1 to 2 tablespoons olive oil

$1/4$ to $1/3$ cup fresh lemon juice

3 to 4 large ripe tomatoes

$1/2$ teaspoon seeded and minced jalapeño (optional)

Salt

$1/2$ pound whole cooked shrimp or 4 ounces fresh crabmeat, picked over for shells and cartilage

GARNISHES

$1/4$ cup peeled, seeded, and chopped cucumber

$1/4$ cup chopped scallions, both white and green parts

$1/4$ cup chopped yellow or green pepper

$1/2$ to $3/4$ cup chopped tomato

$1/4$ cup minced fresh cilantro

Mix together the bread crumbs, garlic, olive oil, and $1/4$ cup of the lemon juice in a nonreactive bowl and let sit for about 15 minutes so that the bread crumbs absorb the other ingredients. Meanwhile, core the tomatoes and cut them into large chunks. Puree in a blender. Put the pureed tomatoes through a sieve or colander. Put the tomatoes, jalapeño, if using, and bread crumb mixture into a blender and process until smooth. (You'll need to do this in two batches. Add $3/4$ cup water if you prefer a thin soup.) Taste and add salt—or additional lemon juice—if needed. Refrigerate in a glass bowl until cold. Just before serving, stir in the shrimp or crabmeat. Serve with the condiments in individual small bowls on the side.

Chilled Salmon and Cucumber Soup

Try this soup as a main course on a steamy summer evening. It is also
a great way to use up leftover salmon.

SERVES 4

1½ pounds salmon fillets

¾ to 1 cup diced onions
(about 1 medium)

3 cups Fish Stock (page 247)

3 cucumbers, peeled, seeded,
and diced

1½ to 2 tablespoons chopped
fresh dill

2½ cups plain yogurt

Salt

Freshly milled black pepper

Steam the salmon until just cooked through, about 10 minutes. Let it cool, then refrigerate.

Combine the onions, fish stock, and cucumbers in a saucepan. Cook over low heat until the cucumbers are tender but not mushy, about 5 minutes. Pulse in a food processor or blender with the fresh dill and yogurt just until combined. Season with salt and pepper to taste. Chill.

Just before serving, flake the salmon and add the pieces to the soup. Garnish with additional chopped cucumbers and dill if you wish.

Butternut Squash Soup with Shellfish

Fall's fresh butternut squash shines in this tasty soup from Legal's Paramus, New Jersey, restaurant. You can vary the shellfish—sliced lobster, whole shrimp, or crabmeat all work nicely.

SERVES 6

2 large butternut squash

$1/3$ to $1/2$ cup olive oil

2 whole leeks

4 stalks celery

2 tablespoons butter

2 bay leaves

6 cups fish or chicken stock

2 cups heavy cream

1 to 2 teaspoons ground nutmeg

1 to 2 teaspoons ground cinnamon

8 ounces to 1 pound cooked lobster meat, peeled and cooked shrimp, or lump crabmeat, picked over for shells and cartilage

Salt

White pepper

Preheat the oven to 400°F.

Halve the squash, brush with oil, and place them on a baking sheet. Roast for 20 to 30 minutes, or until cooked through and golden brown. When the squash are cool, peel, seed, and coarsely chop them. Set them aside.

Clean and dice the leeks and celery. Heat the butter in a large nonreactive skillet and add the leeks and celery. Cook the vegetables over medium heat for about 15 minutes, or until they are soft and translucent. Add them to a large nonreactive pot along with the squash and the bay leaves. Cover with the stock and simmer, uncovered, for 30 minutes over medium heat. Add more stock or water if needed to keep the vegetables covered. Add the cream, nutmeg, and cinnamon. Remove the bay leaves, and blend the soup in a blender or food processor until pureed. (If you're using a food processor, just blend the solids and stir them back into the liquid.) Strain, if desired, and top with the seafood. Season with salt and white pepper to taste.

VARIATION

With maple crème fraîche
Mix together $1/4$ cup each sour cream, cream cheese, and real maple syrup. Season with salt to taste. Omit the seafood and drizzle over the hot soup.

—Chef Stephen Calise

Fish Stock

Some markets now charge you for the frames (the skeleton of the fish). Make sure the gills and the intestines are removed because they will give a bitter, "off" flavor to the stock. Use white-fleshed fish only, such as cod, haddock, or grouper.

MAKES ABOUT 8 CUPS

6 pounds cleaned fish frames

1 stalk celery

1 carrot, sliced

2 onions, sliced

4 peppercorns

Chop the fish frames into pieces. Place them in a large nonreactive pot along with the celery, carrot, onions, and peppercorns. Cover with 3 quarts water. Bring the water to a boil, lower the heat, and simmer, uncovered, for about 30 minutes. Strain off the stock and boil it for 25 to 30 minutes to concentrate the flavor. If you wish, pour it through coffee filters to clarify it before using.

Measure the stock into 1-cup portions and freeze.

Soft-Shell Crab Sandwich

Most crabs come pretrimmed nowadays, but check to insure that the gills and tail are trimmed (if not, see page 33 for instructions). At our restaurants, we coat them with cornmeal and deep-fry them in oil; at home, it's easier to lightly flour the crabs and sauté them in grapeseed or olive oil, bacon fat, or butter.

SERVES 4

8 slices lean bacon

Unbleached all-purpose flour

4 soft-shell crabs, trimmed

Oil, butter, or bacon fat

4 toasted sandwich buns

Mayonnaise

4 slices ripe tomato

Lettuce

In a large skillet, cook the bacon until crisp. Set aside. Flour the crabs, shake to remove any excess flour, and sauté them in the fat of your choice, until cooked through, about 1 minute per side. Spread each bun with mayonnaise, top with tomato, lettuce, 2 slices of bacon, and a crab.

Crabmeat Roll

New Englanders think that Maine crabmeat is the ideal choice for these rolls, but the blue crab is common from Maine to Florida. New Englanders also eat their crabmeat rolls in hot dog buns. Please don't garnish with paprika—it's too harsh for the sweet taste of the crabmeat.

For each roll:

½ cup fresh crabmeat, picked over for shells and cartilage

1 to 2 tablespoons diced celery

1 tablespoon good-quality mayonnaise, such as Hellmann's

Fresh lemon juice

1 hot dog bun spread with butter and toasted

Mix together the crabmeat, celery, and mayonnaise. Taste and season with lemon juice. Stuff a hot dog bun with the mixture.

VARIATIONS

With Cajun Remoulade Sauce (page 273)
Substitute the sauce for the mayonnaise. Add 1 teaspoon chopped fresh dill.

Lobster Rolls
Substitute cooked lobster for the crabmeat.

Crabmeat Melt

This supper or brunch recipe, made with fresh crabmeat, takes about five minutes to prepare. You can toast the English muffins in advance. Be sure the crabmeat is fresh, not frozen. (A sign of frozen crabmeat is a tremendous amount of liquid. If you have purchased frozen crabmeat, add a pinch of dry mustard, and press down on the crabmeat to extract excess liquid before mixing with the mayonnaise.)

SERVES 4

1 teaspoon butter (optional)

4 English muffins, split

Scant $^1/_2$ cup good-quality mayonnaise, such as Hellmann's

1 pound fresh crabmeat, picked over for shells and cartilage

$^1/_4$ teaspoon bottled horseradish

2 large meaty tomatoes, thinly sliced

1 avocado, peeled and thinly sliced

$^1/_2$ cup freshly grated Monterey Jack cheese, or a combination of Monterey Jack and Cheddar cheeses

Preheat the broiler.

Lightly butter the muffins. Heat a large skillet and pan-brown the muffins until lightly browned. Set them aside. (Or you can toast them in a toaster oven, unbuttered.)

Mix together the mayonnaise, crabmeat, and horseradish. Place the muffin halves on a countertop. Layer each half with $^1/_4$ cup of the crabmeat mixture, sliced avocados, tomatoes, and 1 tablespoon of the cheese. Place on a baking sheet and broil for about 3 minutes, or until the cheese melts. Serve immediately.

VARIATIONS

With fried green tomatoes
Omit the avocado and red tomatoes. Thickly slice green tomatoes, dip in cornmeal, and fry in butter. You will need 8 slices. Place on the muffin, top with the crabmeat, and then with the cheese. Proceed as above.

With sweet marjoram
Add $^1/_2$ to 1 teaspoon chopped fresh sweet marjoram to the crabmeat mixture. Proceed as above.

Fish Sandwich

Haddock is delicious, but you can substitute cusk or pollock

SERVES 4

1 recipe Fried Haddock (page 53)

Mayonnaise or Tartar Sauce (page 272)

4 bulkie rolls or hamburger buns

Sliced tomatoes

Lettuce

Prepare the haddock. Spread mayonnaise or tartar sauce on a roll. Add the haddock, and top with the tomatoes and lettuce.

VARIATION

Chilean-style Sandwich

This unusual sandwich, with its spread of avocado and garnish of green beans, is inspired by the Chilean sandwich *chacarero*. Use freshly cooked green beans, or set aside some Middle Eastern–Style Green Beans (page 258).

> *For each sandwich use:*
> **Grapeseed oil**
> **6 ounces white-fleshed fish, such as haddock or cusk**
> **1 large densely textured roll**
> **3 tablespoons mashed avocado**
> **3 slices sliced tomato**
> **1 slice Cheddar or Swiss cheese**
> **6 to 8 fresh green beans**
> **Salt**
> **Freshly milled black pepper**

Heat the grapeseed oil in a skillet to depth of $1/4$ inch and add the fish, skin side down. Sauté on each side for about 3 minutes over medium-high heat. The flesh will become golden and the fish will be cooked through. Drain on a paper bag. Halve the roll and spread with the avocado. Top with the tomato, cheese, green beans, and the fish. Season with salt and pepper to taste.

Grilled Swordfish Tacos

Try these with either soft- or hard-shell tacos. Tuna also works well.

MAKES 4 TO 6 TACOS

2¹/₂ cups peeled and diced avocados

¹/₂ to ³/₄ cup chopped red onions

¹/₄ cup fresh lime juice

Hot pepper sauce

2¹/₂ tablespoons seeded and minced jalapeño

2 cups seeded and coarsely diced plum tomatoes (about 5)

¹/₃ cup chopped fresh cilantro

1 to 2 teaspoons ground cumin

¹/₄ to ¹/₃ cup olive oil, plus more for the fish

¹/₄ cup chopped scallions, both white and green parts

1¹/₂ to 2 pounds swordfish fillets

4 to 6 tacos

Salt

Freshly milled black pepper

8 ounces shredded lettuce

Sour cream

Mix together the avocados, onions, lime juice, and a dash of hot sauce in a nonreactive bowl, and set aside. In another bowl, toss together the jalapeño, tomatoes, cilantro, cumin, olive oil, and scallions. Let sit while you cook the swordfish.

Oil the swordfish. Grill or broil until cooked through, 8 to 10 minutes. Set aside to cool slightly. If you are using soft tacos, warm them on the grill for about 20 seconds on each side. (Or place them in a hot skillet for about 10 seconds.) Diagonally slice the swordfish. Taste both the avocado and the tomato mixtures and season with salt and pepper to taste.

Make an assembly line for the tacos on your countertop. Place all the tacos in a row. Look at the swordfish, avocado mixture, and tomato mixture and see how they can be divided into equal portions. For each portion, place 2 or 3 slices of swordfish on one side of the taco, top with the avocado mixture, then add the tomatoes and shredded lettuce to taste. Fold over and serve with sour cream. (Or you can layer the ingredients in hard taco shells.)

—Executive Chef Rich Vellante

Shrimp Wrap

Many a Logan Airport customer grabs a shrimp wrap to enjoy on the plane. We use flour tortillas, but you could also substitute a toasted bun. Quadruple the recipe for four servings.

MAKES 1 WRAP

1 cup chopped cooked shrimp (about 5 ounces)

1 to 2 tablespoons mayonnaise

2 tablespoons chopped celery (optional)

1 tablespoon chopped scallions

One 10-inch flour tortilla

2 to 3 tomato slices

Lettuce

Mix the shrimp with the mayonnaise, celery, if using, and scallions. Spread on a flour tortilla. Arrange the tomatoes and lettuce on top. Roll up the tortilla. Cut in half diagonally.

—Chef John Compton

Wraps

MOST OF OUR RESTAURANTS offer a lunch special of a cup of chowder and a tortilla flour wrap filled with an assortment of fish and vegetables. Customers racing through Boston's Logan Airport often grab our Shrimp Wrap (page 253), but our chefs prepare dozens of other variations. Here are some suggestions for you to make at home. Each uses a ten-inch flour tortilla as the wrap, or you could also use lavash (Armenian flat bread). The tortilla tastes best if it is warmed in a skillet for a moment or two, or placed on a grill. Remember that wraps are a great way to use up small amounts of sauces and condiments lurking in your refrigerator, as well as leftover fish (use within a day).

- Sauté or grill shrimp: Wrap with a Caesar salad mix and lots of freshly grated Parmigiano-Reggiano cheese.
- Grill mahi mahi or arctic char: Thinly slice and toss with roasted red peppers and bacon. Spread a tortilla with tartar sauce and shredded iceberg lettuce and roll up.
- Sauté haddock or cusk: Slice thickly. Wrap in a tortilla with lettuce, tomato, and mayonnaise mixed with pureed roasted red peppers.
- Thinly slice leftover fish: Marinate for 5 minutes in lemon juice. Drain and wrap with shredded romaine lettuce and Guacamole Sauce (page 278) and sliced red onions.
- Grill or fry squid: Wrap with pickled jalapeños, mayonnaise, and shredded lettuce.
- Sauté swordfish: Thinly slice and wrap with Mango Salsa (page 284) and shredded lettuce.
- Deep-fry popcorn shrimp: Wrap with Fried Rice (page 187) and season with Asian-Style Vinaigrette (page 280).
- Deep-fry catfish fingers and wrap with shredded lettuce, chopped tomatoes, and Cajun Remoulade Sauce (page 273).
- Rub swordfish with a Cajun seasoning mix, grill it, thinly slice, and wrap with lettuce and a good-quality commercial tomato salsa.
- Pan-sear a tuna steak: Thinly slice it and wrap with Fried Rice (page 187) that has extra shredded carrots and scallions.
- Oven-bake salmon in a barbecue sauce: Thinly slice it and wrap with roasted vegetables, such as peppers, summer squash, and onions.
- Rub mahi mahi with a Jamaican jerk seasoning, grill or bake it, thinly slice, and wrap with cole slaw.
- Fry oysters and place in a tortilla with seaweed salad (found at many Asian grocery stores).

Vegetables and Side Dishes

Baked Beans

Add Zesty Fish Cakes (page 185) and you have the makings for New England's traditional Saturday night supper. Substitute maple syrup for the brown sugar, as is done in Vermont, if desired. Usually, beans are soaked overnight to soften them, but sometimes they can start to ferment. Using the method described here, you substitute a longer cooking time for the overnight soak. A deep pot, such as an earthenware bean pot, works best.

MAKES 8 CUPS

1 pound dried Great Northern or navy beans

½ pound salt pork

1 tablespoon dry mustard

4 tablespoons brown sugar

½ cup molasses

2 tablespoons ketchup (optional)

Salt (optional)

Freshly milled black pepper (optional)

Wash the beans, place in a nonreactive pot, and cover with water. Bring to a boil, and boil rapidly for 5 minutes. Cover the pot and let the beans sit while you assemble the remaining ingredients. Drain the beans, saving the water.

Preheat the oven to 300° F.

Cut the salt pork into thin pieces, leaving the skin side whole. Put the beans in a deep baking pot, layering the salt pork pieces every inch or two. Add the dry mustard, brown sugar, and molasses to the liquid, and pour over the beans. Add extra water if needed. Remember that the beans will swell as they cook. Cover the pan and bake for 4 to 6 hours, adding water if needed. If you wish, add 2 tablespoons ketchup during the last hour of cooking. Season with salt and pepper, if desired.

VARIATION

Save some beans for an English breakfast of fried eggs, sausages, halved tomatoes, and baked beans.

Speckled Butter Bean Casserole

Many supermarkets now carry this southern bean in the frozen food section. This casserole stays in good condition for at least four days if refrigerated, and improves as it sits. Serve with baked or broiled plain fish.

SERVES 4 TO 6

1 pound fresh or frozen speckled butter beans

1 cup coarsely chopped sweet onions

2 slices bacon, coarsely chopped

¹⁄₂ cup chopped celery

2 teaspoons light brown sugar

¹⁄₂ cup seeded and chopped tomato

¹⁄₂ cup water, ham stock, or chicken stock

Preheat the oven to 350° F.

Butter an 8-cup nonreactive casserole. Stir in the beans, onions, bacon, celery, sugar, tomato, and water or stock. Cover the pan and bake for 1 to 2 hours, or until the beans are softened.

Middle Eastern—Style Green Beans

These beans are delicious with any kind of plainly prepared fish. Save a few for a Chilean-style fish sandwich (see page 251). Stored in the refrigerator, they will stay in good condition for three to four days.

SERVES 4

1 pound green beans, trimmed

1 tablespoon sliced garlic

$^{1}/_{2}$ cup peeled and chopped Bermuda or sweet onions

$^{2}/_{3}$ cup peeled, seeded, and chopped Italian tomatoes

2 tablespoons olive oil

Cinnamon (optional)

2 tablespoons chopped fresh parsley or mint

1 to 2 tablespoons fresh lemon juice

Salt

Freshly milled black pepper

Put the beans, garlic, and onions in a large, shallow, nonreactive saucepan. Cover with about 4 cups water. Bring the mixture to a boil, lower the heat to medium, and cook, stirring occasionally, for 40 minutes.

Add the tomatoes, olive oil, and a pinch of cinnamon, if desired. Raise the heat and gently boil for 20 minutes, or until almost all of the liquid has evaporated. Stir in the parsley and lemon juice. Season with salt and pepper to taste. Serve at room temperature.

VARIATIONS

With roasted red peppers
Add $^{1}/_{4}$ cup thinly sliced red pepper along with the parsley.

With mussels
Sprinkle with cooked mussels before serving.

Onion Strings

Onion strings have been on our menu virtually since Legal Sea Foods began. Our customers like them because they're more delicate tasting than onion rings. The trick is to cut the onions as thinly as possible, and to soak them in buttermilk before frying. Be sure to serve them immediately, otherwise the onion strings will become soggy.

SERVES 4

2 pounds large yellow or sweet onions, such as Vidalia

3 to 4 cups buttermilk

2 cups grapeseed or vegetable oil

3 to 4 cups Fried Fish Coating (page 286)

Peel the onions and cut a pie-shaped wedge from the top to the bottom of each onion. Place the onion sideways on a counter and hold it tightly with one hand, almost squeezing the onion closed. (This makes it easier to cut thin slices.) Thinly slice the onion and separate out each strand. Continue until all the onions are sliced. Cover the strands with buttermilk and let soak for at least 15 minutes.

Add the oil to a deep fryer, and heat the oil to 360° F. While the oil is heating, drain the onion strands and toss in the Fried Fish Coating. Place a small batch of strings in the heated oil and deep-fry until they are lightly browned and crisp, about 30 seconds per batch. Remove with a slotted spoon, and continue frying the onions until all are cooked. Place the cooked strings on paper bags or several layers of paper towels, and serve immediately.

Mashed Potatoes

We always have mashed potatoes on the menu, usually a mixture of Red Bliss and Yukon Gold varieties. The secret ingredients are trace elements of Monterey Jack cheese and sour cream. We use our steaming ovens to steam the potatoes, but at home it's easier to boil them.

SERVES 4

4 cups peeled and cubed potatoes

3 tablespoons shredded Monterey Jack cheese

$\frac{1}{4}$ cup milk

2 to 4 tablespoons butter

2 to 3 tablespoons sour cream

Salt

Freshly milled black pepper

2 to 3 tablespoons chopped fresh parsley

Place the potatoes in a nonreactive pot, cover with water, and bring them to a boil. Gently boil the potatoes until cooked through, about 15 minutes. Drain the potatoes. Place back in the pot with the cheese, milk, butter, and sour cream. Mash with a potato masher, adjusting the amounts to suit your palate. Season with salt and pepper to taste. Sprinkle with parsley before serving.

Spinach with Pine Nuts

Spinach's beautiful deep color and acidic overtones contrast nicely with most fish. If you wash and stem the spinach ahead of time, the actual preparation takes less than five minutes. Remember that spinach is mostly water, so what might seem like a huge amount of spinach will wilt considerably. Really fresh spinach rarely needs embellishments, but packaged spinach frequently benefits from a splash of Worcestershire or soy sauce.

SERVES 4

2 tablespoons olive oil

3 tablespoons pine nuts or walnuts

1 pound spinach leaves, stemmed, washed, and dried

Worcestershire or soy sauce (optional)

Freshly milled black pepper

Heat the olive oil in a large nonreactive skillet. Add the nuts and sauté them for 2 minutes over medium heat, stirring frequently. Do not let them brown. Remove from the pan with a slotted spoon and set aside. Turn up the heat, add the spinach, and sauté until limp, stirring constantly. This will take 1 to 2 minutes. Remove from the heat, stir in the pine nuts, and taste. If desired, add a dash of Worcestershire or soy sauce and black pepper. Serve immediately.

VARIATION

With dried red pepper flakes
Omit the pine nuts. Add $1/2$ to 1 teaspoon dried red pepper flakes just before serving.

Pureed Butternut Squash

Butternut squash is always on our menu because its beautiful color and rich flavor set off virtually any fish. The fresher the squash, the less sweetener you need. For the driest possible squash, mash right in the colander, and let the squash sit for five minutes before adding the remaining ingredients.

SERVES 4

5 cups peeled and cubed butternut squash (about 2 medium)

3 tablespoons butter

2 tablespoons pancake or maple syrup

Generous dash of ground nutmeg, mace, cardamom, or pumpkin pie spice mixture

Salt (optional)

Place the squash in a large nonreactive saucepan, cover with water, and bring to a boil. Lower the heat to medium and gently boil for 10 to 15 minutes. The time will vary depending upon the age of the squash and the size of the cubes. Drain in a colander placed in a sink. Mash with a potato masher. Put back either into the pan or into a serving dish and stir in the butter, syrup, and a generous dash of the nutmeg. Taste and adjust the seasonings, adding salt, if desired. Let the mixture sit for 10 minutes before serving to meld the flavors.

VARIATIONS

With Chinese chili sauce (mae ploy)
Add 1 teaspoon sweet chili sauce to the mashed squash.

Substitute buttercup squash
Buttercup squash's denser flesh takes longer to cook. Add about 5 minutes to the cooking time and save 2 tablespoons of the cooking liquid to add to the mashed squash. Pumpkin pie spices go particularly well with buttercup squash.

Summer Squash with Cherry Tomatoes

This colorful scramble is best made with summer vegetables that are brimming with vegetable juices. Try it with grilled, assertively flavored fish, such as tuna, salmon, or mackerel. You can vary the flavor by changing the herbs.

SERVES 4 TO 6

1 to 2 tablespoons olive oil

2 cups sliced summer squash (about 4 small)

¼ cup diced roasted red pepper

1 cup cherry tomatoes

1 cup raw corn kernels (about 1 large ear)

⅓ cup sliced celery (optional)

2 tablespoons chopped fresh mint, basil, or lovage

Heat the oil in a large nonreactive skillet. Add the squash and sauté, stirring frequently, for 3 minutes over medium-high heat. Stir in the peppers, tomatoes, corn, and celery, if using. Lower the heat to medium and continue cooking, stirring frequently, for another 5 minutes. The vegetables should be barely cooked through and retain their texture. Stir in the herbs just before serving.

VARIATION
Substitute either fresh or frozen leftover Bi-Colored Plum Tomatoes with Garlic (page 265) for the fresh cherry tomatoes.

Chipotle Sweet Potato Mash

The heat of the chipotle peppers is tempered by the full flavor of the sweet potatoes. At Legal's West Palm Beach restaurant, this mash is served with Citrus Soft-Shell Crabs (page 109) and Grilled Tomato Salsa (page 285). You can prepare the sweet potatoes ahead of time and reheat them in the microwave.

SERVES 4

3 pounds sweet potatoes (about 4)

2 tablespoons canned chipotle peppers in adobo sauce

1 cup light cream

4 tablespoons unsalted butter

Salt

Freshly milled black pepper

1 to 2 tablespoons minced fresh chives

Peel and dice the sweet potatoes into large chunks (about 1½ inches). Place them in a large pot, cover with water, and bring to a boil. Gently boil for 10 to 20 minutes, or until a fork pierces the chunks easily.

Meanwhile, in a separate saucepan, combine the peppers, cream, and butter. Bring the mixture to a boil, lower the heat, and cook over medium heat for 10 minutes, or until the cream is slightly thickened. Drain the potatoes and mash with the cream mixture. Season with salt and pepper to taste. Just before serving, stir in the chives.

—Chef Joe Coletto

Bi-Colored Plum Tomatoes with Garlic

Most farmers' markets and many specialty vegetable markets carry miniature yellow plum tomatoes, which are sweeter and less acidic than most tomatoes. Tossed with red plum, grape, or cherry tomatoes, you have a colorful and tasty accompaniment to full-flavored fish, such as mackerel, bluefish, or tuna. Wait to sauté the tomatoes until just before serving because they soften and wilt slightly as they sit.

SERVES 4 TO 6

1 tablespoon butter or olive oil

1 to 2 tablespoons minced garlic

2 cups miniature yellow plum tomatoes

2 cups miniature red plum, grape, or cherry tomatoes

Sherry vinegar or Worcestershire sauce

Salt (optional)

1 tablespoon chopped fresh parsley or garlic chives

Place the butter in a nonreactive skillet and heat it until it is bubbling. Add the garlic, and stir for 1 minute. Add the tomatoes and cook over medium heat, stirring frequently, for 3 to 4 minutes, or until they are slightly cooked. Add a dash of sherry vinegar or Worcestershire sauce. Season with salt to taste, if desired. Sprinkle with parsley before serving.

Slow-Baked Plum Tomatoes

Long slow baking turns even rock-hard plum tomatoes into a delicious fish accompaniment. Our catering department prepares batches of these tomatoes to add a rich flavor—and beautiful color—to swordfish. Any extra tomatoes are delicious eaten as is, on pizza, or as a topping with smoked salmon and cream cheese on English muffins or bagels.

SERVES 4 TO 6

1½ pounds large plum tomatoes (about 6)

2 to 3 tablespoons olive oil

Dried thyme

1 head garlic (optional)

Salt

2 tablespoons balsamic vinegar

Preheat the oven to 325°F.

Halve the tomatoes and place them, cut sides up, in a nonreactive baking pan. Drizzle with the olive oil. Sprinkle with a generous pinch of thyme, and scatter the garlic cloves, if using, in the pan. Sprinkle with salt. Bake for 25 minutes. Lower the heat to 200°F and cook another 2 hours. After 1 hour, drizzle with the vinegar. Baste occasionally. Remove from the oven, baste again, and let cool.

—Chef Siobhan Magee-Bonifacio

Zipper Peas

In the south, these fresh peas are a summer treat. They're delicious with fried or baked fish and, if refrigerated, stay in good condition for several days. Keep them in the cooking liquid, and reheat before serving. You can buy the peas in supermarkets and farmers' markets throughout the south—and at specialty markets throughout the country. The cooking time depends upon whether you like them slightly firm (northern style) or totally cooked through (southern style).

SERVES 4

1½-inch piece salt pork

2 teaspoons minced garlic

2 cups shelled zipper (or field) peas

Cut the salt pork into pieces. Place in a nonreactive saucepan along with 3 cups water and the garlic. Bring the mixture to a boil, lower the heat, and simmer for 20 minutes. Add the peas, and cook over medium heat, uncovered, for 30 to 60 minutes, depending upon how firm you'd like the peas to be. The cooking time also will vary depending upon the age of the peas. Remove with a slotted spoon before serving.

Corn Bread

Try the jalapeño variation with fried fish.

MAKES ONE 8-INCH PAN

²⁄₃ cup sour cream

¹⁄₂ teaspoon baking soda

1 cup self-rising flour

1 cup medium-grind cornmeal

¹⁄₄ teaspoon salt

1 to 2 teaspoons sugar

¹⁄₂ cup plus 1 tablespoon milk

3 tablespoons grapeseed oil or melted butter

1 large egg

Preheat the oven to 400°F.

Combine the sour cream and baking soda in a glass measuring cup or bowl. Let sit for 10 minutes until the mixture increases slightly in volume. Mix together the flour, cornmeal, salt, and sugar in a large bowl. Stir together the milk, oil, and egg with the sour cream mixture, then pour over the dry ingredients. Gently stir them together. Put into a greased 8-inch baking pan. Bake for 20 to 25 minutes, or until cooked through.

VARIATIONS

With corn
Add 1 cup cooked corn kernels just before baking.

With jalapeños
Add 1 tablespoon minced jalapeños just before baking.

Rhode Island Johnny Cakes

At our Warwick, Rhode Island, restaurant, we serve Johnny cakes with sea scallops or fried oysters. We use locally ground white cornmeal from Usquepaugh (see Note) for these cooked corn cakes, said to have been eaten by itinerant preachers on their travels. (Eventually, the original name of journey cakes evolved into Johnny cakes.) Be sure to use boiling water and serve immediately, because they lose their soft texture upon standing. Johnny cakes also are delicious served with butter and maple syrup for breakfast—or as a brunch dish topped with leftover fish in a sauce or chicken hash.

MAKES 6 CAKES

²/₃ cup stone- or water-ground white cornmeal (see Note)

¹/₈ to ¹/₄ teaspoon salt

²/₃ cup boiling water

¹/₂ teaspoon honey or 1 teaspoon sugar (optional)

1 to 2 tablespoons milk or half-and-half

Butter

Combine the cornmeal and salt in a large bowl. Gradually add the boiling water. Stir in the honey, if using, and milk. You should end up with a batter that's slightly thinner than a pancake batter. (Cornmeals vary in absorption. Add an additional tablespoon of water if necessary.)

Heat a large buttered skillet or griddle and immediately spoon about ¹/₄ cup batter onto the pan for each cake. Do not crowd the pan. Cook the cakes for about 2 minutes until browned, then turn and cook on the other side. Serve immediately.

VARIATIONS

With fried oysters
Serve with deep-fried oysters and bacon strips.

With sautéed sea scallops
Melt butter and sauté sea scallops. Serve over the cakes, sprinkled with chopped fresh chives or sweet marjoram.

Note: A source for stone-ground cornmeal is the Kenyon Corn Meal Company of Usquepaugh, Rhode Island, PO Box 221, West Kingston, RI 02892; 1–800–7–KENYON; www.kenyonsgristmill.com.

Rice Pilaf

The toasted almond garnish adds just the right amount of crunch

to this easy-to-prepare pilaf.

SERVES 4

1 tablespoon butter

3 tablespoons chopped scallions,
both white and green parts

1 cup long-grain rice, such as
jasmine

2 cups chicken or vegetable stock

1 tablespoon dry white wine
(optional)

Salt

Freshly milled black pepper

¼ cup toasted sliced almonds

Melt the butter in a large nonreactive skillet over medium heat, add the scallions, and cook for 1 minute, stirring frequently. Add the rice and cook another 2 minutes, stirring constantly. (The rice will brown slightly.) Add the chicken stock and wine, if using. Season with salt and pepper to taste. Cook the rice over medium heat for 12 to 15 minutes, or until almost cooked through. Cover the pan, turn off the heat, and let sit for another 5 minutes. Place in a serving dish and sprinkle with the almonds.

Sauces and Coatings

Tartar Sauce

Most people consider tartar sauce an obligatory accompaniment to fried clams or fish. It's also a flavorful replacement for mayonnaise in a fish sandwich. Our sauce has a number of ingredients, many of which you probably have on hand.

MAKES ABOUT 1¼ CUPS

1 cup mayonnaise

2 tablespoons minced sweet onion

2 tablespoons finely chopped
kosher dill pickles

2 tablespoons finely chopped
mixed sweet pickles

¼ to ½ teaspoon juice from
sweet pickles

1 tablespoon minced celery

1 tablespoon minced green pepper

1 teaspoon minced garlic
(optional)

1 teaspoon sweet pepper relish

1 teaspoon sweet red pepper
relish

Hot pepper sauce

¼ teaspoon white vinegar

¼ teaspoon dry mustard

1 teaspoon fresh lemon juice

1 teaspoon Dijon mustard,
preferably country style

Combine the mayonnaise, onion, pickles, juice, celery, green pepper, garlic, if using, relishes, a dash of hot sauce, the vinegar, dry mustard, lemon juice, and Dijon mustard in a nonreactive bowl. Let the flavors meld in the refrigerator for an hour or two before serving. Any extra sauce keeps for at least a week refrigerated in a covered container.

Cajun Remoulade Sauce

Use this as a spread in fish sandwiches, as an accompaniment to grilled or fried fish, or as an ingredient in Crabmeat and Mango Salad (page 206). Vary the proportions depending upon how savory you'd like the mixture to taste. The sauce will stay in good condition for three days if refrigerated.

MAKES 1 $\frac{1}{2}$ CUPS SAUCE

1$\frac{1}{2}$ cups mayonnaise

2 tablespoons whole-grain mustard

1$\frac{1}{2}$ to 2 teaspoons bottled horseradish

$\frac{1}{4}$ to $\frac{1}{2}$ teaspoon Worcestershire sauce

Hot pepper sauce

2 tablespoons chopped scallion stems

1 tablespoon chopped fresh parsley

1 tablespoon fresh lemon juice

$\frac{1}{2}$ teaspoon ketchup (optional)

Salt

Freshly milled black pepper

Mix together the mayonnaise, mustard, horseradish, Worcestershire sauce, a dash of hot sauce, the scallion stems, parsley, lemon juice, and ketchup, if using, in a nonreactive bowl. Season with salt and pepper to taste. Let sit for 15 to 30 minutes before serving.

Chilled Horseradish Citrus Cream

This addictive sauce, a specialty at Legal's Burlington, Massachusetts, restaurant, goes particularly well with fish sprinkled with a Cajun or Jamaican jerk rub. Vary the amount of horseradish to suit your taste.

MAKES ABOUT 3 ¼ CUPS

2 cups sour cream
¾ to 1 cup bottled horseradish
¼ cup fresh lemon juice
¼ cup fresh lime juice
2 teaspoons minced garlic
2 tablespoons honey
Freshly milled black pepper
Salt

Mix together the sour cream, horseradish, lemon and lime juices, garlic, and honey in a nonreactive bowl. Season with a generous amount of pepper and salt to taste.

—Chef Michael Lus

Cocktail Sauce

This homemade version has a fresher flavor than commercial preparations. Any leftover sauce will keep for at least five days if refrigerated in a covered container.

MAKES ABOUT ½ CUP

½ cup ketchup
2 teaspoons fresh lemon juice
1 teaspoon bottled horseradish
Worcestershire sauce
⅛ teaspoon dry mustard
Hot pepper sauce

Mix together the ketchup, lemon juice, horseradish, a generous dash of Worcestershire sauce, the dry mustard, and a dash of hot pepper sauce in a nonreactive bowl. Taste, and correct seasonings if desired.

Avocado Cream

You'll need a blender to achieve a smooth, creamy texture for this side dish, which is excellent with grilled fish, such as halibut, or as an ingredient in Shrimp and Avocado Quesadilla (page 198).

MAKES A SCANT ²/₃ CUP

¼ cup plain yogurt

2 teaspoons fresh lime juice

1 tablespoon cream cheese

¾ avocado, peeled

⅛ teaspoon bottled horseradish (optional)

Salt

Place the yogurt, lime juice, cream cheese, avocado, and horseradish, if using, in a blender. Blend at high speed until smooth, stopping the machine at least once to stir the mixture. Season with salt to taste.

VARIATION

With cilantro and hot pepper sauce
Stir in 1 to 2 teaspoons chopped fresh cilantro and a dash of hot pepper sauce before serving.

Sesame Seed Avocado

Goat cheese deepens the avocado's flavor, but you can substitute cream cheese if you wish. Serve this with bluefish or salmon.

MAKES ABOUT 1 CUP

1 ripe avocado

1 to 2 tablespoons softened goat cheese, such as Montrachet

1 tablespoon toasted sesame seeds

1 to 2 tablespoons fresh lime juice

Salt

Cayenne pepper

Mash the avocado flesh and mix with the cheese, sesame seeds, and lime juice in a nonreactive bowl. Season with salt to taste and a pinch of cayenne pepper. Let sit for a few minutes before serving to allow the flavors to meld.

VARIATION

With chili paste
Omit the cayenne pepper and add ¹/₁₆ to ⅛ teaspoon of Chinese chili paste with garlic.

Add-On Barbecue Sauce

The additional ingredients customize any standard barbecue sauce. The sauce is particularly apt with stronger-flavored fish, such as mackerel, bluefish, or salmon. Use it also with Barbecued Shrimp (page 84).

MAKES ABOUT ¾ CUP SAUCE

½ cup dried cherries or cranberries

½ cup red wine, such as Merlot or Pinot Noir

1 cup commercial barbecue sauce

½ to 1 teaspoon Worcestershire sauce

1 tablespoon A1 sauce

Red pepper flakes

1 tablespoon honey

½ tablespoon cider vinegar

In a nonreactive saucepan, cover the dried fruit with water, bring to a boil, lower the heat, and simmer for 10 minutes. Add the wine and gently boil for another 20 minutes, or until all but about 2 tablespoons of the liquid is absorbed. Remove from the heat. Add the barbecue sauce, Worcestershire sauce, A1 sauce, a generous sprinkling of red pepper flakes, honey, and cider vinegar. Place back on the stove, bring the mixture to a boil, lower the heat, and simmer for about 15 minutes. Cool slightly. Place in a blender and blend just long enough to break up the fruit, 10 to 15 seconds.

—Chef Kevin Fisk

Dill Cucumber Sauce

This sauce is particularly tasty with strong-flavored fish such as bluefish or mackerel. Vary the amount of mustard and dill to suit your palate.

MAKES 1 1/3 CUPS

1/2 cup plain nonfat yogurt

1 teaspoon minced lemon zest

1/4 cup fresh lemon juice

1 to 1 1/2 tablespoons Dijon mustard

1 cup peeled, seeded, and chopped cucumber (about 1 medium)

1/3 cup chopped red onion

2 tablespoons chopped fresh dill or mint

Dry mustard

1/2 teaspoon honey (optional)

Salt (optional)

In a nonreactive mixing bowl, combine the yogurt, lemon zest, lemon juice, Dijon mustard, cucumber, onion, dill, and a generous pinch of dry mustard. Refrigerate the sauce for at least 2 hours before serving. Season with honey and salt to taste, if desired.

Guacamole Sauce

This sauce is ideal with spicy fried fish, squid, or shrimp. Adjust the amount
of olive oil and lime juice to suit the consistency you prefer.

2 to 3 tablespoons olive oil

⅓ cup finely chopped sweet
onions or scallions, both white and
green parts

1 tablespoon chopped garlic

1 teaspoon seeded and chopped
jalapeño (optional)

2 cups coarsely chopped avocados
(about 3 medium)

3 to 4 tablespoons fresh lime juice
(about 1½ limes)

1 tomato, peeled, seeded, and
chopped

¼ to ½ teaspoon ground cumin

2 tablespoons chopped fresh
cilantro

Salt

Freshly milled black pepper

Heat the oil in a medium nonreactive saucepan. Stir in the
onions, garlic, and jalapeño, if using. Cook over medium heat,
stirring frequently, for 4 minutes, or until the onions are
wilted. Either place the mixture in a food processor and pulse
the machine on and off for about 30 seconds, or leave as is
for texture. Add the avocados and the lime juice (or mash by
hand with a large spoon). Add the tomato. Season with
cumin, cilantro, salt, and pepper to taste.

VARIATIONS

Spicy Fried Cusk with Guacamole Sauce

Follow the directions for Fried Haddock (page 53), substituting cusk for the haddock and using the spicy variation of the
Fried Fish Coating (page 286). Place the Guacamole Sauce in
the center of a platter and surround with the fried fish.

Fried Shrimp with Guacamole Sauce

Use shrimp following the frying technique described in Fried
Haddock (page 53). The shrimp will cook through in 1 to 1½
minutes, depending upon their size. Follow the serving sug-
gestion for Spicy Fried Cusk (above).

Honey Mustard

This homemade mustard is delicious with smoked salmon or gravlax.

MAKES ABOUT 2 CUPS

1 cup dry mustard

1 cup malt or white vinegar

2 eggs

½ cup mild-flavored honey, or ¼ cup sugar

1 tablespoon fresh orange juice (optional)

2 to 3 tablespoons chopped fresh dill

Beat together the mustard and vinegar in a nonreactive bowl until smooth. Refrigerate, covered, for at least 24 hours. Beat in the eggs, honey, and orange juice, if using. Put the mixture in a double boiler and cook over simmering water until thickened, 8 to 10 minutes. Cool. Stir in the dill. This mustard keeps for several weeks stored in a covered jar in the refrigerator.

Marinara Sauce

We serve this basic sauce in many preparations. Add shrimp or squid and toss with pasta; simmer with smoked tomatoes as an accompaniment for grilled fish; or use in Mussels Marinara (page 226). Freeze any leftover sauce in half-cup portions. If you are making this sauce ahead of time, wait to add salt until assembling the final dish. You'll find that the sauce stays fresh-tasting longer.

MAKES ABOUT 2 CUPS

2 tablespoons olive oil

1 cup chopped onions

2 teaspoons chopped garlic

10 plum tomatoes, peeled, seeded, and chopped

¼ cup chopped fresh basil

Salt

Heat the olive oil in a large nonreactive skillet. Add the onions and garlic and cook over medium heat for about 5 minutes. Add the tomatoes and continue to cook, stirring occasionally, for 10 minutes. Raise the heat and cook for 5 minutes longer, or until the sauce is thick, stirring frequently. Stir in the basil and remove from the heat. Season with salt to taste.

Asian-Style Vinaigrette

A favorite in our West Palm Beach restaurant, this dressing is great tossed with watercress or napa and savoy cabbages. You'll need to whisk it before using because it doesn't stay emulsified. If refrigerated, it lasts for several days. The absence of salt keeps this vinaigrette tasting fresh.

MAKES ABOUT ¾ CUP

1 to 1½ tablespoons chopped shallots

1 to 1½ tablespoons minced garlic

⅓ to ½ cup red wine vinegar

1 to 2 tablespoons sesame oil

2 tablespoons sugar

3 tablespoons Chinese chili sauce (mae ploy)

½ to 1 teaspoon ground fresh chili paste (sambal oelek)

¼ cup mixture of olive and grapeseed oils

Mix together the shallots, garlic, vinegar, sesame oil, sugar, chili sauce, chili paste, and oils in a nonreactive bowl. Taste and correct seasonings if necessary.

—Chef Dave Salzano

Peanut Sauce

Dip shrimp or calamari into this sauce inspired by the Vietnamese peanut sauces served with spring rolls.

MAKES ABOUT ½ CUP

¼ cup chunky peanut butter

1 tablespoon hoisin sauce

2 teaspoons fresh lemon juice

2 to 3 teaspoons rice vinegar

2 teaspoons jalapeño or apple jelly

1 teaspoon finely minced garlic (optional)

¼ teaspoon ketchup

Mix together the peanut butter, hoisin sauce, lemon juice, rice vinegar, 2 teaspoons water, jelly, garlic, if using, and ketchup in a nonreactive bowl. Let sit for at least 30 minutes to let the flavors meld before serving.

Sweet Dipping Sauce

This sweet-and-sour sauce is excellent with fried fish or shellfish, such as squid or shrimp. Any extra sauce keeps for days if stored in a glass jar in the refrigerator.

MAKES 4 SERVINGS

6 tablespoons rice vinegar

3 tablespoons sugar

⅛ teaspoon wasabi powder

½ teaspoon dried red pepper flakes

2 teaspoons diagonally sliced scallions (optional)

Mix together the vinegar, sugar, wasabi, and red pepper flakes in a nonreactive bowl. Let sit for at least 30 minutes. Before serving, stir in the scallions.

Red Pepper Mustard Sauce

Serve this sauce with Crabmeat and Artichoke Hushpuppies (page 78), fried fish, or grilled or broiled mild-flavored fish, such as cod or halibut.

MAKES ABOUT $\frac{1}{3}$ CUP

2 tablespoons chopped roasted red pepper

1 teaspoon Dijon or Creole mustard

$\frac{1}{4}$ teaspoon bottled horseradish

Cayenne pepper

$\frac{1}{4}$ to $\frac{1}{3}$ cup mayonnaise

Salt

Freshly milled black pepper

Fresh lemon juice

Puree the red pepper in a blender or food processor. Mix with the mustard, horseradish, a pinch of cayenne pepper, and the mayonnaise in a nonreactive bowl. Season with salt, pepper, and lemon juice to taste. Let sit for 15 minutes before serving.

White Wine Butter Sauce

A little of this rich sauce goes a long way. You can reduce the wine and cream ahead of time, and just reheat before whisking in the butter. Try it with salmon, halibut, or cod.

1 cup heavy cream

¾ cup white wine

Black peppercorns

4 tablespoons cold butter

Cayenne pepper (optional)

Salt

Place the cream in a small nonreactive saucepan. Bring to a boil, and gently boil until reduced to ½ cup. Set aside. Meanwhile, in another nonreactive saucepan, boil the wine and peppercorns until the wine is reduced to about 1½ tablespoons. Remove the peppercorns, and whisk in first the cream, and then, tablespoon by tablespoon, the butter. Season with a pinch of cayenne pepper, if desired, and salt. Either drizzle over fish or place alongside.

VARIATIONS

With sweet wine
At Legal's Long Wharf restaurant in Boston, a popular special is cashew-encrusted halibut with a sweet champagne sauce. A sweet white wine, such as a Mosel, works equally well.

With capers
Add 1 tablespoon drained capers to the sauce before serving.

With fresh tarragon or chervil
Add 2 to 3 teaspoons minced fresh tarragon or chervil just before serving.

With Dijon mustard
Add ¼ to ½ teaspoon mustard just before serving.

—Chef Peter Dori

Mango Salsa

This zippy salsa, best made with ripe mangoes, marries well with mild-flavored fish, such as red snapper, cod, or haddock.

MAKES 1¾ TO 2 CUPS

2 cups peeled and diced mangoes (about 2)

2 to 3 teaspoons seeded and chopped jalapeño

3 tablespoons minced red pepper

1 tablespoon fresh minced cilantro

2 tablespoons fresh lime juice

1 teaspoon olive oil

Salt

Freshly milled black pepper

In a nonreactive bowl, gently stir together the mangoes, jalapeño, red pepper, cilantro, lime juice, and olive oil. Season with salt and pepper to taste. Let sit, refrigerated, for at least 30 minutes before serving to allow the flavors to meld.

—Chef Kevin Fisk

VARIATIONS

Shrimp and Mango Stuffed Avocado

For each serving, peel and halve an avocado. Drizzle with lime juice to keep the avocado from turning brown. Stuff with 1 to 2 tablespoons of the salsa (depending upon the size of the avocado). Top with a row of cooked shrimp running from top to bottom.

Tropical Salad

On a large round platter, fan out slices of casaba melon or cantaloupe, fresh pineapple, and mango salsa arranged in parallel rows. Leave room in the center for a mound of cooked shrimp or mussels. Garnish with chopped fresh cilantro or parsley.

Grilled Tomato Salsa

At Legal's Boca Raton, Florida, restaurant, this versatile salsa is served with Citrus Soft-Shell Crabs (page 109).

SERVES 4

1 yellow beefsteak tomato

1 red beefsteak tomato

1 small red onion

4 tablespoons olive oil

2 tablespoons seeded and minced jalapeño

¼ cup chopped fresh cilantro

¼ to ⅓ cup fresh lime juice

1 teaspoon minced garlic

Salt

Freshly milled black pepper

Core the tomatoes and halve them. Peel and quarter the onion. Toss with 2 tablespoons of the olive oil. Place on a grill over medium heat, lightly charring the vegetables. This will take anywhere from 5 to 10 minutes, depending upon the heat of the grill. Remove the tomatoes and onion from the grill and let them cool. Then, roughly chop them and place in a nonreactive bowl. Add the jalapeño, cilantro, the remaining 2 tablespoons olive oil, the lime juice, and the garlic. Season with salt and pepper to taste. (If the lime juice makes the salsa too acidic, add 1 tablespoon more oil.) Refrigerate before serving.

—Chef Joe Coletto

Cracker Crumb Mixture

This rich crumb topping keeps for weeks in the refrigerator.

MAKES ABOUT 2 CUPS

$1/4$ pound oyster crackers or saltines

2 tablespoons finely chopped onion

$1/2$ cup melted butter

2 tablespoons minced fresh parsley

$1/2$ teaspoon minced fresh thyme leaves

Whirl the crackers in a food processor or blender until they are evenly ground but retain some texture. Sauté the onion until softened in 1 tablespoon of the butter, and then add to the crumb mixture in a bowl along with the remaining butter, parsley, and thyme. Mix thoroughly. If the mixture hardens in the refrigerator, place it in a microwave oven for 5 to 10 seconds before using.

Fried Fish Coating

All of our fried fish is coated with a flour and cornmeal mixture we prepare at our central commissary. You can approximate it at home using the finest grind of cornmeal available. (White cornmeal gives the best results.) This recipe makes enough for several batches. Store in a plastic zipper bag in the refrigerator, which keeps the mixture dry and makes it easy to shake before using. You can also divide the basic mixture to make both plain and spicy coatings by adding half the spices in the variation to half of the mixture.

MAKES 2 CUPS

1 cup white cornmeal

1 cup unbleached all-purpose flour

$1/2$ teaspoon dry mustard

$1/2$ teaspoon salt

Place the cornmeal, flour, dry mustard, and salt in a blender. Blend at medium speed until thoroughly combined, 20 to 30 seconds.

VARIATION

Spicy Fish Coating
Add $1/8$ teaspoon cayenne pepper and 2 to 3 teaspoons Old Bay Seasoning.

Desserts

Blueberry and Peach Crumble

Blueberries and peaches come into season together. You can substitute pears, apples, or apricots for the peaches and blueberries.

SERVES 4 TO 6

5 peaches or nectarines, peeled and thinly sliced

1 cup blueberries

¹/₃ cup fresh orange juice

2 teaspoons minced orange zest

³/₄ cup unbleached all-purpose flour

¹/₃ to ¹/₂ cup packed brown sugar

3 tablespoons butter

Heavy cream (optional)

Preheat the oven to 325°F.

Mix together the peaches, blueberries, orange juice, and orange zest. Place the fruit in a buttered 9-inch pie or square pan, and set aside.

Combine the flour and brown sugar, then cut in 2 tablespoons of the butter with a pastry blender until the mixture forms crumbs about the size of small peas. Sprinkle the flour mixture over the fruit, and dot with the remaining 1 tablespoon butter.

Bake until the peaches are cooked through, the top is slightly browned, and the mixture is bubbling, about 30 minutes. Serve either hot or cold, with heavy cream, if desired, to pour over the crumble.

Key Lime Pie

Everyone loves a good key lime pie; it is one of Legal's most popular desserts. Many gourmet shops now sell the small, yellow, intensely flavored key limes, but if you can't find them, use green Persian limes.

MAKES ONE 9-INCH PIE

3 large eggs

One 14-ounce can sweetened condensed milk

3/4 cup fresh lime juice, preferably from key limes

2 teaspoons minced lime zest

A lightly baked 9-inch pie shell

Whipped cream (optional)

Preheat the oven to 350°F.

Separate the eggs, and place the yolks in a mixing bowl. Beat them together with the condensed milk for 3 minutes. Combine with the lime juice and lime zest, and set aside. Beat the egg whites until they are soft but not stiff. Gently fold them into the lime juice mixture. Spoon into a cooked 9-inch pie shell. Bake on the middle rack of the oven for 20 to 30 minutes, or until the center is firm. Remove and cool on a cake rack. Chill in the refrigerator before serving. Top with whipped cream, if desired.

Mango and Strawberry Shortcake

Adding pureed fresh mango to the yellow cake batter adds a tropical touch to an old-fashioned dessert. If fresh mangoes are in short supply, substitute orange juice for the mango puree. This type of dense-textured yellow cake was popular in the 1950s, when Legal Sea Foods was founded. If you wish, omit splitting and filling the cake and top with ice cream and fruit, such as fresh peach or mango ice cream accompanied by peaches, raspberries, or blackberries.

MAKES ONE 9-INCH CAKE

$^1/_2$ cup butter

$^3/_4$ cup plus 2 tablespoons sugar

1$^1/_2$ mangoes

$^1/_2$ lemon

2 tablespoons minced orange zest

2 eggs

1$^1/_4$ cups self-rising flour

1 pint strawberries

1 cup whipping cream

Preheat the oven to 350°F.

Cream together the butter and $^3/_4$ cup sugar in a large mixing bowl until light, about 2 minutes. In a blender or food processor, process half a peeled mango and the lemon. You should end up with about $^1/_2$ cup mango juice. If not, add orange juice to make $^1/_2$ cup total. Set the mixture aside.

Add the orange zest and the eggs, one by one, to the butter and sugar mixture. Beat only long enough to combine. Alternately stir in the flour and the mango puree. Pour the batter into a greased, deep 9-inch cake pan. Bake for 35 minutes, or until a cake tester inserted into the center comes out clean. Cool the cake on a rack for 5 minutes before removing from the pan. Cool completely before assembling.

Meanwhile, peel the remaining mango and dice the flesh. This will be a messy process, so do it over a bowl so that any juice that drips from the mango is saved. Stem and slice the strawberries, saving 3 or 4 for a garnish. Toss the mango and strawberries with 2 tablespoons sugar and set aside.

Just before serving, whip the cream and fold in the fruit. Split the cake and fill with half the whipped cream mixture, top with the remaining cake, and top with the remaining whipped cream and fruit. Halve the reserved strawberries and arrange on top.

VARIATIONS

With blueberries
Add $1/3$ cup whole blueberries to the fruit filling.

Coconut Cake
Substitute $1/2$ cup canned coconut milk and $1/2$ cup shredded packaged coconut for the mango puree. Add 1 teaspoon vanilla extract. Proceed as above.

Orange Apricot Cheesecake Pie

Top off a simple fish dinner with this exceptionally easy-to-prepare cheesecake pie made with a prepared crust. The orange zest is essential. Skip the crust and bake the cheesecake in a buttered pie plate, if desired.

MAKES ONE 9-INCH PIE

Two 8-ounce packages cream cheese

$^1/_2$ cup sugar

2 teaspoons minced orange zest

2 eggs

$^1/_4$ cup fresh orange juice

2 tablespoons apricot or orange preserves

9-inch prepared graham cracker pie crust

Orange slices

Preheat the oven to 350°F.

Mix together the cream cheese, sugar, and orange zest until well blended. Add the eggs, mix again, then beat in the orange juice and preserves. Pour into a prepared pie shell. Bake for 35 to 40 minutes, or until the center is almost set. Cool. Refrigerate for several hours or overnight. Before serving, garnish with thinly sliced oranges.

Mango Cream

At Legal's south Florida restaurants, we use mangoes in both main dishes and desserts. This easy dessert uses super-ripe mangoes. When they're in season (usually June in Florida), make and freeze several batches of this cream for fall meals. The amount of lime juice depends on how tart you'd like the mixture to taste.

SERVES 4 TO 6

1 cup mango pulp and juice (about 2 mangoes)

½ cup sugar

1 to 2 tablespoons fresh lime juice

1 cup sour cream

Blueberries, blackberries, or raspberries (optional)

Place the mango pulp in a food processor or blender and process until pureed. Add the sugar, lime juice, and sour cream, and run the machine for a few seconds to combine the ingredients. Pour the cream into a freezer bowl or tray. Freeze until hard. Remove from the freezer about 15 minutes before serving to soften the cream slightly. Garnish each serving with blueberries, blackberries, or raspberries, or a mixture of these soft fruits, if desired.

VARIATION

Peach Cream
Substitute peaches for the mangoes.

The Cigar Exception

ONE OF MY ALL-TIME FAVORITE customers is Red Auerbach, the former coach, general manager, and now president of the Boston Celtics. A few years ago, I put a notice in the menu that there would be no cigar or pipe smoking in the restaurants . . . with the exception of Red Auerbach. Well, one night, Red had finished dinner and all of a sudden lit up a cigar. The wait staff was horrified and immediately went over to ask him to put it out. "I can smoke here," he said, holding up the menu. "Roger said I could. It's right here on the menu."

Peach Mango Ice Cream

We make all the ice creams and sorbets served at Legal's restaurants. Depending upon the season, you can find special fruit flavors as well as old favorites such as chocolate—or a vanilla-bean vanilla. The season for mangoes and peaches overlaps. Using both fruits creates an intense flavor. If you're using one of the ice cream freezers that operate with a frozen bowl, remember that you need to plan in advance because the bowl must be placed in the freezer several hours ahead of time.

SERVES 6

4 peaches

1 mango

2 tablespoons fresh lime juice

1 cup milk

2 cups heavy cream

$^3/_4$ to $^7/_8$ cup sugar

3 tablespoons commercial orange juice with pineapple (optional)

Peel the peaches and mango. Dice coarsely and place in a blender along with the lime juice. Blend in short bursts so that chunks of the peaches and mango are intact. Pour into a refrigerator dish and place in the coldest part of the refrigerator.

Heat the milk, cream, and sugar in a nonreactive saucepan, stirring frequently, until the sugar dissolves, about 3 minutes. Remove from the heat before the mixture boils, at the point when bubbles are forming on the sides. Cool, then refrigerate for about 1 hour.

Stir the peach and cream mixtures together. Taste and add the orange juice, if desired. Freeze in an ice cream freezer, following the manufacturer's directions. The ice cream will taste best if you let it "ripen" overnight. Let soften at room temperature for about 20 minutes before serving.

VARIATION

With orange zest and whiskey
Add 2 tablespoons grated orange zest and whiskey to taste. Remember that alcohol hinders the freezing process, so use only 1 to 3 teaspoons.

Pears and Cantaloupe with Ice Cream

Try this refreshing dessert when pears and cantaloupes are in season.

SERVES 4 TO 6

5 tablespoons butter

$^1/_4$ cup sugar

6 large medium-ripe pears, peeled and sliced

1 tablespoon dark rum

2 tablespoons fresh orange or lime juice

$^1/_2$ large cantaloupe, peeled and sliced

Vanilla ice cream

Place the butter and sugar in a large nonreactive skillet and heat, stirring constantly, until the sugar dissolves. Add the pears and cook for about 5 minutes, or until they start to become transparent. Add the rum and fruit juice and cook 3 to 5 minutes longer, depending upon the ripeness of the pears.

Stir in the cantaloupe and continue to cook, stirring constantly, until the syrup thickens and coats the fruit, about 4 minutes. Taste and add additional citrus juice if desired. Serve over vanilla ice cream.

Tropical Bruschetta

This splashy dessert can be multiplied and used as a cocktail party or buffet dessert.
The fruit and chocolate sauces also go nicely over pound cake or ice cream.

SERVES 4

³/₄ cup peeled ripe mango, cut into
¹/₂-inch pieces

1 cup fresh pineapple, cut into
³/₄- to 1-inch pieces

2 star fruit, sliced approximately
¹/₂ inch thick

1 to 2 teaspoons rum or
hazelnut syrup

1 tablespoon cream of coconut,
such as Coco Lopez

1 tablespoon fresh orange juice

8 slices toasted brioche or French
bread, sliced diagonally

1 recipe Chocolate Sauce
(page 298)

Mix together the mango, pineapple, star fruit, rum, cream of coconut, and orange juice in a nonreactive bowl. Let sit for at least 15 minutes. Place the toasted bread on a platter and brush with the chocolate sauce. Arrange the star fruit on top and fill in with the mango and pineapple.

Chocolate Sauce

takes just minutes to make, is ideal with Tropical Bruschetta (page 297) or spooned over ice cream. This sauce can be refrigerated in a covered dish for three days and reheated. If you use sweetened cocoa, reduce the amount of sugar to taste.

MAKES ABOUT ¾ CUP

1 tablespoon butter

3 tablespoons unsweetened cocoa, such as Hershey's

3 tablespoons heavy cream

1 teaspoon brandy or dark rum

3 tablespoons sugar

Put the butter, cocoa, cream, brandy, sugar, and 1 tablespoon water in a small nonreactive saucepan. Bring the mixture to a boil, whisking constantly, and cook for about 2 minutes or until the mixture thickens and the cocoa is dissolved. (If the mixture is too thick, thin with cream or water.)

Butterscotch Coconut Sauce

Try this over coconut or vanilla ice cream, or as a topping for cooked bananas or pears. It's an easy way to use up coconut milk left over from Tropical Shrimp and Scallops (page 150).

MAKES ABOUT ½ CUP

4 tablespoons brown sugar

½ cup coconut milk

¼ teaspoon dark rum

Heat 4 tablespoons water in a small saucepan and add the brown sugar. Cook together over high heat until the sugar dissolves and browns, forming a glaze. Immediately add the coconut milk and rum. Serve warm.

Index

Guacamole sauce, 278
    wraps with, 254
Gumbo, shellfish, 243

H

Haddock, 15, 16, 19, 20. *See also* Scrod
    corn and green bean chowder, 237
    easy baked haddock, 113
    escabeche, with carrots, 114
    fish sandwich, 251
    fried, 53
    with herb and bread crumb topping, 115
    seafood casserole, 142
    seafood seviche, 82
    and vegetable stew, 240
    wrap, 254
Halibut, 16, 20–21
    with fruit salsa, 116
    grilled, 56
    with lobster vinaigrette, 209
    with pico de gallo salsa, 94
Hash, shrimp, 148
Health benefits of seafood, 17
Hepatitis, 11, 30
Herb(s). *See also specific herbs*
    and bread crumb topping, haddock with, 115
    as garnishes, 225
    potato salad with, 203
    sautéed sole or flounder with, 65
    shellfish and herb pasta, 229
    striped bass with garlic and, 95
    and tomato salsa, glazed salmon with, 137
Hog snapper Pepe, 157
Honey mustard, 279
Hoppers, 30, 43
Horseradish. *See also* Wasabi
    chilled horseradish citrus cream, 274
    cod with lemon and, 102
    crusty sole with, 161
Hushpuppies, crabmeat and artichoke, 78

I

Ice cream
    peach mango, 295
    pears and cantaloupe with, 296
Imitation crabmeat, 33

J

Jalapeño
    chutney, mahi mahi with pear and, 121
    corn bread, 268
    jalapeño jelly glaze, salmon with, 138

mayonnaise, spicy fried grouper with, 111
    and salmon nachos, 191
Jambalaya, shrimp and oyster, 230
Jasmine special, 221
Jerk seasoning
    jerked shrimp with watermelon coulis, 147
    mahi mahi wrap with, 254
    tropical shrimp and scallops, 150–51
Johnny cakes, Rhode Island, 269

K

Kabobs, scallop and shrimp, 141
Kale and tomato sauce, bluefish in, 96
Key lime pie, 289

L

Latkes, fish, 188
Leftovers, 182–98
    arctic char burritos, 182
    Chinese-American egg rolls, 183
    corn and green bean chowder, 237
    deviled eggs with shrimp, 196
    easy fish curry, 186
    easy shellfish tart, 194
    egg foo yung, 184
    fish and vegetable soup, 238
    fish latkes, 188
    fried rice, 187; tuna or shrimp wrap with, 254
    green Thai-style fish curry, 151
    mushroom-and-fish-stuffed crepes, 189
    salmon and jalapeño nachos, 191
    salmon frittata, 192
    salmon with asparagus and ravioli, 227
    savory turnovers, 193
    shrimp and avocado quesadilla, 198
    shrimp bruschetta, 195
    stuffed grape leaves, 88
    Thai-style shrimp with noodles, 197
    wraps, 254
Lemon(s). *See also* Citrus fruit
    cod with horseradish and, 102
    shad roe with chives and, 143
    shrimp with garlic and, 152
    sole with capers and, 164
Lemongrass, stir-fried monkfish with beans and, 124–25
Lemon sole, 27. *See also* Sole
Lime. *See also* Citrus fruit
    key lime pie, 289
    swordfish in rosemary lime sauce, 166
Linguine with littlenecks, 222
Listeria, 11

red, with pineapple and peppers, 159;
steamed, with ginger and scallions, 158;
tomato, pepper, and mango snapper, 160
sole: crusty, 161; easy baked, 162; with
lemons and capers, 164; microwaved, 58;
and salmon lattice, 134–35; sautéed, 65;
stuffed with crabmeat, 163
swordfish: with onion jam, 170; in rosemary
lime sauce, 166; sautéed, with citrus
scallion sauce, 165; stir-fry, 167
trout: balsamic roasted, 171; with mandarin
oranges, 174; microwaved, 58; sage-
infused, 172; stuffed, 173
tuna: broiled, with tomatillos and peppers,
176; with cucumber garnish, 175
wolffish with peppers and mushrooms, 177
Mako shark, 15, 27
Mandarin oranges, rainbow trout with, 174
Mango
crabmeat and mango salad, 206
cream, 293
glaze, salmon with, 139
mahi mahi Barbados, 122
peach mango ice cream, 295
salmon with pear, mango, and jalapeño
chutney, 121
salsa, 284; summer flounder in butter sauce
with, 110; swordfish wrap with, 254
shrimp and mango stuffed avocado, 284
steeped shrimp with fruit, 212
and strawberry shortcake, 290–91
tomato, pepper, and mango snapper, 160
tropical bruschetta, 297
Marinara sauce, 279
mussels marinara, 226
Marinated grilled shrimp, 149
Marinated shellfish, 144
Marinated shrimp and cucumbers, 210
Mayonnaise
Cajun remoulade sauce, 273
jalapeño, spicy fried grouper with, 111
tartar sauce, 272
Mediterranean shrimp, 232
Mercury, 27
Microwaving, 57–59
Middle Eastern–style green beans, 258
Monkfish, 16, 22
fish chowder, 239
stir-fried, with beans and lemongrass,
124–25
Mushrooms
cod with peppers and, 101, 103

crabmeat with morel mushrooms, 108
mushroom-and-fish-stuffed crepes, 189
oyster and mushroom casserole, 127
scallops and mushroom bowtie pasta, 228
shad roe with bacon, tomatoes, and, 143
wolffish with peppers and, 177
Mussel(s), 30, 36–37
au gratin, 79
easy shellfish tart, 194
marinara, 226
marinated shellfish, 144
Middle Eastern–style green beans with, 258
oven-roasted, 123
pizza, 87
salads: curried mussel salad, 211; mussel
tabbouleh, 213; potato salad with mussels,
202; steeped shrimp and mussels with
fruit, 212; tropical salad, 284
in salmon Milan, 131
shellfish and herb pasta, 229
steamed, 80
three-way, 241
Mustard
and bread crumbs, salmon with, 115
honey mustard, 279
red pepper mustard sauce, 282
salmon with bacon and, 140

N

Nachos, jalapeño and salmon, 191
Noodles. *See also* Pasta
soba noodle salad, 216
Thai-style shrimp with, 197

O

Ocean catfish. *See* Wolffish
Oils, for frying and sautéing, 66
Old Bay Seasoning, 66
Olive topping, cod with, 104
Omega-3 fatty acids, 17, 18–19, 21, 23, 25, 37
Onions
onion jam, swordfish with, 170
onion strings, 259
Orange(s). *See also* Citrus fruit
orange apricot cheesecake pie, 292
orange marmalade glaze, 136
Oven-steaming, 62–63
Oyster(s), 30, 38–41
fried, 54; with Johnny cakes, 269
and mushroom casserole, 127
scalloped, 128
and scallop stew, 242